The Complete Florida Beach Guide

Wild Florida

UNIVERSITY PRESS OF FLORIDA
Florida A&M University, Tallahassee
Florida Atlantic University, Boca Raton
Florida Gulf Coast University, Ft. Myers
Florida International University, Miami
Florida State University, Tallahassee
New College of Florida, Sarasota
University of Central Florida, Orlando
University of Florida, Gainesville
University of North Florida, Jacksonville
University of South Florida, Tampa
University of West Florida, Pensacola

University Press of Florida
Gainesville · Tallahassee · Tampa · Boca Raton
Pensacola · Orlando · Miami · Jacksonville · Ft. Myers · Sarasota

The Complete Florida Beach Guide

Mary and Bill Burnham

Foreword by M. Timothy O'Keefe

WILD FLORIDA
edited by M. Timothy O'Keefe

Books in this series are written for the many people who visit and/or move
to Florida to participate in our remarkable outdoors, an environment rich in
birds, animals and activities, many exclusive to this state. Books in the series
will offer readers a variety of formats: Natural history guides, historical outdoor
guides, guides to some of Florida's most popular pastimes and activities, and
memoirs of outdoors folk and their unique lifestyles.

*30 Eco-trips in Florida: The Best Nature Excursions and How to Reduce
your Impact on the Environment,* by Holly Ambrose (2005)

A Hiker's Guide to the Sunshine State, by Sandra Friend (2005)

*Fishing Florida's Flats: A Guide to Bonefish, Tarpon, Permit, and Much
More,* by Jan S. Maizler (2007)

50 Great Walks in Florida, by Lucy Beebe Tobias (2008)

*Hiking the Florida Trail: 1,100 Miles, 78 Days, Two Pairs of Boots, and One
Heck of an Adventure,* by Johnny Molloy (2008)

The Complete Florida Beach Guide, by Mary and Bill Burnham (2008)

13 12 11 10 09 08   6 5 4 3 2 1

Library of Congress Cataloging-in-Publication Data
Burnham, Mary (Mary K.)
The complete Florida beach guide / Mary and Bill Burnham ;
foreword by M. Timothy O'Keefe.
p. cm.—(Wild Florida)
ISBN 978-0-8130-3221-4 (alk. paper)
    1. Florida—Guidebooks. 2. Beaches—Florida—Guidebooks. 3.
Parks—Florida—Guidebooks. 4. Recreation areas—Florida—Guide-
books. I. Burnham, Bill, 1969– II. Title.
F309.3.B87   2008
917.5904'6409146—dc22   2007032166

The University Press of Florida is the scholarly publishing agency
for the State University System of Florida, comprising Florida A&M
University, Florida Atlantic University, Florida Gulf Coast University,
Florida International University, Florida State University, New College of Florida, University of Central Florida, University of Florida,
University of North Florida, University of South Florida, and University of West Florida.

University Press of Florida
15 Northwest 15th Street
Gainesville, FL 32611-2079
http://www.upf.com

Contents

Foreword xxi
Preface xxiii
Acknowledgments xxv
List of Icons xxvii
Introduction 1

East Coast 13

Amelia Island
Fort Clinch State Park 15
Fernandina Main Beach 16
Seaside Park 18
South Fernandina Beach Accesses 19
Peter's Point Beachfront Park 20
Scott Road Beach Access 20
American Beach 21
Burney Beachfront Park 22
South End Walkover 23
Amelia Island State Park 23

Jacksonville Area
Big Talbot Island State Park 25
Little Talbot Island State Park 26
Huguenot Memorial Park 27
Kathryn Abbey Hanna Park 28
Atlantic Beach 29
Neptune Beach 30
Jacksonville Beach 31
Oceanfront Park 32

Ponte Vedra–Vilano Beaches
Mickler's Landing Beach 33

Guana-Tolomato-Matanzas National Estuarine Research
   Reserve 33
Usina Beach 34
North Beach Park 35
Nease Beachfront Park 35
Surfside 36
Vilano Beach 37

St. Augustine Area

Anastasia State Park 38
St. Augustine Beach 39
Frank Butler Park East 40
Crescent Beach Park 41
Matanzas Beach 42

Flagler Beach Area

River to Sea Preserve 43
Washington Oaks Gardens State Park 44
Malacompra County Park 46
Old Salt Road Park 46
Jungle Hut Road Park 47
Varn Beach Park 47
Flagler Beach 48
Gamble Rogers Memorial State Recreation Area 49

Daytona Beach Area

North Peninsula State Park 50
Bicentennial Park 50
Tom Renick Park 51
Ormond Beach 51
Daytona Beach 52
Frank Rendon Park 54
Wilbur-By-The-Sea 54
Winterhaven Park 55
Lighthouse Point Park 55

New Smyrna Beach Area

Smyrna Dunes Park 57
Flagler Avenue Park 58
Mary McLeod Bethune Beach Park 59

Canaveral National Seashore

Apollo Beach, Canaveral National Seashore   60

Klondike Beach, Canaveral National Seashore   61

Playalinda Beach, South District Canaveral National Seashore   63

Cape Canaveral–Cocoa Beach

Jetty Park   64

Cape Canaveral and Avon-by-the-Sea   65

Cherie Down Park   66

Cocoa Beach   67

Alan Shepard Park   68

Sidney Fischer Park   68

Lori Wilson Park   69

Robert P. Murkshe Memorial Park   69

Patrick Air Force Base   70

South Patrick Shores   71

Melbourne Beach Area

Pelican Beach Park/Satellite Beach   72

Richard G. Edgeton Bicentennial Park   72

Millennium Park   73

Irene H. Canova Park   73

Canova Beach Park   74

Howard E. Futch Memorial Park/Paradise Beach   74

Sunrise Park   75

James H. Nance Park   75

Ocean Avenue Park   76

Spessard Holland North and South Beach Parks   76

Coconut Point Park   77

Juan Ponce de Leon Landing   78

Bonsteel Park   79

Sebastian Inlet State Park   79

Sebastian Inlet State Park South Beach Access   80

North Hutchinson Island

Amber Sands Beach Access   81

Treasure Shores Park   81

Golden Sands Beach Park   82

Wabasso Beach   82

Wabasso Causeway Park   83
Sea Grape Trail Access   84
Turtle Trail Beach Access   84
Tracking Station Park   85
Jaycee Park   85
Sexton Beach   86
Humiston Park   87
Riomar Beach   87
South Beach Park   88
Round Island Oceanside Park   88
Avalon State Park   89
Pepper Beach Park   89
Ft. Pierce Inlet State Park   90

Hutchinson Island

Seaway Drive   91
South Jetty Park   91
Ft. Pierce Beach Public Accesses   92
South Beach Boardwalk   93
Kimberly Bergalis Memorial Drive and Surfside Park   94
Coconut Drive Beach   94
John Brooks Park   95
Frederick Douglass Memorial Beach   96
Middle Cove Access   97
Blind Creek Park   97
Turtle Beach   98
Walton Rocks Beach   99
Ocean Bay Natural Area   99
Herman's Bay Access   100
Normandy Beach Access   100
Dollman Park   101
Waveland Beach   101
Glasscock Beach   102
Jensen Sea Turtle Beach   102
Bob Graham Beach   103
Beachwalk/Pasley Park   104
Bryn Mawr Beach Access   104
Virginia Forrest Access   105

Tiger Shores Beach   105
Stuart Beach   106
Santa Lucea Beach and Fletcher Beach   106
Ross Witham Beach Access (House of Refuge Beach)   107
Chastain Beach/The Rocks   108
Bathtub Reef Beach Park   109

Jupiter Island
St. Lucie Inlet Preserve State Park   110
Hobe Sound National Wildlife Refuge   111
Hobe Sound National Wildlife Refuge Headquarters   111
Hobe Sound Beach   112
Blowing Rocks Preserve   113
Coral Cove Park   114

South Florida   115

Palm Beach Area
Dubois Park   117
Jupiter Beach County Park   117
Carlin Park   118
Jupiter Beach   119
Juno Beach Park and Pier   119
Loggerhead Park   120
John D. MacArthur Beach State Park   121
Ocean Reef Park   121
Riviera Municipal Beach   122
Palm Beach Shores Park   123
Midtown Beach   123
Phipps Ocean Park   124
Richard G. Kreusler Park   124
Lake Worth Municipal Beach   125
Lantana Public Beach   126
Ocean Inlet Park   127
Ocean Ridge Hammock Park   128
Boynton Beach Oceanfront Park   128
Gulfstream County Park   129
Delray Municipal Beach   129

Atlantic Dunes Park   130
Spanish River Park   131
Red Reef Park   132
South Beach Park   133
South Beach Pavilion   133
South Inlet Park   134

Fort Lauderdale Area

Deerfield Public Beach   135
North Ocean Park   135
Pompano Public Beach   136
Lauderdale-By-The-Sea Public Beach   137
Fort Lauderdale City Beach   137
Canine Beach   139
Hugh Taylor Birch State Park   139
John U. Lloyd Beach State Park   140
Dania Beach Ocean Park   141
Hollywood North Beach Park   142
Hollywood Beach   142
Hallandale Beach   144

Miami Area

Samson Oceanfront Park   145
Haulover Park   145
Oleta River State Park   146
Bal Harbour   147
Surfside   147
North Shore Open Space Park Beach   148
North Miami Beach   149
Lummus Park   149
Marjory Stoneman Douglas Ocean Beach Park   150
South Pointe Park   151
Rickenbacker Causeway/Hobie Beach   152
Virginia Key Beach   153
Historic Virginia Key Beach Park Trust   154
Crandon Park   154
Bill Baggs Cape Florida State Park   155
Matheson Hammock County Park   157

Homestead Area

Biscayne National Park 158
Homestead Bayfront Park 158
Everglades National Park 159

Florida Keys 161

Key Largo

North Nest Key 164
John Pennekamp Coral Reef State Park 165
Harry Harris County Park 166

Islamorada

Founder's Park 167
Islamorada Library Park 167
Robbie's Marina 168
Anne's Beach 169

Layton

Long Key State Park 171
Curry Hammock State Park 171

Marathon

Coco Plum Beach 173
Sombrero Beach 173

Lower Keys

Veterans Memorial Park 175
Bahia Honda State Park 175
Long Beach Drive 176
Boca Chica Beach 177

Key West

Smathers Beach 178
C. B. Harvey Rest Beach Park 178
Higgs Beach 179
Dog Beach 180
South Beach 181
Fort Zachary Taylor Historic State Park 181
Simonton Street Beach 182
Dry Tortugas National Park 183

Perdido Key

Perdido Key State Park 187
Johnson Beach 188
Big Lagoon State Park 189

Santa Rosa Island

Fort Pickens, Gulf Islands National Seashore 191
Quietwater Beach 192
Pensacola Beach/Casino Beach 193
Opal Beach, Santa Rosa Unit of Gulf Islands National
 Seashore 194
Navarre Park 196
Navarre Beach 197

Okaloosa Island

Okaloosa Island Beach Accesses 199
Newman C. Brackin Wayside Park and Okaloosa Pier 200
John Beasley County Park 201
Okaloosa Unit, Gulf Islands National Seashore 201
Eglin Air Force Base 202

Destin

Destin Public Beach Access 203
Clement Taylor Park 204
Henderson Beach State Park 205
James Lee County Park 205

Beaches of South Walton

Miramar Beach 207
Topsail Hill Preserve State Park 208
South Walton Beach Access Points 209
Grayton Beach 211
Grayton Beach State Park 213
Van Ness Butler Regional Beach Access 214
Seagrove Beach 215
Deer Lake State Park 216

Inlet Beach Regional Access 217
Camp Helen State Park 218

Panama City Beach

Panama City Beach 219
St. Andrews State Park 221
Shell Island 221
Crooked Island 223

St. Joseph Bay Area

Mexico Beach 224
St. Joe Beach 225
St. Joseph Peninsula State Park 226
Cape Palms Park 227
Stumphole Beach Access 227
Cape San Blas Lighthouse 228
Salinas Park 229
Indian Pass Beach 230

Apalachicola Area

St. Vincent National Wildlife Refuge 231
Little St. George Island 233
St. George Island 234
St. George Island State Park 235
Dog Island 236
Carrabelle Beach 237
Bald Point State Park 237

Nature Coast 241

Wakulla County

Mashes Sands County Park 243
Shell Point Beach 244

Taylor County

Hodges Park at Keaton Beach 245

Dixie County

Butler and Douglas Community Park/Horseshoe Beach 246
Shired Island County Park 247

Levy County

Cedar Key City Park   248
Cedar Keys National Wildlife Refuge   248
Yankeetown Park   250

Citrus County

Fort Island Gulf Beach   251

Hernando County

Alfred A. McKethan Pine Island Park   252
Rogers Park   253

Pasco County

Robert J. Strickland Memorial Park   254
Robert K. Rees Park   254

Southwest Coast   257

Tarpon Springs Area

Anclote River Park   259
Anclote Key Preserve State Park   259
Fred H. Howard Park   261
Sunset Beach   262
Crystal Beach Live Oaks Park   262

Dunedin Area

Dunedin Causeway   263
Honeymoon Island State Park   264
Caladesi Island State Park   264
Three Rooker Bar   266

Clearwater–St. Petersburg Area

North Clearwater Beach   267
Clearwater Beach   268
Sand Key County Park   269
Bellair Beach Access   270
Indian Rocks Beach Access   270
Indian Rocks Beach   272
Indian Shores   272

Redington Shores Beach Access 273
North Redington Beach Access 273
Madeira Beach 274
John's Pass Park 274
City of St. Petersburg Municipal Beach 275
Treasure Island Beach Accesses 276
Sunset Beach 277
Upham Beach 278
St. Pete Beach Access 278
Pass-a-Grille Beach 279
Shell Key Preserve 280
Fort De Soto County Park 280
Egmont Key State Park 282
E. G. Simmons County Park 282

Bradenton Area
Palma Sola Causeway Park 284
Bayfront Park 284
Anna Maria Beach Accesses 285
Holmes Beach Accesses 286
Manatee Public Beach 286
Katie Pierola Park 287
Cortez Beach 288
Coquina Beach 289
Greer Island Beach 289
Longboat Key Accesses 290
Quick Point Nature Preserve 291

Sarasota Area
North Lido Beach 292
Lido Beach/Coolidge Park 292
South Lido Park 293
Siesta Key North Beach Accesses 294
Siesta Key Public Beach 295
Crescent Beach/Point of Rocks 296
Turtle Beach 296
Nokomis Beach 297
North Jetty Park 298

Venice Area

South Jetty 299
Venice Municipal Beach 299
Service Club Park 300
Venice Fishing Pier 301
South Brohard Paw Park 302
Caspersen Beach Park 302
Manasota Beach 303
Blind Pass Beach 304

Port Charlotte Area

Chadwick Park at Englewood Beach 305
Stump Pass Beach State Park 305
Don Pedro Island State Park 306
Boca Grande Public Access 306
Gasparilla Island State Park 307

Ft. Myers–Sanibel Area

Cayo Costa State Park 309
North Captiva Island 310
Captiva Beach North 311
Turner Beach 312
Bowman's Beach 313
Tarpon Bay Road Beach 314
Gulfside City Park/Algier's Beach 314
Lighthouse Beach Park 315
Sanibel Causeway Beach 316
Bunche Beach 316
Bowditch Point Regional Park 317
Ft. Myers Beach 318
Lynn Hall Memorial Park 318
Lovers Key State Park 319
Bonita Beach Dog Park 320
Little Hickory Beach Access 321
Bonita Beach Public Accesses 322
Bonita Beach Park 322

Naples Area

Barefoot Beach Access   323
Barefoot Beach Preserve   323
Delnor-Wiggins Pass State Park   324
Bluebill Beach Access   325
Vanderbilt Beach Park   325
Clam Pass Park   326
Gulfshore Boulevard Beach Access   326
North Gulf Shore Beach Access   327
Lowdermilk Park   327
Naples Beach Public Access   328
Naples Municipal Beach and Pier   329
Tigertail Beach County Park   330
S. Marco Beach Access   331
Cape Romano   331
Ten Thousand Islands National Wildlife Refuge   333

Index   335

Foreword

Already ranked as one of the most populous states, Florida absorbs hundreds of thousands of new residents every year. It seems impossible that truly wild places can remain anywhere in such a densely inhabited region. In spite of the tremendous influx of people to the Sunshine State, significant sections of the original natural Florida do still endure, including more of our famous coastline than most residents or visitors ever realize.

The University Press of Florida celebrates the diversity of the state's outstanding beaches in its broad-ranging series *Wild Florida* with *The Complete Florida Beach Guide*. Written by the dynamic husband and wife team of Bill and Mary Burnham, *The Complete Florida Beach Guide* is the most definitive work of its type.

You'll find this a useful and valuable book, with descriptions of all the state's beaches based entirely on the Burnhams' own personal visits, not on brochures provided by local tourist boards. Bill and Mary traveled 1,600 miles by kayak, ferry, and automobile to gather material, leaving their footprints on sands all over Florida, from wild uninhabited barrier islands in the Panhandle to heavily populated, party-driven places like Miami's famed South Beach.

The Complete Florida Beach Guide should be viewed as a perennial supplement to the annual list of "America's Best Beaches" compiled by Stephen Leatherman (Dr. Beach), who always ranks Florida's beaches among the country's best. Any place Dr. Beach chooses that you haven't heard about, you'll find described here, including directions, hours, facilities, fees, and contact information.

It's about time that the sandy Atlantic and Gulf of Mexico coastlines of Florida receive their due recognition. Florida beaches are catnip for people, responsible for luring most visitors to vacation in Florida and then move here. According to some sources, almost 75 percent of Florida's entire population is concentrated in coastal communities, and the trend is steadily increasing, despite hurricane threats. More than 30 percent of Florida's total population is concentrated from Palm Beach southward into Miami-Dade. (Palm Beach County currently holds the distinction of being one of only four U.S. counties with a population of one million or more: in Palm Beach, 1.1 million were counted during the last census.)

Bill and Mary Burnham's *The Complete Florida Beach Guide* will show you how to legally bypass seemingly impenetrable barriers of condominiums and hotels guarding the beaches. The Florida Constitution guarantees public access to every beach below the high tide mark. So, like those who enjoy a bird's-eye view from their oceanfront properties, you have the right to stroll the surf line, look for shells, or take a refreshing swim.

The Complete Florida Beach Guide will direct you to the entry point for every Florida beach, from gorgeous Perdido Key State Park to the seven remote islands of Dry Tortugas National Park. This is an invaluable resource for both locals and tourists, for anyone of any age who has ever enjoyed playing in a sandbox. If you think you've found your favorite beach, you probably haven't looked far enough. Enjoy the discovery! Bill and Mary Burnham certainly did.

M. Timothy O'Keefe
Series Editor

Preface

Welcome to Florida's Beaches

Walking on Naples Beach.

A pelican armada glides just feet above the ocean in tight formation. Offshore, dolphins break the emerald green water in graceful arcs. The cries of seagulls blend with the delighted shrieks of children dodging the surf.

Here in the Sunshine State, beachgoing is an art form—and with literally hundreds of public beaches from which to choose, there's one for every temperament. Whether you yearn to walk a deserted barrier island or strut your stuff in South Beach, this brand new guide lists every coastal beach—and, yes, we visited every single one.

We tell you how the beaches were formed, from the white crystalline sand of the Gulf of Mexico to coarse coral sand of the Keys, and whether there are lifeguards, whether the beach is handicapped accessible, and whether pets are allowed. Directions, parking conditions, hours, facilities (restrooms, showers, picnic shelters), fees, and contact information are provided.

When you get bored with lying on the sand, your beach guide tells you what else you can do, no matter which beach you're enjoying: fishing, boating, volleyball, nature trails, camping, beach driving, or horseback riding. We even tell you whether you'll have good luck looking for shells.

We've kayaked to remote offshore islands in search of wild beach experiences, sometimes setting up our tent at night. Even in urban areas, you might encounter native plants and wildlife, and we tell you where.

As for the human variety of wildlife, we tell you whether this is a Spring Break party beach, a family beach, or a clothing-optional beach.

The guide is designed for both visitors and locals. We've been to the hot tourist spots, and we've also found lesser-known accesses where the crowds thin out.

Just steps off the sand, fun watering holes and eateries, nature centers, and preserves can also be found, and they're all listed here.

We hope you'll have as much fun reading this as we had doing the research. Wear sunscreen, bring plenty of water, and always remember to leave no trace.

Acknowledgments

Thanks to all the local parks departments and lifeguards who provided information on amenities at each park, and to all the visitor and convention bureaus who helped us with research and lodging.

We are especially indebted to Florida State Parks personnel (Carlene Barrett, in particular) who arranged for us to camp at or near the finest beaches in the country.

Many thanks to our editors at the University Press of Florida, John Byram and Michele Fiyak-Burkley, series editor M. Timothy O'Keefe, our proofreader, Martha Steger, and our map maker, Bill Nelson.

Driving on the beach.

Icons

The following icons have been used to indicate which amenities are available at each beach:

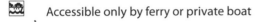 Accessible only by ferry or private boat

   Handicapped accessible

$ Fee charged

Restrooms

Showers

Swimming

No swimming allowed

Lifeguards

Concession

Playground

Boat ramp

Fishing

Camping

Good shelling

Beach driving allowed

Horseback riding allowed

Pets allowed

No pets

Introduction

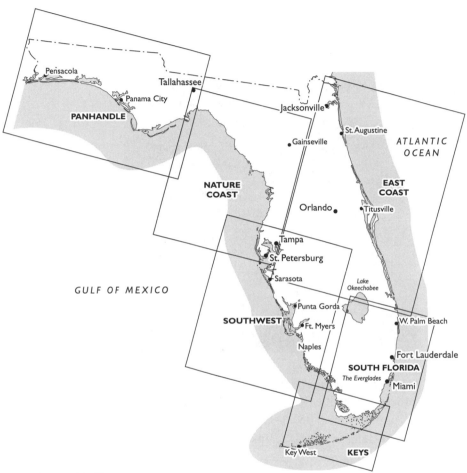

Leave No Trace

It should go without saying that you should take from the beach what you bring. We like to tuck a plastic grocery bag in a pocket so we can pick up a few extra pieces of trash. Please don't bring glass containers on the beach, and pick up after your pet, where pets are allowed.

The aftermath of a hurricane clearly shows that where a healthy dune system exists, damage to property is minimized. The seemingly

Remember to
leave no trace.

innocent act of climbing up or walking on top of a dune starts a long
process of decline that can lead to erosion and eventually blowouts.
It's important that people stay off the dunes and beach vegetation. In
fact, picking sea oats is against state law and getting caught results in
a stiff fine.

Digging in the sand is a primal pleasure enjoyed by all ages, but
please avoid digging during sea turtle nesting season, March through
October, and don't allow your pet to dig either. You might disturb the
eggs. During this season, lights should be kept dim along beaches
where sea turtles nest.

Bringing home a special shell is as integral a beach experience
as sunbathing. All we ask is to remember: it's quality, not quantity.
Please ask children, especially, to limit their haul. A valuable lesson

can be learned by asking that, for every shell, a child find and remove a piece of trash.

Primitive camping requires knowledge of practices to minimize human impact on the water and on fragile coastal habitats. Please visit Leave No Trace, www.lnt.org, the Web site of the Center for Outdoor Ethics, for proper practices on a range of subjects, from washing dishes to managing human waste.

The Beach Belongs to Us All

Below the high tide line, that is. The Florida State Constitution grants: "the title to lands under navigable waters, within the boundaries of the state, which have not been alienated, including beaches below mean high water lines, is held by the state, by virtue of its sovereignty, in trust for all the people."

So, clearly, we can walk, swim, and play on any beach we want to, right? Not exactly. It's *getting* to the beach that's the hard part. In many of the most developed areas of Florida, hotels, condos, and large private communities have gobbled up all the land bordering the beach. In others, the local county or city has deemed access a priority, whether it's expansive public parks, or simply pedestrian paths through the high-rises. It varies tremendously by municipality, so if you're thwarted in one town, simply head up or down the coast to the next, and don't let anyone tell you to stay off a "private beach." It belongs to us all.

Beach Safety

There's been much ado about shark attacks of late, but your chances of drowning are exponentially greater. Follow these precautions when swimming:

1. Obey the colored flag if posted on the beach: red means to avoid any water contact; yellow cautions of strong currents or rough water; green means, go for a swim.
2. If you have children or are an unsure swimmer, choose a beach with a lifeguard.

3. Be aware of rip current danger. If you are caught in a rip current, relax and swim parallel to shore until you can ride incoming waves to land.
4. Do not swim in channels or in the passes between islands, where strong currents may overpower you.
5. Swim with a buddy, or at least have someone on shore keeping an eye out for you.
6. Always use a dive flag when snorkeling or diving (it's state law).
7. Do not swim in areas with boats or personal watercraft.

Sun and Heat

Unless there's a stand of that pesky nonnative species, the Australian pine, few Florida beaches offer shade. Some have concessions that rent umbrellas or cabanas. If not, bring your own, and don't forget sunscreen, sunglasses, a hat, and plenty of water.

Beach safety.

Avoid sunburn, wrinkles, and future skin cancers by using a high-SPF broad-spectrum sunscreen, preferably one that contains a physical barrier as well. New variations on the once-gunky zinc oxide are much more pleasant to use. Avoid exposure from 11 a.m. to 3 p.m., or at least wear lightweight clothing to cover up.

When venturing onto a wild beach, hike by the clock. Halve the amount of time you have and turn around at the halfway point. This will ensure you can get back before dark. Primitive campers should follow the Leave No Trace ethic (www. LNT.org), and bring at least one gallon of water per person per day.

> Ten times more fatalities from dog attacks than from shark attacks have been recorded. Drowning is by far the biggest risk at the beach. (According to the *International Shark Attack File*, maintained by the Florida Museum of Natural History, University of Florida.)

Sharks and Alligators

Attacks from these sharp-toothed creatures get a lot of sensational press, but let's put things into perspective. Over the past half century, about 30 fatalities have occurred in Florida from shark and alligator attacks combined; however, there have been hundreds of attacks resulting in injury. The best course is avoidance. Here are some tips for avoiding sharks:

1. Do not swim at twilight or after dark, which is feeding time for sharks.
2. Don't wear shiny jewelry or metallic bathing suits.
3. Don't swim if you are bleeding from a wound or menstruating.
4. Do swim in groups and don't go too far from shore.
5. Avoid sharp drop-offs and areas off sandbars, which are favorite hang-outs for sharks.

Of the hundreds of species of sharks, only a handful have been known to attack humans. The gray bull shark is fairly common in Florida and quite aggressive. But you're most likely to encounter the docile nurse shark, identifiable because it is the only shark that can sit on the bottom without moving. It's dark brown in color. No matter the species, it's safest to steer clear of all sharks, as any can bite.

The American alligator is Florida's official state reptile and is legally protected. In the course of hiking and paddling the entire coast of Florida, we rarely encountered 'gators in the wild. They don't like salt water and, frankly, they don't like humans or any prey that's bigger than they are. However, in populated areas, alligators become accustomed to humans and can become a nuisance and a danger. If you see an alligator posing a threat, contact authorities; do not try to divert it to another area or kill it. It is a violation of state law to feed alligators; this acclimates them to human contact, often leading to aggression.

Bottom line, sharks and alligators have been in Florida far, far longer than humans. Think of them as our living dinosaurs.

Alligator or Crocodile?

Alligators live in freshwater (although they can venture into salt water for brief periods and have been seen on beaches), and crocodiles live in salt water. There are fewer than 1,000 of the endangered American crocodile, which rarely venture out of the Everglades and the Florida Keys.

Hurricanes and Lightning

With today's minute-by-minute weather reporting, we're presuming everyone knows when a hurricane is coming and will act accordingly—that is, stay off the beach. (Of course, there's that recalcitrant breed of surfer, windsurfer, and kiteboarder who lives for an impending perfect storm.)

A much more common threat for beachgoers exists from lightning. Especially in summer, Florida thunderstorms rise up quickly, sometimes with only a few minutes' warning.

The National Lightning Safety Institute (www.lightningsafety

.com) advises avoiding water and open spaces during thunderstorms—places like the beach.

Let's say you hear boomers far off over the horizon, but you're still enjoying a fine sunny day at the beach. When do you have to scramble for shelter? Here's an easy rule of thumb: Count the seconds between the flash of light and the bang of thunder ("one-one-thousand, two-one-thousand . . ."). Five seconds means the storm is one mile away. If the time gets shorter between boomers, the storm is heading your way. If the time is 30 seconds or less, seek shelter in a substantial building, not under a picnic shelter or tree, which could fall on you. No shelter around? Seek ditches or low ground, clumps of shrubs or trees of uniform height, crouch down and say a few Hail Marys.

If you're going to be out on a remote beach for the day, and especially when boating or camping, consider investing in a handheld weather band radio. Not only will it give you very localized weather in any hazardous conditions, you can "may day" for help on channel 16 if you're lost or injured. The U.S. Coast Guard, marinas, commercial vessels, and most pleasure boaters monitor this channel.

> **Storm Damage**
>
> Hurricanes and tropical storms can wreak havoc on public beach accesses. Rest assured that for the most part, state and local authorities diligently repair boardwalks and facilities as soon as they can. Sometimes the permitting process is what takes the longest. If you find an access is closed, we hope you'll find another one nearby from the listings in the guide, and please write and tell us; we'd love your feedback (www.BurnhamInk.com).

Red Tide

Despite the name, it doesn't always turn the water red. It can appear perfectly normal, you may never know it's there, and it poses no problem for most beachgoers. Red tides occur most commonly on the gulf coast of Florida. An area may go for years without a bloom, and then experience a succession for no apparent reason. The higher-than-normal concentration of a microscopic alga, also know as an algal bloom, produces a toxin that can kill all sea life, producing a foul odor, and you may see dozens of dead fish washed up on the beach during a bloom. There may be a ban on eating mollusks (clams, oysters, and scallops), but it is okay to eat shrimp, crab, lobster and fish. The toxin becomes airborne and can cause coughing, sneezing, and watery eyes in some people. For this reason, people with severe or chronic respiratory conditions such as emphysema or asthma should avoid areas affected by red tide. Those with plant allergies may be more sensitive to the irritation and find a red tide area quite unpleasant. Others experience no effects at all.

Visit http://research.myfwc.com or 866-300-9399 for red tide conditions throughout the state. From outside Florida, call 727-552-2448.

Jellyfish and Stingrays

A sting from a jellyfish is typically an excruciating nuisance for about an hour. In such an instance, rinse the affected area with salt water (freshwater will only release more toxin), and then wash the area again with vinegar. However, if you are stung by the Portuguese man-of-war, characterized by a floating blue "bubble," you may need medical attention. The sting is very painful and can even cause death. The bubble is quite beautiful, and you may be tempted to get a closer look. But steer clear, its tentacles hang down and behind in the water for many feet; even when a Portuguese man-of-war is dead on the beach, its tentacles may still have venom.

Most Florida rays are harmless, but the stingray does have a barbed venomous tail that can cause pain and even death in the rare instance of a deep puncture to the chest, head, or artery. The shocking death of Crocodile Hunter Steve Irwin, who was stabbed in the heart by a stingray tail, shows that a fatal encounter, though rare, is possible. To avoid stepping on the barbed tail of a stingray, shuffle your feet along in the water rather than high-stepping. If you are jabbed, soak your foot in hot water for an hour to neutralize the venom. If the barb breaks off in your flesh, see a doctor to remove it and prevent infection.

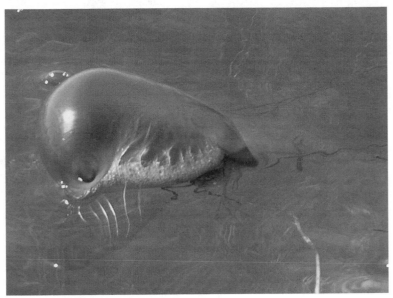

Portuguese man-of-war jellyfish.

The Nature of Florida's Beaches

Beachcombing

Walking on a ribbon of sand, picking up shells, beach glass, sea beans, and the like, has to be one of the best forms of slow-down therapy known to man. Florida's beaches are literally an outdoor classroom in sea life. In that line of washed-up seaweed, called the "wrack," you'll find evidence of all kinds of tiny creatures and plants. Look for the curlicue egg casings of the whelk, and the mermaid's purse, which harbors a tiny skate inside. Sea beans make their way on the Gulf Stream from South America. Look for the aptly named hamburger bean and the sea heart. You may see dead coral, sponges, worm shells, and snails washed up on the beach.

Conchology—the study of shells, not of the animals that once lived inside—is a fascinating endeavor, and Florida's beaches are a treasure trove. You may find giant cockles and mussels, sand dollars, and scallops of every hue from orange to black. Whelks of all sizes are common, but if you find a queen conch shell you're very lucky.

Fill a small bag or bucket, but leave some for the next beach-comber, and be sure no living sea creatures are inside the shells you take. The queen conch is protected by Florida state law.

Beach Wildlife

From a beach crawling with a sea of tiny fiddler crabs to a refuge for red wolves, Florida's beaches offer fascinating wildlife moments. We've watched hundreds of shorebirds feeding in the surf at dusk, dolphins rushing the shore fishing for mullet, and pelicans diving head-first into water from three stories high, and we've heard the telltale cry of the bald eagle.

Each beach season has its own story to tell. In spring, osprey nest in tall perches while young eagles test their wings. In summer, five kinds of sea turtles crawl up on Florida's beaches to lay their eggs. Fall brings migrations of waterfowl, shorebirds, tropical songbirds, mon-arch butterflies, and dragonflies. In winter, the giant, slow-moving,

Nature of Florida's
beaches, sand dollar.

Roseate spoonbill (by permission of the U.S. Fish and Wildlife Service).

endangered manatee makes its way to the warmer waters of coastal estuaries and shallow rivers.

Plants and Trees

In addition to being our first line of defense against erosion and storms, Florida's coastal dunes harbor an incredible diversity of plant life. Don't let the delicate blooming of woody goldenrod and golden asters fool you; every plant on the dune is adapted to withstand the harsh elements of wind, salt, and sun.

What may appear to be simply shrubs on the dunes are often full-sized slash pines and southern magnolias, their trunks covered with sand and only their tops protruding. Salt spray and wind shape live oaks and other trees into twisted forms.

Gently swaying stalks of sea oats are a familiar beach image, and you may think their oatlike panicles would look great in your dried arrangement at home. But sea oats are protected by state law because their extensive root systems are so vital to maintaining the structure of the dunes. Simply put, these plants bind sand and, by doing so, help build dunes. As the plants grow, they capture more windblown sand. Foot traffic is very destructive to sea oats, and picking them is illegal.

In addition to dunes, ecological communities of mangrove, pine forest, estuarine marsh, and coastal dune lakes characterize Florida's coast. Look for a park with a boardwalk trail through these habitats, with signs identifying the plants and trees.

Suggested Reading

The Nature of Florida's Beaches Including Sea Beans, Laughing Gulls and Mermaids' Purses, by Cathie Katz
Florida's Living Beaches: A Guide for the Curious Beachcomber, by Blair and Dawn Witherington

East Coast

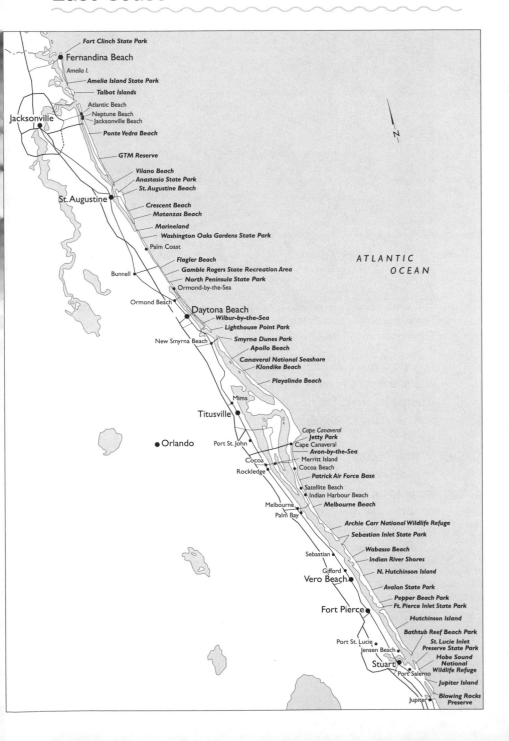

Family fun on Daytona Beach (by permission of the Daytona Beach Area Convention and Visitors Bureau).

Daytona, space shuttle launches, the oldest city in the nation, and one of the world's most important sea turtle nesting sites—these are landmarks along famous Route A1A, a local road that hopscotches barrier islands and helped to pioneer Florida's beach tourism industry.

It isn't all strip malls and high-rise condominiums. State parks, a national seashore, and wildlife refuges protect pockets of wild beachfront. From the Talbot Islands to Hobe Sound, modern beachcombers can visit these for a sense of what coastal Florida looked like before Europeans stepped ashore.

While development pressures along this section of Florida coastline are keen, the public access provided by local government has, with a few notable exceptions of exclusivity, ensured that Florida's beaches are open to all who care to visit. Even Jupiter Island, one of the wealthiest zip codes in America, has a free public beach.

Whether you seek the excitement of Daytona's Beach Street or the seclusion of Canaveral National Seashore's 12 miles of sand accessible only by foot, you'll find it on Florida's East Coast.

Amelia Island

John Sayles' film *Sunshine State*, which fictionalized the challenges to old Florida towns facing development, was filmed in the Victorian railroad town of Fernandina Beach and other spots on Amelia Island. A mile from the restored Olde Town find a gem of a state park and a five-mile public beach with generous public access, including notable efforts to create handicapped accessibility. The small town swells to 150,000 for the Isle of Eight Flags Shrimp Festival during the first weekend in May.

Fort Clinch State Park

Special features: Outdoor shower · Picnic shelters · Developed campground · Fishing pier · Beach fishing · Nature trails

Driving the three-mile entrance road through this park is like a meditation: ancient live oaks draped with Spanish moss and resurrection fern form a shady tunnel over the roadway, inspiring a sense

Fort Clinch has a long, wild beach for walking.

of calm and peace. The 1,120-acre state park, one of Florida's first, preserves the northern tip of Amelia Island. It is bordered by the Amelia River, Cumberland Sound (Georgia is straight across), and the Atlantic Ocean, and the entire shoreline is fringed with beaches. On the Atlantic side, a gorgeous, intact dune system stretches for nearly a mile along a usually uncrowded beach. Camp here among the dunes within earshot of the surf; for more shelter from wind and sun, use the shady River Area Campground near the Civil War fort. Go north of the jetty for twice as much beach overlooking the sound. Several nature trails and a mountain bike trail wind through a shady coastal hardwood hammock.

Details: The oceanside beach has a large paved parking lot, with a five-to-ten-minute walk on a level boardwalk to the beach and restrooms. Handicapped-accessible picnic tables with umbrellas line the way. This parking lot also gives access to a half-mile-long fishing pier.
Beach Length: 2.7 miles
Pets: Allowed on a leash in park and campground, but not on the beach.
Directions: From I-95 exit 373 (Fernandina/Callahan), go 16 miles east on A1A and turn right on Atlantic Avenue. It is 2 miles to the park entrance on left.
Hours: 8 a.m. to sunset; visitor center 9 a.m. to 5 p.m. daily.
Fee: $5 per vehicle (up to eight people)
Contact: 904-277-7274
www.floridastateparks.org/fortclinch

Fernandina Main Beach

Special features: Outdoor shower · Picnic shelters · Beach fishing

This expansive, sunny park has miniature golf, volleyball, and a waterslide. Parking is in three large paved lots at Atlantic Avenue and Trout and Dolphin streets. There's a handicapped-accessible beach

City of Fernandina main beach.

walkover and viewing area. Call ahead to reserve a beach wheelchair. North of here, there's pedestrian access only along Ocean Avenue for one mile. At N. Fletcher Avenue and E. 9th Street, North Beach Park has a small parking lot with a handicapped-accessible boardwalk to the beach, and outdoor showers, but no facilities. A sea oat replanting project has preserved a piece of the beach's wild character.

> **Prehistoric Treasure**
>
> When beachcombing for seashells on Amelia Island, keep an eye out for fossilized sharks' teeth. They're usually black or gray and range from the size of a pin to five inches long. They came from sharks of 10 to 20 million years ago. The largest was the megalodon shark, which grew to 65 feet, more than twice as long as our great white.

Beach Length: The park has 500 feet of beachfront, but you can walk north more than a mile to Fort Clinch State Park, or south for several miles.

Pets: Allowed on a leash.

Directions: From I-95 exit 373 (Fernandina/Callahan), go 16 miles east on A1A and turn right on Atlantic Avenue for 2.5 miles to the beach on N. Fletcher Avenue.

Hours: 8 a.m. to 9 p.m.

Fee: None

Contact: City of Fernandina Beach Parks and Recreation, 904-277-7350

www.fernandinabeachflorida.org

Seaside Park

Special features: Outdoor shower · Picnic shelters · Beach fishing

This small park offers free beach parking two miles south of Main Beach, at S. Fletcher Avenue (A1A) and Sadler Road. Restrooms are at nearby businesses, which include the Seaside Café and the Beach Store.

Beach Length: 4.5 miles total.

Pets: Allowed on a leash.

Hours: 8 a.m. to 9 p.m.

Fee: None

Contact: City of Fernandina Beach Parks and Recreation, 904-277-7350

www.fernandinabeachflorida.org

South Fernandina Beach Accesses

Special features: Beach fishing

The beach crowds thin out as you travel south on S. Fletcher Avenue (A1A) and condos become modest beach homes. Along 4.5 miles of beach are 46 numbered accesses, 21 of them with small parking areas. Matanzas Avenue in the southern part of the city is handicapped accessible. There are no facilities.

Beach Length: 4.5 miles.
Pets: Allowed on a leash.
Hours: 8 a.m. to 9 p.m.
Fee: None.
Contact: City of Fernandina Beach Parks and Recreation, 904-277-7350
www.fernandinabeachflorida.org

Beach Driving and Camping

Nassau County residents can drive on the beach in certain designated areas (not the entire length of the beach). Camping in small campers and tents is allowed, but for no more than 24 hours. Out-of-county residents must obtain a county permit to drive onto the beach, available at Hall's Beach Store on S. Fletcher Ave. (A1A) at Sadler Road, for $5 per day or $25 for the season. Four-wheel drive is strongly recommended. There is no beach driving allowed within Fernandina Beach city limits (904-548-4600, www.nassauclerk.org; Hall's Beach Store: 904-261-7007).

Peter's Point Beachfront Park

Special features: Outdoor shower · Indoor shower · Picnic shelters · Beach fishing · Primitive camping · Four-wheel drive recommended

Several Nassau County beaches offer a fun place to drive, ride horses, and even camp. This large, open park has plenty of parking, including one parking lot for horse trailers. County ordinance requires that horse trailers have a decal from the public works department. Vehicles and horses must stay off the dunes and out of swimming areas. RV parking is available for county residents only. Lifeguard on duty from May 1 through Labor Day.

Beach Length: The park contains 400 feet of beachfront; you can walk for miles in either direction and drive 0.5 mile north along the beach.
Pets: Allowed on a leash.
Directions: Located 1 mile south of Fernandina Beach city line on S. Fletcher Avenue (A1A), just north of the intersection of Amelia Island Parkway.
Hours: Open 24 hours.
Fee: None.
Contact: Nassau County Parks and Recreation, 904-548-4689 www.nassaucountyfl.com

Scott Road Beach Access

Special features: Beach fishing · Primitive camping · Four-wheel drive recommended

This large paved parking lot provides public access to Summer Beach, which is otherwise flanked by a private community and the Ritz-Carlton. There are no facilities, but a handicapped-accessible boardwalk and vehicle access are available. Lifeguard on duty from May 1 through Labor Day. See Beach Driving and Camping, above.

Beach Length: Vehicles restricted to about 400 feet of beach.
Pets: Allowed on a leash.
Directions: 0.5 mile south of S. Fletcher Avenue (A1A) on Amelia Island Parkway
Hours: Open 24 hours.
Fee: None.
Contact: Nassau County Parks and Recreation, 904-548-4689 www.nassaucountyfl.com

American Beach

Special features: Beach fishing · Four-wheel drive recommended

This historic African American resort community, a national historic district, remains a quiet holdout amid development encroaching from all sides. The struggle was fictionalized in the film *Sunshine State*. Founded in the 1930s by the Afro-American Insurance Company for its employees to freely enjoy the beach, it remained a popular black resort until the 1970s. Nassau County in partnership with the Trust for Public Land has proposed a $1 million historic park and the renovation of the former Rendezvous Club into a museum and cultural center, pending funding. Restrooms are at Burney Beachfront Park at the southern end of American Beach. There's pedestrian access at the end of Burney Road, and a vehicle ramp at the end of Lewis Street. Noncounty residents need a permit to drive on the beach, which is open for about a half mile south (see Beach Driving and Camping, above). Free parking along Gregg Street.

Beach Length: 0.5 mile.
Pets: Allowed on a leash.
Directions: 3.3 miles north of George Grady Bridge (the southern

tip of Amelia Island), go east on Burney Road 0.6 mile and turn left on Gregg Street, which parallels the beach.
Hours: Open 24 hours.
Fee: None.
Contact: Nassau County Parks and Recreation, 904-548-4689
www.nassaucountyfl.com

Burney Beachfront Park

Special features: Indoor shower · Outdoor shower · Picnic shelters ·
Beach fishing · Primitive camping · Four-wheel drive recommended

This large paved parking lot has a handicapped ramp to the beach. Camping is permitted no more than 24 hours; permit required for out-of-county residents (see Beach Driving and Camping, above). Lifeguard on duty from May 1 through Labor Day.

Beach Length: You can drive about 0.5 mile north to American Beach, or walk miles in either direction.
Pets: Allowed on a leash.
Directions: 3.3 miles north of George Grady Bridge (at the southern tip of Amelia Island), go east on Burney Road 0.6 mile and turn right into park.
Hours: Open 24 hours.
Fee: None.
Contact: Nassau County Parks and Recreation, 904-548-4689
www.nassaucountyfl.com

Amelia Island Plantation

This 1,350-acre secluded hideaway on the southern end of Amelia Island offers luxury hotel rooms, beach villas, golf, tennis, swimming pools, a spa, shopping and dining, and, of course, gorgeous beaches on the Atlantic. 888-261-6161, www.aipfl.com

South End Walkover

Special features: Beach fishing

This small, shady parking lot in the midst of Amelia Island Plantation is easy to miss. There are stairs over the dunes to the beach. No
facilities.

Beach Length: About 1.5 miles; you can go south to the tip of the
island, or north to the golf course. Stay on the beach, however, as this
is a private, gated community.
Pets: Allowed on a leash.
Directions: 1 mile north of George Grady Bridge (southern end of
island) on A1A.
Hours: Open 24 hours.
Fee: None.
Contact: Nassau County Parks and Recreation, 904-548-4689
www.nassaucountyfl.com

Amelia Island State Park

*Special features: Fishing pier · Beach fishing · Four-wheel drive rec-
ommended*

This 200-acre park at the southern tip of Amelia Island is not a great
swimming or sunning beach, but it is popular with beach drivers,
horseback riders, and fishermen. Fishing opportunities include the
surf and the handicapped-accessible George Grady Bridge fishing
pier. Steer clear of areas marked off for bird nesting, and when driving be aware that there may be very little beach at high tide. The sand
is soft, so four-wheel drive is required. There are two large paved
parking lots. The park is not staffed, and there are no facilities.

Beach Length: 1.6 mile.

Pets: Not allowed.

Directions: A1A on the southern tip of Amelia Island at the George Grady Bridge.

Hours: Open 24 hours.

Fee: $1 per person (honor box). No beach driving permit needed.

Contact: Talbot Islands Ranger Station, 904-251-2320
www.floridastateparks.org/ameliaisland

Kelly Seahorse Ranch offers four guided horseback rides daily, reservation by credit card required: 904-491-5166
www.kellyranchinc.com

Sea Islands vs. Barrier Islands

The Talbot islands more closely resemble the Georgia sea islands to the north than Florida's barrier islands. They're part of the same Pleistocene Ridge running from Charleston to Jacksonville deposited during the last ice age. When the water rose, it broke through the ridges, leaving only the highest land exposed as islands. The Talbot islands are growing and moving north to south as the ocean shifts the sand. Beach crowds are spread out here among several wonderful parks.

Jacksonville Area

Big Talbot Island State Park

$

Special features: Portable toilets only · Picnic shelters · Beach fishing ·
Nature trails

This is a fascinating wild beach, hammered by wind and erosion that has carved out a 20-foot bluff and "boneyard beach" littered with the skeletons of ancient live oak and cedar trees. These remains make beach walking a bit tough in places, especially at high tide, and swimming is prohibited because of underwater hazards. The bluff is a nice spot for picnicking. Drive one mile south of the picnic area to find a half-mile hiking trail to Blackrock Beach, an unusual Florida beach of black humus stone. Watch your step—the surface is slippery when wet. You can also reach Blackrock Beach by walking one mile south along the beach from the picnic area.

Details: The picnic area has a medium-sized dirt parking lot with a handicapped-accessible platform and benches. From there it's 0.2 mile north on a wide, graded trail to the beach. The trailhead for Blackrock Beach has a small roadside parking area.
Beach Length: 0.5 mile.
Directions: From I-95 north of Jacksonville, take exit 358A (Heckscher Drive/Route 105) and travel east for 22 miles. Note: At 15 miles, Route 105 becomes A1A at the St. Johns River ferry.
Pets: Allowed on the nature trails, but not on the beach.
Hours: 8 a.m. to sunset.
Fee: $2 honor box.
Contact: Talbot Islands Ranger Station, 904-251-2320
www.floridastateparks.org/bigtalbotisland

Little Talbot Island State Park

Special features: Outdoor shower · Picnic shelters · Beach fishing · Developed campground

This gem of a park has a long swath of wild Atlantic beach, nature trails, and kayaking in the marshes of Myrtle Creek. The campground is across A1A from beach facilities and has large, tree-shaded sites. For a scenic route and some exercise, hike the four-mile trail from the entrance station through a maritime hammock of ancient dunes out onto the beach, where a right (south) turn leads a mile and a quarter back to the main beach parking lot.

Details: A large paved parking lot serves beachgoers, with two sets of restrooms and a handicapped-accessible boardwalk over the dunes.

A handicapped ramp leads to the wind-driven, constantly changing, six-mile beach at Little Talbot Island State Park.

Free beach wheelchairs are available. Swimming is permitted only in the area accessible from this parking lot. There are no lifeguards. Swimming is dangerous at the southern end of the island because of strong currents. This park has the best recycling program we've seen at a state park, with bins for nearly everything at the entrance station.

Beach Length: Between Nassau Sound and Ft. George Inlet there are 5.5 to 6 miles of beach depending on storms and tides.

Pets: Allowed on the trails and in the campground, but not on the beach, shoreline, or boardwalks.

Directions: From I-95 north of Jacksonville, take exit 358A (Heckscher Drive/Route 105) and travel east for 17 miles. Note: At 15 miles, Route 105 becomes A1A at the St. Johns River ferry.

Hours: 8 a.m. to sunset.

Fee: $4 per vehicle (2 to 8 passengers); $3 for cars with 1 passenger; $1 for pedestrians and cyclists.

Contact: 904-251-2320
www.floridastateparks.org/littletalbotisland
Kayak Amelia for guided paddling tours and rentals: 888-30-KAYAK
www.kayakamelia.com

Huguenot Memorial Park

Special features: Outdoor shower · Picnic shelters · Good beach for small children · Beach fishing · Developed campground · Four-wheel drive recommended

This unusual park has camping in dunes on a beach at the mouth of the St. Johns River. You can drive on the Atlantic beach at low tide and also make a unique two-mile loop around a spit of sand. Beware of soft sand and rising tide.

Details: There's a shady picnic area near the entrance, a surfing area, and a family beach swim area on a lagoon sheltered from waves and beach driving. Beach wheelchairs available.

You can camp right on the beach at Huguenot Memorial Park.

Beach Length: Between 2 and 4 miles, fluctuating with tides and sand movement.

Pets: Allowed on a leash.

Directions: From I-95 north of Jacksonville, take exit 358A (Heckscher Drive/Route 105) and travel east for 16 miles. Note: At 15 miles, Route 105 becomes A1A at the St. Johns River ferry.

Hours: 8 a.m. to 6 p.m. (open until 8 p.m. April through October).

Fee: 50¢ per person.

Contact: City of Jacksonville Department of Parks and Recreation, 904-251-3335

www.coj.net

Kathryn Abbey Hanna Park

Special features: Indoor shower Outdoor shower · Picnic shelters · Beach fishing · Nature trails · Developed campground

This large, shady park has a long beach and many recreational opportunities. Hike or bike some of the 20 miles of nature trails, kayak on Hanna Park Lake, surf, fish, or swim in the Atlantic, then stay the night in the campground or one of the cozy cabins.

Beach Length: 1.5 mile.

Pets: Allowed on a leash.

Directions: From A1A in Mayport, go east 1 mile on Wonderwood Road to end.

Hours: 8 a.m. to sunset.

Fee: $3 per vehicle.

Contact: City of Jacksonville Department of Parks and Recreation, 904-249-4700

www.coj.net

Atlantic Beach

Special features: Outdoor shower · Beach fishing

This pleasant beach village of brick shops and restaurants has about two miles of white beach. Atlantic Boulevard is the center of activity, with free on-street parking if you can find it. There are private parking lots as well (fees usually $5). North of Atlantic Boulevard along Beach Avenue is a quiet residential neighborhood with streets numbered 1 through 19, most with pedestrian access and very limited on-street parking. All access points have outdoor showers, except for 16th Street, and are handicapped acces-

Atlantic Beach is a pleasant beach community with two miles of sand.

sible. Beach Avenue eventually becomes very narrow with many bikers and walkers. There are public restrooms at Bull Memorial Park, a short walk off the beach at 7th Street and Ocean Boulevard. The beach has a lifeguard from Memorial Day through Labor Day.

Beach Length: 2 miles.
Pets: Allowed on a leash.
Directions: From Jacksonville, take Arlington Expressway to Atlantic Boulevard and go to the end, a total of about 10 miles.
Hours: Open 24 hours.
Fee: None.
Contact: Atlantic Beach Recreation Department, 904-247-5828
www.ci.atlantic-beach.fl.us

Neptune Beach

Special features: Beach fishing

There are restaurants and shops at Town Center on Atlantic Boulevard, the dividing line between Neptune Beach and Atlantic Beach. This is primarily a residential community, with no public restrooms or beach parking lots. Along the beach, Strand Street can be driven only north to south, with many speed bumps to discourage cruising. There are pedestrian accesses at nearly every street ending, and free on-street parking where you can find it. The best parking is on Atlantic and Florida boulevards. There's handicapped parking at Atlantic Boulevard and at Hopkins, Davis, and Lemon streets.

Beach Length: 0.5 mile.
Pets: Allowed on a leash, but only between 5 p.m. and 9 a.m.
Directions: On A1A just north of Jacksonville Beach, from Atlantic Boulevard south to 20th Avenue.
Hours: Open 24 hours.
Fee: None.
Contact: Neptune Beach Public Works Department, 904-270-2423
www.ci.neptune-beach.fl.us

Jacksonville Beach

Special features: Outdoor shower · Fishing pier · Beach fishing

First Street runs along the ocean with an unobstructed view of the wide, white beach. Beach Boulevard is the hub of activity, with numbered avenues running both north and south from here. There's a one-mile boardwalk with public restrooms at 2nd, 5th, and 19th avenues North, and free, paved parking lots at most avenues between 20th Avenue North and 16th Avenue South. There's a handicapped-accessible 1,300-foot fishing pier with restrooms at North 1st Street (open 6 a.m. to 10 p.m., 904-241-1515), and large public parking lots between North 3rd and 4th avenues. The beach has a lifeguard year-round.

Handicapped access: There are ramps to the beach at 5th Avenue North and 6th Avenue South, and at the boardwalk at Beach Boulevard and 1st Street. Beach wheelchairs are available at the lifeguard station (904-249-9141 or 904-247-6236).

Jacksonville Beach has a 1,300-foot fishing pier, handicapped accessible.

Beach Length: 2 miles.
Pets: Allowed on a leash 5 p.m. to 9 a.m.
Directions: From Jacksonville, take SR 228/Hart Bridge Expressway East to Beach Boulevard, which ends at the beach. Total: about 17 miles.
Hours: Dawn to dusk.
Fee: None.
Contact: Jacksonville Beach Recreation Department, 904-247-6236 www.jacksonvillebeach.org

Oceanfront Park

Special features: Portable toilets only · Picnic shelters · Beach fishing

Jacksonville Beach's two-acre oceanfront park on First Street South between 5th and 6th avenues South has volleyball, a handicapped-accessible dune walkover, and beautiful landscaping. A bronze statue of a boy riding a dolphin symbolizes the city's dedication to preserving public beach access (although it's not such a great model for interaction with sea mammals!). The beach has a lifeguard on duty year-round.

Beach Length: The park has 300 feet of beachfront, with access to 2 miles of beach.
Pets: Allowed on a leash 5 p.m. to 9 a.m.
Directions: From Jacksonville, take SR 228/Hart Bridge Expressway East to Beach Boulevard, which ends at the beach. Turn right on First Street South and go 5 blocks to the park. Total: about 18 miles.
Hours: Dawn to dusk.
Fee: None.
Contact: Jacksonville Beach Recreation Department, 904-247-6236 www.jacksonvillebeach.org

Ponte Vedra–Vilano Beaches

Mickler's Landing Beach

Special features: Outdoor shower · Beach fishing

This very popular park has a large paved parking lot that fills quickly on nice days. A long boardwalk ramp leads to the beach, with one step down at the end. Orange-pink coquina sand is visible on the dunes, while the beach sand has a fine, almost ashy consistency.

Beach Length: 500 feet.
Pets: Allowed on a leash.
Directions: 4 miles south of Ponte Vedra Beach on Route 203; 0.2 mile north of intersection with A1A.
Hours: Open 24 hours except during sea turtle nesting season, May 15 to Oct. 15, when the beach is closed from 10 p.m. to 5 a.m.
Fee: None.
Contact: St. Johns County Division of Beach Management, 904-209-0336
www.co.st-johns.fl.us/BCC/Parks_1_Recreation/Beaches.aspx

Guana-Tolomato-Matanzas National Estuarine Research Reserve (formerly Guana River State Park)

Special features: Portable toilets only · Beach fishing · Nature trails

Travel south of Mickler's Landing on A1A and enjoy the drive to a pristine beach without interruption by development. The reserve's spectacular new Environmental Education Center opened in 2005 and its top-notch displays showcase the natural environment and animals found in this 55,000-acre reserve. Much of the reserve is located offshore, preserving wetland, marsh, ocean, and the northernmost mangrove habitat on the East Coast. The center is 7.5 miles north of Vilano Beach, just off A1A on Guana River Road. It is open daily, 9 a.m. to 4 p.m.

Details: Within the preserve are three beach access points. The large paved parking lots are located on the west side of A1A, so be alert crossing A1A to the dune walkovers. There are no facilities other than portable toilets, and payment for parking is made in honor boxes. The South Beach Access is handicapped accessible.
Beach Length: 4 miles.
Pets: Allowed on the hiking trails, but not on the beach.
Directions: North Beach Access is 3.2 miles south of Route 203 on A1A; Middle Beach Access is 2.3 miles further south; South Beach Access is another mile south of that (and 11 miles north of Vilano Beach).
Hours: 8 a.m. to sunset.
Fee: $3 per vehicle; $1 for pedestrians and bicyclists.
Contact: 904-823-4500
http://nerrs.noaa.gov/GTM/welcome.html

Usina Beach

Special features: Portable toilets only · Beach fishing · Four-wheel drive recommended

Small parking lot with vehicle access to beach. Limited facilities. The vehicle access is not maintained, so four-wheel drive is a must. Located near The Reef Restaurant, offering oceanside dining.

Beach Length: 100 feet of access to miles of beach.
Pets: Allowed on a leash.
Directions: 2.5 miles north of Vilano Beach on A1A, just north of Euclid Avenue.

Hours: Open 24 hours except during sea turtle nesting season, May 15 to Oct. 15, when the beach is closed from 10 p.m. to 5 a.m.
Fee: $5 beach driving permit (obtain at Vilano Beach). Free for pedestrians.
Contact: St. Johns County Division of Beach Management, 904-209-0336
www.co.st-johns.fl.us/BCC/Parks_1_Recreation/Beaches.aspx

North Beach Park

Special features: Picnic shelters · Beach fishing

A large sand parking lot and restrooms in an open air, shingled building are the only facilities. A pedestrian bridge with 33 steps going up crosses A1A to the beach.

Beach Length: 420 feet.
Pets: Allowed on a leash.
Directions: 1.7 miles north of Vilano Beach on A1A at Twenty-fourth Street on the west side of the road.
Hours: Open 24 hours except during sea turtle nesting season, May 15 to Oct. 15, when the beach is closed from 10 p.m. to 5 a.m.
Fee: None.
Contact: St. Johns County Division of Beach Management, 904-209-0336
www.co.st-johns.fl.us/BCC/Parks_1_Recreation/Beaches.aspx

Nease Beachfront Park

Special features: Picnic shelters · Beach fishing · Nature trails

This new park will feature beach access, restrooms, a picnic pavilion, and nature trail. A parking lot is on the land side of A1A with a crosswalk to beach.

Beach Length: Undetermined at this time.

Pets: Allowed on a leash.

Directions: Parking on the west side of A1A, 0.4 mile north of Vilano Beach.

Hours: Open 24 hours except during sea turtle nesting season, May 15 to Oct. 15, when the beach is closed from 10 p.m. to 5 a.m.

Fee: None.

Contact: St. Johns County Division of Beach Management, 904-209-0336

www.co.st-johns.fl.us/BCC/Parks_1_Recreation/Beaches.aspx

Surfside

Special features: Outdoor shower · Picnic shelters · Beach fishing · Four-wheel drive recommended

A century ago visitors arrived by yacht at the Surfside Dance Hall, which was located on this site until the 1970s. Today there are funky hippie beach cottages among the condos and large homes. Some of the cottages have art studios and secondhand shops inside. This park was a bit rough around the edges when we were there, but new restrooms, parking lot, and picnic pavilion are being built in 2007. You can drive onto the beach and go a third of a mile south to Vilano Beach. Because of erosion, the beach is quite narrow, so stay close to the dunes. Four-wheel drive is a must.

Beach Length: 160 feet of access to miles of beach.

Pets: Allowed on a leash.

Directions: On A1A, 0.3 mile north of Vilano Beach.

Hours: Open 24 hours except during sea turtle nesting season, May 15 to Oct. 15, when the beach is closed from 10 p.m. to 5 a.m.

Fee: $5 beach driving permit (obtain at Vilano Beach). Free for pedestrians.

Contact: St. Johns County Division of Beach Management, 904-209-0336

www.co.st-johns.fl.us/BCC/Parks_1_Recreation/Beaches.aspx

Vilano Beach

Special features: Outdoor shower · Picnic shelters · Beach fishing · Four-wheel drive recommended

This is a pleasant beach community with a public beach on the oceanside, and a boat ramp and fishing pier on the Intracoastal Waterway. Beach driving is allowed for 0.75 mile south of the access around the tip of the peninsula, and 0.3 mile north to Surfside. Four-wheel drive is a must on the soft coquina sand. There's a nice blue pavilion with picnic tables and a fun water spray feature for the kids. Small paved parking lot.

Beach Length: 1 mile.
Pets: Allowed on beach.
Directions: From St. Augustine, take A1A north across bridge 1.7 mile to the island. Turn right on Coastal Highway, go 0.1 mile to a T (Vilano Road). Turn right to public boat ramp and fishing pier, or left to reach the beach.
Hours: Open 24 hours except during sea turtle nesting season, May 15 to Oct. 15, when the beach is closed from 10 p.m. to 5 a.m.
Fee: $5 to drive on beach (permit required). Pedestrians free.
Contact: St. Johns County Division of Beach Management, 904-209-0336
www.co.st-johns.fl.us/BCC/Parks_1_Recreation/Beaches.aspx

St. Augustine Area

Anastasia State Park

Special features: Outdoor shower · Picnic shelters · Beach fishing · Nature trails · Developed campground

This is one the few Florida beaches that's actually getting larger. The process began when the Army Corps of Engineers moved St. Augustine Inlet in the 1940s. Sand has since filled in the historic inlet, making Conch Island a peninsula growing out from Anastasia Island like a bunion. The wide, hard-packed beach is great for walking, biking, jogging, bird watching, and surf fishing. Shelling gets better the farther you go toward the point. Currents and riptides can be dangerous, so swimmers should stick close to the area watched by a lifeguard behind Island Joe's Restaurant. Good surfing can be

Conch Island, off Anastasia State Park, continues to grow with drifting and deposited sand.

had the length of the beach, but Salt Run, once the historic inlet to St. Augustine, is now a quiet water lagoon. Its near shore waters are shallow and clear, ideal for kayaking, and the park has a launch and rental hut located here. Paddle past the beautiful lighthouse and moored sailboats and land on the northern tip of the island to have a wild beach all to yourself.

EAST COAST

Beach Length: 4.5 miles.
Pets: Allowed on a leash throughout the park, but not on the beach.
Directions: From US 1 in St. Augustine, turn east on SR 312, then north on A1A, 1.5 mile to the park entrance.
Hours: 8 a.m. to sundown.
Fee: $5 per vehicle; $3 with a single occupant.
Contact: 904-461-2033
www.floridastateparks.org/anastasia
Surf report: 904-824-9855
www.blueskysurfshop.com

St. Augustine Beach

*Special features: Outdoor shower · Picnic shelters · Beach fishing ·
Fishing pier · Four-wheel drive recommended*

This fun, hopping beach community offers another kind of "wild" beach compared with the neighboring state park. Enjoy beachside bars and eateries, surf shops, parasailing, and beach driving. The St. Johns County Fishing Pier is the main entry to the beach. There's a visitor center, plentiful free parking, a bocce court, and tackle shop ($2 to fish on the pier, 50¢ to sightsee). There are numerous access points at street ends with free on-street parking, and beach ramps for vehicles at A Street (northernmost, can only go south from here), Ocean Trace, Dondanville Road, Matanzas Avenue, Mary Street, and Crescent Beach. A 10 mph speed limit is strictly enforced and a $5 daily pass is required. Four-wheel drive may be required depending on conditions. There are portable toilets at most beach ramps. The

EAST COAST

beach has a lifeguard from the fishing pier south to the Ft. Matanzas access, Memorial Day through Labor Day.

Beach Length: 2 miles.
Pets: Allowed on a leash.
Directions: 4 miles south of St. Augustine on A1A Beach Boulevard, a business spur off A1A.
Hours: Open 24 hours except during sea turtle nesting season, May 15 to Oct. 15, when the gates are locked from 10 p.m. to 5 a.m.
Fee: None; $5 to drive on beach (obtain permit at fishing pier).
Contact: St. Johns County Division of Beach Management, 904-209-0336
www.co.st-johns.fl.us/BCC/Parks_1_Recreation/Beaches.aspx

St. Augustine

This city's settlement by Spain in 1565 preceded James-town, Virginia, by nearly a half century. Take a break from the beach to explore America's oldest tourist destination on foot (www.visitoldcity.com).

Frank Butler Park East

Special features: Picnic shelters · Beach fishing · Four-wheel drive recommended

The free parking lot in Crescent Beach has a long boardwalk with stairs over the dunes. Across A1A, Frank Butler Park West has a boat ramp on the Intracoastal Waterway. A vehicle ramp to the beach is located just north of the park at Minnie Street.

Beach Length: 500 feet.
Pets: Allowed on a leash.

Directions: On A1A 1 mile north of Crescent Beach, between Minnie and Dune streets.
Hours: Open 24 hours except during sea turtle nesting season, May 15 to Oct. 15, when the gates are locked from 10 p.m. to 5 a.m.
Fee: None; $5 to drive on beach (obtain permit at St. Johns County Fishing Pier).
Contact: St. Johns County Division of Beach Management, 904-209-0336
www.co.st-johns.fl.us/BCC/Parks_1_Recreation/Beaches.aspx

Crescent Beach Park

Special features: Outdoor shower · Beach fishing · Four-wheel drive recommended

There's a free parking lot with vehicle access to beach. Dine outside for lunch or dinner with a view of the ocean at South Beach Grill.

Beach Length: 800 feet.
Pets: Allowed on a leash.
Directions: On A1A, just south of its intersection with Route 206.
Hours: Open 24 hours except during sea turtle nesting season, May 15 to Oct. 15, when the gates are locked from 10 p.m. to 5 a.m.
Fee: None; $5 to drive on beach (obtain permit at St. Johns County Fishing Pier).
Contact: St. Johns County Division of Beach Management, 904-209-0336
www.co.st-johns.fl.us/BCC/Parks_1_Recreation/Beaches.aspx

EAST COAST

Matanzas Inlet is popular for surf fishing.

Matanzas Beach

Special features: Portable toilets only · Beach fishing · Four-wheel drive recommended

Use the free parking lot, or drive onto the beach (four-wheel drive highly recommended). There's only a portable toilet, but a quarter mile north on the west side of A1A, Ft. Matanzas National Monument has restrooms, a visitor center, and free boat tours out to the island fort. At Matanzas Inlet, there are free beach accesses with limited parking on both sides of the highway.

Beach Length: 3 miles.
Pets: Allowed on a leash.
Directions: Just north of Matanzas Inlet.
Hours: 5 a.m. to 10 p.m.
Fee: $5 to drive on beach.
Contact: St. Johns County Division of Beach Management, 904-209-0336
www.co.st-johns.fl.us/BCC/Parks_1_Recreation/Beaches.aspx

Flagler Beach Area

River to Sea Preserve

*Special features: Outdoor shower · Fishing jetty · Beach fishing ·
Nature trails*

This 90-acre preserve offers nature trails, fishing on the jetties, and a canoe/kayak launch on the Intracoastal Waterway. The handicapped-accessible boardwalk overlook has stairs down to the beach, where you'll find some coquina rock formations. There's a large paved parking lot at the beach.

Beach Length: 1 mile.
Pets: Allowed on a leash.
Directions: On both sides of A1A in Marineland. Beach access is immediately south of the Marineland Aquarium.
Hours: Dawn to 11 p.m.
Fee: None.
Contact: Flagler County Parks and Recreation, 386-437-7490
www.flaglerparks.com/riversea/preserve.htm

> Beach driving was banned in Flagler County on December 21, 2004. Try biking instead. A 19-mile path runs from River to Sea Preserve in Marineland southward to the Volusia County line. It follows A1A with unobstructed views of the ocean.

Washington Oaks Gardens State Park

 $

Special features: Picnic shelters · Beach fishing · Nature trails

The 425-acre park runs from the ocean to the Matanzas River. The beach features one of the best examples of coquina rock outcrops, which are ancient shells bound together to form a hard rock. Here, relentless waves form blowholes and fantastic formations in the bedrock. Because of the rock hazard, swimming is not permitted, but surf fishing is popular.

Coquina rock formations create tidal pools at Washington Oaks Gardens State Park.

Tidal pools at Washington Oaks Gardens State Park harbor myriad organisms.

Details: The oceanside entrance has a portable toilet only. There's handicapped access to an overlook, but not to the beach. Across A1A, the main park has full facilities, beautiful gardens, and nature trails.
Beach Length: 2,000 feet.
Pets: Allowed in the picnic area and on trails, but not on the beach or in the gardens.
Directions: 2 miles south of Marineland on A1A.
Hours: 8 a.m. to sunset.
Fee: $4 per vehicle, $3 for single occupant; $1 for pedestrians and cyclists; honor box
Contact: 386-446-6780
www.floridastateparks.org/washingtonoaks

Malacompra County Park

Special features: Beach fishing · Nature trails

This quiet park has a small parking lot where we saw a gopher tortoise ambling across the road. There's a playground at nearby Hammock Community Center.

Beach Length: The access point is perhaps 50 feet wide, but leads to miles of beach.
Pets: Allowed on a leash.
Directions: Off A1A at the end of Malacompra Road in Hammock.
Hours: Dawn to 11 p.m.
Fee: None.
Contact: Flagler County Parks and Recreation, 386-437-7490
www.flaglerparks.com/recreation/beach.htm

Old Salt Road Park

Special features: Outdoor shower · Beach fishing

A small parking lot nestled between the private property of Ocean Hammock Lodge Golf and Swim Club.

Beach Length: Narrow access to many miles of beach.
Pets: Allowed on a leash.
Directions: Off A1A at the end of 16th Street in Hammock.
Hours: Dawn to 11 p.m.
Fee: None.
Contact: Flagler County Parks and Recreation, 386-437-7490
www.flaglerparks.com/recreation/beach.htm

Jungle Hut Road Park

Special features: Outdoor shower · Beach fishing

The small free parking lot is bounded by private communities.

Beach Length: 100-foot access to miles of beach.
Pets: Allowed on a leash.
Directions: Off A1A at the end of Jungle Hut Road in Hammock.
Hours: Dawn to 11 p.m.
Fee: None.
Contact: Flagler County Parks and Recreation, 386-437-7490
www.flaglerparks.com/recreation/beach.htm

Varn Beach Park

Special features: Outdoor shower · Beach fishing

Small free parking lot has a handicapped-accessible boardwalk over healthy dunes covered with saw palmettos and other native vegetation. Surf fishing is very popular here. At the southern end of Beverly Beach find some free on-street parking with stairs down to the beach, but no facilities.

Beach Length: 500-foot access to miles of beach.
Pets: Allowed on a leash.
Directions: On A1A in Beverly Beach.
Hours: Dawn to 11 p.m.
Fee: None.
Contact: Flagler County Parks and Recreation, 386-437-7490
www.flaglerparks.com/recreation/beach.htm

EAST COAST

Flagler Beach

Special features: Picnic shelters · Fishing pier · Beach Fishing

Outside the busy town center, this is a quiet beach community with no development on the oceanside, making for a nice view as you drive along A1A or walk the beautiful six miles of beach. There are lifeguards from 7th Street North to 7th Street South. Below 10th Street South, the beach gets quite narrow at high tide and a seawall has been built. The orange coquina sand is a bit coarse on bare feet (good exfoliation!) but great for shelling.

Details: At the intersection of Route 100 (Moody Boulevard) and A1A, find free on-street parking, seafood restaurants, and a fishing pier ($6 to fish, $1.50 to walk out). There's a sand ramp for handicapped access just north of the fishing pier. Call 386-517-2436 to reserve a beach wheelchair. There are many pedestrian accesses along A1A via stairs, but only a few have parking.

Beach Length: 6 miles.

Pets: Prohibited between 10th Street North and 10th Street South. Beyond those areas, they must be on a leash.

Directions: From I-95 exit 284, take SR 100 east 4 miles to the beach.

Hours: Open 24 hours (lifeguard on duty 9 a.m. to 5 p.m.).

Fee: None.

Contact: City of Flagler Beach, Beach Services, 386-517-2031 www.cityofflaglerbeach.com

Gamble Rogers Memorial State Recreation Area

Special features: Outdoor shower · Picnic shelters · Beach fishing · Nature trails · Developed campground

The park is on both sides of A1A, with a small parking area, restrooms, and campground on a steep bluff overlooking the beach. There's a handicapped ramp and beach wheelchairs are available. On the other side of the highway, the park has nature trails, a boat ramp, and kayaking on the Intracoastal Waterway (rentals: 386-561-8509). South of here there's no development at all for several miles on either side of A1A; it's all state park land.

Beach Length: 2,000 feet.
Pets: Allowed in the campground, but not on the beach.
Directions: 3 miles south of Flagler Beach, on A1A.
Hours: 8 a.m. to sunset.
Fee: $4 per vehicle (honor box at beach).
Contact: 386-517-2086
www.floridastateparks.org/gamblerogers

Daytona Beach Area

North Peninsula State Park

Special features: Picnic shelters · Beach fishing · Nature trails

This park provides access to a long wild beach that's great for bird watching and surf fishing. There's a small parking area at the beach, but no facilities. Turn west on Highbridge Road and go 0.2 mile to reach Smith's Creek Landing, which has restrooms, picnic area, kayak launch, and nature trail through a coastal strand habitat.

Beach Length: 2 miles.
Pets: Not allowed.
Directions: 4 miles south of Flagler Beach on A1A.
Hours: 8 a.m. to sunset.
Fee: None.
Contact: Gamble Rogers Memorial State Recreation Area, 386-517-2086
www.floridastateparks.org/northpeninsula

Bicentennial Park

Special features: Picnic shelters · Beach fishing · Nature trails

Located in the laid-back beach community of Ormond-By-The-Sea, most of this 40-acre park's facilities are on the west side of A1A, with beach access to the Atlantic.

Beach Length: 500 feet.
Pets: Not allowed.

Directions: On the west side of A1A, between Sandra and Rivocean drives in Ormond-By-The-Sea. Be careful crossing the highway.
Hours: Park open sunrise to sunset. The beach is open 24 hours.
Fee: None.
Contact: Volusia County Beach Services, 386-239-7873
www.volusia.org/beach/

Tom Renick Park

Special features: Outdoor shower · Picnic shelters · Beach fishing

Just north of this new park is Beach Patrol headquarters, which has free parking and a portable toilet. South of here, there's free parking and handicapped access at Standish Drive and Neptune Avenue.

Beach Length: 500 feet.
Pets: Not allowed.
Directions: At Rivershore Drive on A1A in Ormond-By-The-Sea, 5 miles north of Daytona Beach.
Hours: Sunrise to sunset; beach open 24 hours.
Fee: None.
Contact: Volusia County Beach Services, 386-239-7873
www.volusia.org/beach/

Ormond Beach

Special features: Outdoor shower · Beach fishing

This community has become an extension of Daytona Beach, with the good and the bad of that area: lots of places to stay, with spill-over crowds from events like Spring Break, Bike Week, and Speed Week. Three miles of beach have about a dozen pedestrian accesses with parking only at Harvard Drive. There are public restrooms at Cardinal and Harvard drives, Williams Avenue, and Riverview and Glenview boulevards. Beach driving is allowed south of Granada Boulevard.

Beach Length: 3 miles.
Pets: Not allowed.
Directions: Just north of Daytona Beach on A1A.
Hours: Open 24 hours.
Fee: None.
Contact: Volusia County Beach Services, 386-239-7873
www.volusia.org/beach/

Daytona Beach

Special features: Beach fishing · Fishing pier

From A1A, you can't see the beach for all the high-rise buildings, but you can drive on it. This tradition dates back a century to land-speed record-setting on the hard-packed sand. More recently, the hotels and businesses offering nonstop fun have made this a legendary Spring Break and motorcycle capital.

Beach Driving: Allowed from Ormond Beach in the north (Granada Boulevard) to Emilia Avenue in the south. No vehicles are allowed in the Main Street Pier area, between Seabreeze and International Speedway boulevards, and at Wilbur-By-The-Sea, a natural beach management zone. Obey the 10 mph speed limit and watch out for pedestrians and wildlife. Park seaward of the conservation area (marked with posts) either facing the dunes or facing the sea. At high tide, sections may be too narrow to drive on, but normally the sand is hard packed so that four-wheel drive is not required.
Handicapped accessibility: Surf wheelchairs, complete with fishing pole holder, can go in soft sand even into the surf. They can be borrowed at most of the beach parks.

Aerial scene of Daytona Beach (by permission of the Daytona Beach Area Convention and Visitors Bureau).

Details: Public restrooms and off-beach parking at International Speedway Boulevard, Sunsplash Park (at Braddock Avenue), and Silver Beach Avenue. There's also some limited off-beach parking at most beach ramps, and on the beach for a $5 fee. Alcohol and glass containers are prohibited on the beach.

Beach Length: 5 miles.

Pets: Not allowed on beach.

Directions: From I-95 take exit 261 and follow US 92 east for 5 miles.

Hours: Open 24 hours for pedestrians and bicyclists. For vehicles: sunrise to sunset, Nov. 1 to April 30; 8 a.m. to 7 p.m. rest of year.

Fee: None for pedestrians and bicyclists. $5 per day for vehicles, Feb. 1 to Nov. 30; free rest of year. $20 season pass for county residents; $40 for nonresidents.

Contact: Volusia County Beach Services, 386-239-7873
www.volusia.org/beach/

Frank Rendon Park

Special features: Beach fishing · Outdoor shower · Picnic shelters

A 2003 addition to this park provided a new beach access in Daytona Beach Shores. There are also public restrooms at Simpson Avenue and at Dunlawton Avenue, which has handicapped access.

Beach Length: 5.5 miles.
Pets: Not allowed.
Directions: On A1A at 2705 S. Atlantic Avenue in Daytona Beach Shores.
Hours: Sunrise to sunset.
Fee: None.
Contact: Volusia County Beach Services, 386-239-7873
www.volusia.org/beach/

Wilbur-By-The-Sea

Special features: Portable toilets only · Beach fishing

The crowds thin out in this quiet beach community, where beach driving is prohibited. From Emilia Avenue south nearly to Lighthouse Point Park is a natural beach management area with no vehicles allowed on the beach. There's public parking at Demotte and Toronita avenues.

Beach Length: 2 miles.
Pets: Not allowed.
Directions: 6 miles south of Daytona Beach on A1A.
Hours: Open 24 hours.
Fee: None.
Contact: Volusia County Beach Services, 386-239-7873
www.volusia.org/beach/

Winterhaven Park

Special features: Picnic shelters · Beach fishing

This small public park provides free beach access. There's also public parking and access at Oceanview and Inlet Harbor.

Beach Length: 2.5 miles.
Pets: Not allowed.
Directions: On A1A in Ponce Inlet.
Hours: Sunrise to sunset.
Fee: None.
Contact: Volusia County Beach Services, 386-239-7873
www.volusia.org/beach/

Lighthouse Point Park

Special features: Outdoor shower · Picnic shelters · Good beach for small children · Fishing jetty · Beach fishing · Nature trails

This large, 55-acre park encompasses the southern tip of the peninsula along Ponce de Leon Inlet. There is a sheltered swimming beach along the inlet, about 100 yards from the parking lot, and a rocky, heavily eroded ocean beach, reached by a half-mile handicapped-accessible boardwalk. There is a free parking lot just outside the gate if you are willing to walk in. The beautiful red lighthouse is a landmark for miles. It is actually outside the park, with separate admission.

Beach Length: 0.7 mile.
Pets: Allowed on a leash on the inlet side beach, but not on the oceanside beach.
Directions: On A1A on the north end of Ponce de Leon Inlet.

Hours: 6 a.m. to 9 p.m.
Fee: $3.50 per vehicle
Contact: Volusia County Beach Services, 386-756-7488
www.volusia.org/parks/lighthouse.htm

Ponce de Leon Inlet lighthouse.

New Smyrna Beach Area

Smyrna Dunes Park

  $

*Special features: Outdoor shower · Picnic shelters · Beach fishing ·
Nature trails*

This large, lush park on the south side of Ponce de Leon Inlet benefits
from sand that drifts from Lighthouse Point Park across the inlet.
From the small paved parking lot, it's a good 15-minute walk on a
boardwalk to the ocean beach, a hike that eager surfers are glad to
brave for some of the best waves in the county. The 1.5-mile boardwalk makes a round trip through the park. The closer beach, on the
inlet, is handicapped accessible.

Beach Length: 1 mile.
Pets: Allowed on the inlet beach.
Directions: 2 miles north of Flagler Avenue in New Smyrna Beach,
the end of North Peninsula Avenue.
Hours: Sunrise to sunset.
Fee: $3.50 per vehicle.
Contact: Volusia County Beach Services, 386-424-2935
www.volusia.org/beach/

Beach Driving

Allowed from the jetty at the border of Smyrna Dunes Park
south to 27th Avenue in New Smyrna Beach. There are ramps
at Beachway, Crawford, Flagler, and 27th avenues. Fee: $5 per
day, annual passes available. Hours for driving: Sunrise to
sunset, Nov. 1 to April 30; 8 a.m. to 7 p.m. rest of year (because
of sea turtle nesting). Except during high tide or after a storm,
four-wheel drive is normally not required. Observe marked
natural areas off-limits to vehicles.

EAST COAST

Flagler Avenue Park

Special features: Outdoor shower · Beach fishing

Much of New Smyrna Beach's 10 miles of beach has been recently replenished with an off-white, silky sand, quite different from the coarse coquina sand to the south at Cape Canaveral. Flagler Avenue is the center of all things beachy, with shops and restaurants, a large sand parking lot, and restrooms. North of here on A1A, North Beach Community Park at Crawford Avenue has portable toilets, outdoor showers, and a nature trail. The southern terminus of vehicle access is at 27th Avenue Park, which has restrooms and a playground.

Beach Length: 300-foot park; 10 miles of beach.
Pets: Not allowed.
Hours: Beach open 24 hours; parks open sunrise to sunset.
Fee: None; $5 to drive on beach.
Contact: Volusia County Beach Services, 386-423-3373
www.volusia.org/beach/

Mary McLeod Bethune Beach Park

Special features: Outdoor shower · Picnic shelters · Beach fishing

This big open park has a large sand parking lot, three picnic pavilions, and Stan's Snack Shack. There's a boardwalk parallel to the beach with a handicapped ramp. Surf fishing is very popular here.

Beach Length: 3 miles.
Pets: Allowed in the park, but not on the beach.
Directions: From A1A in Bethune Beach, turn east on Kingfish Avenue, then right on S. Atlantic Avenue.
Hours: Sunrise to sunset.
Fee: None.
Contact: Volusia County Beach Services, 386-423-3373
www.volusia.org/beach/

EAST COAST

Canaveral National Seashore

Apollo Beach, Canaveral National Seashore

Special features: Beach fishing · Nature trails · Primitive camping

Dunes covered in saw palmetto turn red in the spring from blooms of coral bean. Thousands of sea turtles nest here from May through October. Outside of nesting season, you can ride horseback on the beach or even set up your tent at one of two beach campsites. Fall asleep to the sound of the Atlantic and wake to sunrise over the sea.

Details: Five beach parking lots, each about a mile apart, have portable toilets and outdoor showers. Lots #1A and 5 have handicapped ramps to the beach, and lot #1 has lifeguards Memorial Day through Labor Day. A boat ramp just past the entrance gives access to Mosquito Lagoon. The visitor center, a half mile past the guard shack, has exhibits and restrooms. Turtle Mound Archeological Site has a

Sunset at camp on Canaveral National Seashore.

quarter-mile boardwalk to the top of a mound built of discarded shells by generations of Timucuan Indians.

Primitive camping: Allowed Nov. 1 to April 15 only. Obtain a permit at the visitor's center; reservations are recommended. Be forewarned: there is no shade or shelter from wind on these beach campsites. You must carry all gear and water for a tenth of a mile to the first campsite.

Unofficial nude beach: Located south of the last parking lot. Official eyes are averted if naturists stay south of the last parking lot and eschew the lewd.

Beach Length: 7 miles.

Pets: Allowed on a leash on the lagoon side of the park, but not on beach.

Directions: 9 miles south of New Smyrna Beach on A1A.

Hours: 6 a.m. to 6 p.m. in winter; open until 8 p.m. in summer.

Fee: $3 per person.

Contact: 386-428-3384 ext. 10

www.nps.gov/cana

> Canaveral National Seashore is a national treasure, with 24 miles of federally protected barrier island beach. The pinkish orange coarse coquina sand is the perfect texture for nesting sea turtles, as many as 4,500 each summer. Apollo, Klondike, and Playalinda beaches provide an idyllic habitat for human beachgoers as well.

Klondike Beach, Canaveral National Seashore

Special features: Beach fishing

This section of Canaveral National Seashore is inaccessible by road, but it's possible to walk 12 miles of wild beach backcountry between Apollo and Playalinda beaches. A backcountry permit is required from either Apollo Beach or Playalinda Beach ranger stations. Camping is not allowed. There are no facilities and no freshwater.

Klondike Beach is 12 miles of road-less backcountry beach in Canaveral National Seashore.

Beach Length: 12 miles.

Pets: Not allowed.

Directions: From the north, use the national seashore's southern-most parking lot (#6) at Apollo Beach. From the south use the north-ernmost lot (#13) at Playalinda Beach.

Hours: 6 a.m. to 6 p.m. in winter; open until 8 p.m. in summer.

Fee: $3 per person entrance fee into the national seashore, plus $2 per person backcountry permit.

Contact: 321-867-4077

www.nps.gov/cana

Playalinda Beach, South District Canaveral National Seashore

Special features: Beach fishing · Fishing pier · Nature trails

The healthy dunes behind this wild beach are covered with sea oats and railroad vines. One beautiful Saturday morning, we passed one empty parking lot after another until we reached Lot #13, which was overflowing. We'd stumbled on the unofficial nude area, where a lively volleyball game was going on amid a sea of umbrellas. The county ordinance prohibiting nudity is not enforced here, as long as it's kept north of Lot #13. There's no shade at all, so if you're headed this way, apply sunscreen accordingly.

Details: There are 13 numbered parking lots with restrooms, and lifeguards at Lot #8 from Memorial Day through Labor Day; handicapped ramps at the Eddy Creek parking lot and Lot #8; a beach wheelchair is available on request. Eddy Creek boat ramp has restrooms, a fishing pier, and kayak launch to Mosquito Lagoon.
Beach Length: 4 miles.
Pets: Allowed on a leash on the lagoon side, but not on the beach.
Directions: From Titusville, take Route 406 (Garden St.) across the drawbridge to Merritt Island, veer right on Route 402 to its end.
Hours: 6 a.m. to 6 p.m.; 8 p.m. in summer.
Fee: $3 per person at guard station, several miles before the beach.
Contact: 321-867-4077
www.nps.gov/cana

Cape Canaveral–Cocoa Beach

Jetty Park

Special features: Outdoor shower · Fishing pier · Developed campground

This park in the midst of Port Canaveral is a great spot to watch huge cruise ships coming and going. The beach is wide and composed of gray, silken sand. The 1,200-foot fishing pier is handicapped accessible, and there is a ramp to the wide, 4.5-acre beach. The Jetty Pavilion has a snack bar and elevator-accessed observation deck where

Jetty Park is a great place to camp, fish, and watch ships coming and going from Port Canaveral.

you can eat overlooking the inlet and ocean. A nice paved exercise trail meanders through the shade of sea grape and other native trees to George King Boulevard. The campground fills quickly in season, but has a tent overflow area. No sites are on the water. The camp store has bait and tackle and some groceries.

Beach Length: 600 feet.

Pets: Allowed in designated campsites only, not on the beach or in any day-use areas.

Directions: From Route 1 in Cocoa, take FL 528 east over bridge to Merritt Island and another bridge across the Banana River (total 8 miles). Exit at George King Boulevard and Port Canaveral South Shore Terminals. Go 1.4 mile until the road ends at the park.

Hours: Open 24 hours.

Fee: $5 per vehicle.

Contact: 321-783-7111

www.portcanaveral.org/recreation/beaches.php

> The Beach Trolley bus line runs from Port Canaveral to South 13th Street in Cocoa Beach. Rides are $1.25, half-price for seniors, students, and handicapped. Daily service from 7 a.m. to 9 p.m., Sundays 8 a.m. to 5 p.m. You can bring your bikes and surfboards along. Operated by Space Coast Area Transit (SCAT): 321-633-1878, www.ridescat.com.

Cape Canaveral and Avon-by-the-Sea

Special features: Beach fishing

These quiet beach neighborhoods are nestled between commercial Cocoa Beach and the Port Canaveral ship terminals. Ridgewood Avenue runs along the ocean, parallel to and a few blocks east of the main drag, North Atlantic Avenue. You'll find small, free lots at the ends of most streets, which are named for U.S. presidents (they're in order, which makes this stretch a fun driving quiz). Most access points are handicapped accessible. The Beach Trolley runs along Ridgewood Avenue. The only public restrooms are at Cherie Down Park on Ridgewood Avenue (see below).

Beach Length: 2.3 miles.
Pets: Not allowed.
Directions: From N. Atlantic Avenue in Cape Canaveral, head east on Washington Avenue to Ridgewood Avenue.
Hours: 7 a.m. to sunset.
Fee: None.
Contact: Cape Canaveral Public Works Department, 321-868-1240

Cherie Down Park

Special features: Outdoor shower · Picnic shelters · Beach fishing

This quiet neighborhood park has a lifeguard on duty from April through Labor Day.

Beach Length: The park is 600 feet long; total beach is 2.3 miles.
Pets: Not allowed.
Directions: From N. Atlantic Avenue in Cape Canaveral, head east on Washington Avenue to Ridgewood Avenue.
Hours: Open 7 a.m. to 10 p.m.
Fee: None.
Contact: Brevard County Parks and Recreation, Beach Operations, 321-455-1380
www.Brevardparks.com

Cocoa Beach

Special features: Fishing pier · Beach fishing

The city of Cocoa Beach is six miles long on a mile-wide barrier island. It is the closest beach to Orlando, which is an hour west. North Cocoa Beach is a tad tacky, with "gentlemen's" clubs, adult video stores, and surf shops. South Cocoa Beach is more residential, with numerous public access points. This is a beachgoer's paradise and the surfing is legendary. All told, there are 40 beach access points with metered parking at street-ends off Ocean Beach Boulevard and Atlantic Avenue. The Cocoa Beach Pier at Meade Avenue and Ocean Beach Boulevard has metered parking and a paid parking lot ($7) adjacent to Oh Shucks Seafood Bar. South Cocoa Beach has metered parking lots at the ends of nearly all streets, from South 1st to South 15th. Four parks have public restrooms, listed below. Cocoa Beach Pier has a lifeguard from April through Labor Day. The beach trolley runs the length of the city.

Beach Length: 6 miles.
Pets: Not allowed.
Directions: From I-95, take SR 520 east for 10 miles.
Hours: Open 24 hours
Fee: 25¢ for 15 minutes, 6-hour limit.
Contact: Cocoa Beach Parks Department, 321-868-3252, 321-868-3274
www.cityofcocoabeach.com

EAST COAST

Alan Shepard Park

Special features: Outdoor shower · Picnic shelters · Beach fishing

Named for the astronaut, this five-acre park has large sandy parking lots, picnic pavilion, and Capt. J's Ocean Deck restaurant. Lifeguard on duty from Easter through Labor Day.

Beach Length: 1,000 feet of park.
Pets: Not allowed.
Directions: East end of SR 520 (Cocoa Beach Causeway) at E. Ocean Beach Boulevard.
Hours: Sunrise to 8 p.m.
Fee: $5, must pay at machine for gate to open.
Contact: Cocoa Beach Parks Department, 321-868-3258
www.cityofcocoabeach.com

Sidney Fischer Park

Special features: Picnic shelters · Beach fishing

This 10-acre park is open and grassy. It's named for a mayor of Cocoa Beach from 1956 to 1960. Lifeguard on duty from Easter through Labor Day.

Beach Length: 250 feet of park.
Pets: Not allowed.
Directions: 1 mile south of the SR 520 Bridge on A1A in Cocoa Beach.
Hours: Sunrise to 8 p.m.
Fee: $5; must pay at machine for gate to open.
Contact: Cocoa Beach Parks Department, 321-868-3258
www.cityofcocoabeach.com

Lori Wilson Park

Special features: Outdoor shower · Beach fishing · Nature trails

This lush, shaded park has a quarter-mile nature trail through a semitropical maritime hammock on a raised boardwalk that's handicapped accessible. There are two large paved parking lots, six boardwalks across the dunes (four are handicapped accessible), and picnic tables under the shade. Several handicapped-accessible picnic pavilions overlook the wide beach and ocean. Lifeguard on duty from Easter through Labor Day.

Beach Length: 1,200 feet of park.
Pets: Not allowed.
Directions: 1.4 mile south of SR 520 bridge on A1A in Cocoa Beach
Hours: 7 a.m. to sunset.
Fee: None.
Contact: Brevard County Parks and Recreation, 321-455-1380
www.brevardparks.com

Robert P. Murkshe Memorial Park

Special features: Outdoor shower · Picnic shelters · Beach fishing

This small park is very popular with surfers. There's a small, paved lot and stairs to a nice, wide beach. No lifeguards.

Beach Length: 350 feet of park.
Pets: Not allowed.
Directions: At South 16th Street on A1A, 2.1 miles south of Minuteman Causeway in Cocoa Beach.
Hours: 7 a.m. to sunset.
Fee: None.

EAST COAST

Contact: Brevard County Parks and Recreation, 321-455-1380
www.brevardparks.com

South of Cocoa Beach along A1A there's
free parking for a few cars at the ends
of Summer, Fern, Crescent Beach, and
S. 30th, then pedestrian accesses only
until you get to Patrick Air Force Base.

Patrick Air Force Base

Special features: Outdoor shower · Picnic shelters · Beach fishing

This open base has wonderful beach access along a refreshingly un-developed oceanfront. Free parking lots begin on A1A four miles north of SR 404 (Pineda Causeway), where there's a large paved lot with facilities. Then about every half mile there's a free lot (no fa-cilities), about six of them, all the way to the causeway. They're all open to the public. Just be sure not to park in a space marked for officers. Here's a beach rule we hadn't seen before, but it makes sense: "No kites or kite-boarding due to low-flying aircraft." Surfing is very popular here. No lifeguards.

Beach Length: 4 miles.
Pets: Not allowed.
Directions: From I-95 take Exit #191 and go south on Wickham Road for 6 miles, then east on Pineda Causeway for 4.5 miles to A1A.
Hours: Sunrise to sunset.
Fee: None.
Contact: Patrick AFB Outdoor Recreation, 321-494-9692
www.patrick.af.mil/

South Patrick Shores

Special features: Outdoor shower · Beach fishing

This residential beach community has two small beach parking lots on A1A. Seagull Park, a half mile south of Pineda Causeway (SR 404), has picnic tables. The local residents' association maintains a lot at Berkeley Street with a memorial to the Challenger shuttle mission, which exploded in air in 1986, killing seven astronauts. No facilities.

Beach Length: 2 miles.
Pets: Not allowed.
Directions: On A1A, at SE 1st Street and at Berkeley Street in South Patrick Shores.
Hours: 7 a.m. to sunset.
Fee: None.
Contact: Brevard County Parks and Recreation, Beach Operations, 321-255-4400
www.brevardparks.com

Melbourne Beach Area

Pelican Beach Park/Satellite Beach

Special features: Outdoor shower · Picnic shelters · Beach fishing

This pleasant park has a large paved lot, clubhouse, volleyball nets, picnic pavilion, and a handicapped-accessible ramp to the beach (which has rocks, so be careful swimming). There's also free beach parking (no facilities) at the ends of a half dozen streets between Grant in the north and Palmetto in the south. No facilities.

Beach Length: 2 miles.
Pets: Not allowed.
Directions: In Satellite Beach on A1A at Royal Palm Boulevard, 0.2 mile north of Desoto. Parkway to mainland.
Hours: Dawn to dusk.
Fee: None.
Contact: City of Satellite Beach Recreation, 321-773-6458 www.satellitebeach.org

Richard G. Edgeton Bicentennial Park

Special features: Portable toilets only · Outdoor shower · Picnic shelters · Beach fishing

Amid the condos along the beachfront of this small city of Indian Harbour Beach is a little oasis of green. The large paved lot provides free beach access and is frequented by surfers.

Beach Length: 1 mile.
Pets: Not allowed.

Directions: On A1A at Ocean Dunes Drive in Indian Harbour Beach.
Hours: 7 a.m. to 10 p.m.
Fee: None.
Contact: Indian Harbour Beach Parks & Recreation, 321-773-0552.

Millennium Park

Special features: Portable toilets only · Outdoor shower · Picnic shelters · Beach fishing

This small community park at the south end of Indian Harbour Beach has picnic shelters, playground, and beach access.

Beach Length: 1 mile.
Pets: Not allowed.
Directions: On A1A, 0.2 mile north of Eau Gallie Boulevard (SR 518) at Golden Beach Boulevard.
Hours: 7 a.m. to 10 p.m.
Fee: None.
Contact: Indian Harbour Beach Parks & Recreation, 321-773-0552.

Irene H. Canova Park

Special features: Outdoor shower · Picnic shelters · Beach fishing

Plans for this new 3.3-acre park include a community center, picnic pavilions, and playground.

Beach Length: N/A.
Pets: Not allowed.
Directions: On A1A, 0.1 mile north of the eastern end of Eau Gallie Boulevard (SR 518) in Canova Beach.

Hours: 7 a.m. to sunset.
Fee: None.
Contact: Brevard County Parks and Recreation, Beach Operations, 321-255-4400
www.brevardparks.com

Canova Beach Park

Special features: Outdoor shower · Picnic shelters · Beach fishing

This nine-acre community park has a small paved lot and three boardwalks over the dunes, one of which is handicapped accessible. There is also limited parking with no facilities at Wallace Avenue (just north the park) and another parking area 0.2 mile south of the park.

Beach Length: 500 feet.
Pets: Not allowed.
Directions: On A1A at the eastern end of Eau Gallie Boulevard (SR 518) in Canova Beach.
Hours: 7 a.m. to sunset.
Fee: None.
Contact: Brevard County Parks and Recreation, Beach Operations, 321-255-4400
www.brevardparks.com

Howard E. Futch Memorial Park/Paradise Beach

Special features: Outdoor shower · Picnic shelters · Beach fishing

This 12-acre regional park has volleyball courts, a large paved lot, and two handicapped-accessible dune walkways. Lifeguard on duty from April through Labor Day.

Beach Length: 800 feet.
Pets: Not allowed.
Directions: On A1A at Paradise Beach, 1 mile south of Eau Gallie Parkway
Hours: Dawn to dusk.
Fee: None.
Contact: Brevard County Parks and Recreation, Beach Operations, 321-255-4400
www.brevardparks.com

Sunrise Park

Special features: Picnic shelters · Beach fishing

The small paved lot with metered parking has no facilities, but this doesn't stop the surfers who frequent this beach. There's also metered street parking with dune boardwalks along Wavecrest Avenue from 4th to 11th streets.

Beach Length: 200 feet.
Pets: Not allowed.
Directions: On A1A at Watson Drive in Indialantic.
Hours: 6 a.m. to 9 p.m.
Fee: 25¢ for 20 minutes, up to 4 hours.
Contact: Indialantic Town Hall, 321-723-2242
www.indialantic.com

James H. Nance Park

Special features: Outdoor shower · Picnic shelters · Beach fishing

This park has a large metered parking lot and volleyball court.

Beach Length: 500 feet.
Pets: Not allowed.
Directions: On A1A between 3rd and 4th avenues in Indialantic.
Hours: 6 a.m. to 1:30 a.m.
Fee: 25¢ for 20 minutes, up to four hours.
Contact: Indialantic Town Hall, 321-723-2242
www.indialantic.com

Ocean Avenue Park

Special features: Picnic shelters · Outdoor shower · Beach fishing

This park has a small paved lot with volleyball court and handi-capped ramp to beach. No restrooms. South of here, there's limited parking in sand lots at the ends of numbered streets.

Beach Length: 0.5 mile.
Pets: Not allowed.
Directions: At east end of Ocean Avenue on A1A in Melbourne Beach.
Hours: 7 a.m. to sunset.
Fee: None.
Contact: Town of Melbourne Beach, 321-724-5860
www.melbournebeachfl.org

Spessard Holland North and South Beach Parks

Special features: Indoor shower · Outdoor shower · Picnic shelters · Beach fishing

Two large paved lots provide access to beachgoers and surfers. The south lot has a handicapped boardwalk to beach. Lifeguard on duty from April through Labor Day.

Beach Length: 0.7 mile

Pets: Not allowed.

Directions: 3 miles south of the Melbourne Causeway (US 192) on A1A in Melbourne Beach.

Hours: 7 a.m. to sunset.

Fee: None.

Contact: Brevard County Parks and Recreation, Beach Operations, 321-255-4400

www.brevardparks.com

Coconut Point Park

Special features: Outdoor shower · Picnic shelters · Beach fishing

Within Archie Carr National Wildlife Refuge, this 37-acre park is a splendid undeveloped stretch of sea grape and other native trees. There's a paved parking lot and handicapped ramp all the way to the beach. This is one of the East Coast's most important sea turtle nesting sites; the refuge is named for a conservation biologist who advocated tirelessly for their protection. Surfing and fishing are popular here.

Beach Length: 0.4 mile.

Pets: Not allowed.

Directions: 5.5 miles south of the Melbourne Causeway (US 192) on A1A in Melbourne Beach.

Hours: 7 a.m. to dusk.

Fee: None.

Contact: Brevard County Parks and Recreation, Beach Operations, 321-255-4400

www.brevardparks.com

EAST COAST

Juan Ponce de Leon Landing

Special features: Picnic shelters · Beach fishing · Nature trails

This new 25-acre park is a challenge to the history we've been taught for years. Some historians and county officials believe Ponce de Leon, the Spanish explorer credited with naming "La Florida," first landed here in 1513, not some 125 miles to the north near St. Augustine as is often claimed. A new state historic marker at this park proclaims as much. There's a medium-sized paved lot and a handicapped-accessible boardwalk to beach. It is within Archie Carr National Wildlife Refuge and directly across A1A from Coconut Point Sanctuary's hiking trail.

Beach Length: 500 feet.
Pets: Not allowed.
Directions: On A1A 6.2 miles south of Melbourne Causeway (US 192).
Hours: 7 a.m. to dusk.
Fee: None.
Contact: Brevard County Parks and Recreation, Beach Operations, 321-255-4400
www.brevardparks.com

Archie Carr National Wildlife Refuge extends from south of Melbourne Beach for 20 miles to Wabasso Beach. It is the most important nesting area for loggerhead sea turtles in the western hemisphere, with densities of up to 1,000 nests per mile. Several beach access points, maintained by local parks departments and Sebastian Inlet State Park, allow for swimming, walking, and fishing in the refuge. Please stay off dunes, use only established accesses, don't walk at night, and never approach a sea turtle or its nest. The season is May through September. Nighttime sea turtle watch programs are offered in June and July. Pets are not allowed in the refuge. Call 772-562-3909 ext. 275 for details, or visit www.fws.gov/archiecarr/

Bonsteel Park

Special features: Portable toilets only · Beach fishing

This beautiful park has a medium-sized dirt lot and handicapped-accessible dune walkway.

Beach Length: 600 feet.
Pets: Not allowed.
Directions: On A1A 2.4 miles north of Sebastian Inlet
Hours: 7 a.m. to sunset.
Fee: None.
Contact: Brevard County Parks & Recreation, 321-255-4400
www.brevardparks.com

Sebastian Inlet State Park

Special features: Outdoor shower · Picnic shelters · Beach fishing · Fishing jetty · Nature trails · Developed campground

This idyllic park straddles Sebastian Inlet with expansive ocean views along three miles of beach. Fishing and surfing are outstanding; the jetties are handicapped accessible. On the other side of the barrier island is boat access to the Indian River Lagoon with a marina, eco-tours, and kayaking. Rangers give guided sea turtle walks at night on the beach in June and July. The beach has a lifeguard on duty in summer only.

Beach Length: 1 mile north of inlet and 2 miles south of it.
Pets: Allowed in campground, but not on beach or on jetties.
Directions: From US 1 in Wabasso, go 2.6 miles east on CR 510 over the Indian River to A1A. Go north 7 miles to the park's entrance and

campground on the northern tip of Orchid Island. Cross the inlet and go 1 mile to the park's north entrance and marina.

Hours: Open 24 hours.

Fee: $5 per vehicle; $3 for single occupant; $1 pedestrians and bicyclists.

Contact: 321-984-4852

www.floridastateparks.org/sebastianinlet

Sebastian Inlet State Park South Beach Access

Special features: Outdoor shower · Beach fishing

Large paved parking within Sebastian Inlet State Park, providing access to the park's undeveloped, two-mile stretch of beach and Archie Carr National Wildlife Refuge. A handicapped-accessible boardwalk runs over healthy dunes.

Beach Length: 2 miles.

Pets: Not allowed.

Directions: On A1A on Orchid Island, 0.2 mile south of Sebastian Inlet State Park's southern entrance.

Hours: 8 a.m. to sunset.

Fee: None.

Contact: 321-984-4852

www.floridastateparks.org/sebastianinlet

In 1715 a hurricane wrecked a fleet of Spanish treasure ships off the Florida coast. McLarty Treasure Museum is on the site of the survivor's camp at the southern boundary of Sebastian Inlet State Park. 772-589-2147.

North Hutchinson Island

Amber Sands Beach Access

Special features: Beach fishing

This small county parking lot is within the Archie Carr National Wildlife Refuge. No facilities.

Beach Length: 100 feet of access to miles of beach.
Pets: Not allowed.
Directions: 4.4 miles north of Wabasso Causeway (CR 510) on A1A, on Orchid Island.
Hours: Sunrise to sunset.
Fee: None.
Contact: Indian River County Recreation Department, 772-567-8000 ext. 1732
www.ircrec.com

Treasure Shores Park

Special features: Outdoor shower · Picnic shelters · Beach fishing

This park is a real treasure, beautifully landscaped and virtually deserted the day we visited. Gorgeous vegetation of saw palmetto and sea oats covers the low dunes. The picnic area and playground are nestled under the shade of towering sabal palms. There are paved and sand handicapped-accessible routes to the beach.

Beach Length: 600 feet.
Pets: Not allowed.

Directions: 2.6 miles north of Wabasso Causeway (CR 510) on A1A, on Orchid Island.
Hours: Sunrise to sunset; lifeguard on duty 9:15 a.m. to 4:50 p.m.
Fee: None.
Contact: Indian River County Recreation Department, 772-567-8000 ext. 1732
www.ircrec.com

Golden Sands Beach Park

Special features: Outdoor shower · Picnic shelters

This pleasant park has a handicapped-accessible overlook with one large step down to the beach and then a steep drop down. No fishing or surfing allowed.

Beach Length: 500 feet.
Pets: Not allowed.
Directions: 1.4 mile north of Wabasso Causeway (CR 510) on A1A, on Orchid Island.
Hours: Sunrise to sunset.
Fee: None.
Contact: Indian River County Recreation Department, 772-567-8000 ext. 1732
www.ircrec.com

Wabasso Beach

Special features: Portable toilets only · Beach fishing

This access was devastated by hurricanes in 2005, but should be rebuilt by 2008. Try Boppy's Wabasso Beach Market and walk-up window for ice cream and snacks. Next door is the posh Disney's Vero Beach Resort.

Beach Length: 300-foot access to miles of beach.
Pets: Not allowed.
Directions: At end of Wabasso Causeway (CR 510), off A1A, on Orchid Island.
Hours: Sunrise to sunset.
Fee: None.
Contact: Indian River County Recreation Department, 772-567-8000 ext. 1732
www.ircrec.com

Wabasso Causeway Park

Picnic shelters · Good beach for small children · Beach fishing · Fishing pier

Two small islands along the causeway (CR 510) to Orchid Island have public beaches. The sheltered swimming area on the north side is a good place to let the little ones splash around, or to launch kayaks to explore Pelican Island National Wildlife Refuge. A boat ramp, fishing pier, and restrooms are on the south side of the highway.

Beach Length: 1,500 feet total for both beaches.
Pets: Not allowed.
Directions: From Wabasso, head east on the Wabasso Causeway (CR 510) to Orchid Island.
Hours: Sunrise to sunset.
Fee: None.
Contact: Indian River County Recreation Department, 772-567-8000 ext. 1732
www.ircrec.com

Sea Grape Trail Access

Special features: Beach fishing

There's a small paved lot with a turnaround, and a boardwalk with stairs down to the beach. No facilities.

Beach Length: 300 feet.
Pets: Not allowed.
Directions: 1.5 miles south of Wabasso Causeway (CR 510) on A1A on North Hutchinson Island.
Hours: Sunrise to sunset.
Fee: None.
Contact: Indian River County Recreation Department, 772-567-8000 ext. 1732
www.ircrec.com

Turtle Trail Beach Access

Special features: Beach fishing

This one is very similar to Sea Grape Trail access, with a sand path and stairs to the beach. From here south are large, private communities and beach clubs, with no commercial businesses.

Beach Length: 300 feet.
Pets: Not allowed.
Directions: 2.3 miles south of Wabasso Causeway (CR 510) on A1A on North Hutchinson Island.
Hours: Sunrise to sunset.
Fee: None.
Contact: Indian River County Recreation Department, 772-567-8000 ext. 1732
www.ircrec.com

EAST COAST

Tracking Station Park

Special features: Outdoor shower · Picnic shelters · Beach fishing

This quiet park, tucked at the end of 46th Place, has three small paved lots with two ramps over the dunes. Each has one step down to the secluded beach.

Beach Length: 1,200 feet.
Pets: Not allowed.
Directions: 1.8 mile north of Beachland Boulevard (Route 60) on A1A in Indian River Shores
Hours: Sunrise to sunset.
Fee: None.
Contact: Indian River County Recreation Department, 772-567-8000 ext. 1732
www.ircrec.com

Jaycee Park

Special features: Outdoor shower · Picnic shelters · Beach fishing

This park has two large parking lots, a large, shady picnic area, and the Seaside Grill, serving breakfast, sandwiches, and yummy Blue Bell ice cream. There's a handicapped-accessible ramp to the beach. The boardwalk continues from Jaycee Park for several blocks south, with on-street parking to just past Indian Lilac Road.

Beach Length: 0.3 mile
Pets: Not allowed.
Directions: Cross to North Hutchinson Island on Beachland Boulevard (Route 60), turn north on A1A, and go 1 mile to Mango Road.
Hours: Sunrise to sunset.

Jaycee Park in Vero Beach has a nice boardwalk for strolling, and the Seaside Grill.

Fee: None.
Contact: City of Vero Beach, 772-567-2144
www.covb.org

Sexton Beach

Special features: Beach fishing

This is the center of beach activity for Vero Beach. Seafood restaurants flank the parking lot. Nearby are expensive and trendy shops along Ocean Drive. There are no lifeguards and no public restrooms, except for those in area restaurants. There are stairs to the beach.

Beach Length: 130-foot access to miles of beach.
Pets: Not allowed.
Directions: At the east end of Beachland Boulevard (Route 60) along Ocean Drive in Vero Beach.
Hours: Sunrise to sunset.
Fee: Some parking spaces are free for 2 hours; others are metered.
Contact: City of Vero Beach, 772-567-2144
www.covb.org

Humiston Park

Special features: Outdoor shower · Beach fishing

This park has a grassy picnic area under palms, with stairs to the beach. There are restaurants and shops nearby, and the fun, casual Driftwood Resort is just north of the park, with live music, an open-air bar, and beach access.

Beach Length: 400 feet.
Pets: Not allowed.
Directions: East end of Easter Lily Lane off Ocean Drive in Vero Beach.
Hours: Sunrise to sunset.
Fee: None.
Contact: City of Vero Beach, 772-567-2144
www.covb.org

Riomar Beach

Special features: Beach fishing

This small access has paved parking for five cars and is popular with surfers. No handicapped access and no facilities.

Beach Length: 100-foot access to miles of beach.
Pets: Not allowed.
Directions: At the east end of Riomar Drive off A1A in Vero Beach; 0.9 mile north of E. Causeway Boulevard (17th Street).
Hours: Sunrise to sunset.
Fee: None.
Contact: City of Vero Beach, 772-567-2144
www.covb.org

EAST COAST

EAST COAST

South Beach Park

Special features: Outdoor shower · Picnic shelters

This nice park has a large paved lot and a large overflow lot across the street. No fishing or surfing allowed. Of the three boardwalks over vegetated dunes, the middle one is handicapped accessible, and a beach wheelchair is available.

Beach Length: 500 feet.
Pets: Not allowed.
Directions: At the east end of E. Causeway Boulevard (17th Street) on Ocean Drive in Vero Beach.
Hours: Sunrise to sunset.
Fee: None.
Contact: City of Vero Beach, 772-567-2144
www.covb.org

Round Island Oceanside Park

Special features: Picnic shelters · Outdoor shower · Beach fishing

Just north of the Indian River County line, this park has facilities on both sides of A1A. There's a handicapped ramp to the beach, and across A1A are a canoe/kayak launch, boat ramp, playground, and more restrooms.

Beach Length: 800 feet.
Pets: Not allowed.
Directions: On A1A, 5.5 miles north of Ft. Pierce Inlet State Park.
Hours: Sunrise to sunset.
Fee: None.
Contact: Indian River County Recreation Department, 772-567-8000 ext. 1732
www.ircrec.com

Avalon State Park

Special features: Outdoor shower · Picnic shelters · Beach fishing

This new state park preserves an invaluable stretch of undeveloped coast where sea turtles lay their eggs from May through October. Swimmers and snorkelers should beware of underwater debris from amphibious exercises conducted during World War II. A paved lot and picnic pavilions offer gorgeous views of the ocean. The park is not staffed.

Beach Length: 1 mile.
Pets: Not allowed.
Directions: On A1A, 4 miles north of Ft. Pierce Inlet State Park, at the tip of North Hutchinson Island.
Hours: Sunrise to sunset.
Fee: None.
Contact: Ft. Pierce Inlet State Park, 772-468-3985
www.floridastateparks.org/avalon

Pepper Beach Park

Special features: Picnic shelters · Beach fishing

This large park straddles A1A with restrooms on both sides. Oceanside is a large, paved lot with handicapped-accessible ramps to the beach, tennis and volleyball nets, and baseball fields. Across A1A is Wildcat Cove with a canoe/kayak launch and trail.

Beach Length: 1,200 feet.
Pets: Not allowed.
Directions: 0.6 mile north of the point where A1A makes a sharp left, north of Ft. Pierce Inlet State Park.

EAST COAST

Hours: Open 24 hours.
Fee: None.
Contact: St. Lucie County Recreation Office, 772-462-1521; Marine Safety, 772-462-2355
www.stlucieco.gov/leisure/beaches.htm

Ft. Pierce Inlet State Park

Special features: Picnic shelters · Beach fishing · Nature trails

This park on the southern end of North Hutchinson Island has both ocean and inlet beaches, about a half mile all together. Surfing is popular on the ocean, and fishing on the inlet. Go 1.5 mile north on A1A to find Jack Island Preserve, which is part of the park. There are no facilities or beach, but there's a nice nature trail around a wooded island preserve.

Beach Length: 0.5 mile.
Pets: Allowed on the inlet side of the park, but not on the beach.
Directions: From US 1 in Fort Pierce, take the North Causeway for 2.2 miles to the park on A1A.
Hours: 8 a.m. to sunset.
Fee: $5 per vehicle; $3 with single occupant.
Contact: 772-468-3985
www.floridastateparks.org/fortpierceinlet

Hutchinson Island

Seaway Drive

Special features: Picnic shelters · Beach fishing

This long, narrow beach is on the approach road to the north end of Hutchinson Island, on Ft. Pierce Inlet. There is absolutely no swimming allowed; it's on the busy inlet and the Coast Guard will ticket you. But it is a great place to fish or launch a boat. Adjacent is the St. Lucie County Marine Center, which has public restrooms on the back of the building and wonderful exhibits about marine life inside (420 Seaway Dr., 772-462-FISH).

Beach Length: 0.7 mile.
Pets: Not allowed.
Directions: From Route 1, go 0.5 mile west on Seaway Drive (A1A) across the bridge to Hutchinson Island. The beach is on the left.
Hours: Sunrise to sunset.
Fee: None.
Contact: St. Lucie County Recreation Office, 772-462-1521; Marine Safety, 772-462-2355
www.stlucieco.gov/leisure/beaches.htm

South Jetty Park

Special features: Outdoor shower · Picnic shelters · Fishing jetty

On windy days, this park on the northeastern tip of Hutchinson Island is very popular with kiteboarders. There's a handicapped-accessible paved path to great fishing on the inlet jetty, a paved

EAST COAST

On windy days, South Jetty Park is popular with kiteboarders.

lot, and street parking (both free). There is absolutely no swimming allowed in the inlet, only in the ocean.

Beach Length: 400 feet.
Pets: Not allowed.
Directions: From Route 1, go east on Seaway Drive (A1A), across bridge to Hutchinson Island for 2.5 miles. Where A1A veers sharply south, you'll see the park straight ahead.
Hours: Sunrise to sunset.
Fee: None.
Contact: St. Lucie County Recreation Office, 772-462-1521; Marine Safety, 772-462-2355
www.stlucieco.gov/leisure/beaches.htm

Ft. Pierce Beach Public Accesses

Special features: Beach fishing

Just past the point where A1A veers south on Hutchinson Island, access points with limited free parking can be found at the ends of

St. Lucie Court, Porpoise Avenue, and Gulfstream Avenue. All have stairs to the beach, but at Porpoise they have been covered with sand, so beach wheelchair access is possible. There are no facilities.

Beach Length: 0.5 mile.
Pets: Not allowed.
Directions: Cross Seaway Drive (A1A) to Hutchinson Island; veer right on A1A.
Hours: Sunrise to sunset.
Fee: None.
Contact: St. Lucie County Recreation Office, 772-462-1521; Marine Safety, 772-462-2355
www.stlucieco.gov/leisure/beaches.htm

South Beach Boardwalk

Special features: Outdoor shower · Beach fishing

The "boardwalk" part of this park washed away in a hurricane, but the name remains. There's a thousand feet of paved public parking and handicapped beach access via sand paths. There are food vendors in season.

Beach Length: 1,000 feet.
Pets: Not allowed.
Directions: In Ft. Pierce Beach, 0.6 mile south of the point where A1A veers south.
Hours: Sunrise to sunset.
Fee: None.
Contact: St. Lucie County Recreation Office, 772-462-1521; Marine Safety, 772-462-2355
www.stlucieco.gov/leisure/beaches.htm

Kimberly Bergalis Memorial Drive and Surfside Park

Special features: Picnic shelters · Outdoor shower

Combined, these adjacent city parks are two-tenths of a mile long and nicely landscaped with grass and trees, and they sport a decidedly different look from the island's county parks. A sand path to the beach is handicapped accessible. The memorial park has a paved parking lot; Surfside has parking on an access road parallel to A1A. There's handicapped access to the boardwalk, but not down to the beach. Lifeguard on duty in summer months only.

Beach Length: 1,000 feet.
Pets: Not allowed.
Directions: In Ft. Pierce Beach, 1 mile south of where A1A veers south.
Hours: Sunrise to sunset.
Fee: None.
Contact: St. Lucie County Recreation Office, 772-462-1521; Marine Safety, 772-462-2355
www.stlucieco.gov/leisure/beaches.htm

Coconut Drive Beach

Special features: Beach fishing

This small, out-of-the-way access assures you'll have a quiet beach experience. There's a small paved parking lot and a sand path over the dunes; no facilities.

Beach Length: 350 feet.
Pets: Not allowed.

Directions: 1.6 miles south of the point where A1A veers south, go left on Coconut Drive to its end, then right on Surfside to park.
Hours: Sunrise to sunset.
Fee: None.
Contact: St. Lucie County Recreation Office, 772-462-1521; Marine Safety, 772-462-2355
www.stlucieco.gov/leisure/beaches.htm

EAST COAST

> Bear Point Sanctuary, on Hutchinson Island, 2.8 miles south of where A1A veers south, is on the lagoon side of Hutchinson Island. While there's no beach, a kayak launch and nature trail were built on a dike that borders Bear Point. No facilities. Call 772-462-1692.

John Brooks Park

Special features: Beach fishing

This small access has a handicapped-accessible ramp over healthy dunes, a small sand parking lot, and no facilities.

Beach Length: 150-foot access to miles of beach.
Pets: Not allowed.
Directions: 3.7 miles south of the point where A1A veers south.
Hours: Sunrise to sunset.
Fee: None.
Contact: St. Lucie County Recreation Office, 772-462-1521; Marine Safety, 772-462-2355
www.stlucieco.gov/leisure/beaches.htm

EAST COAST

Frederick Douglass Memorial Beach

Special features: Outdoor shower · Picnic shelters · Beach fishing

This secluded park has no development around for miles. It's one of the few Florida beaches offering horseback riding. The private concessionaire, a real Florida cowboy named Alan Hayes, is gentle with his horses and good with timid riders. With your own horse and a permit you can ride south of the park, below the high tide line. Lifeguard on duty summer only.

Beach Length: 1,000 feet.
Pets: Not allowed.
Directions: 4 miles south of the point where A1A veers south.

The authors take a ride on Hutchinson Island.

Hours: Sunrise to sunset.
Fee: None; $35 for 1-hour horseback ride (772-468-0101)
Contact: St. Lucie County Recreation Office, 772-462-1521; Marine Safety, 772-462-2355
www.stlucieco.gov/leisure/beaches.htm

Middle Cove Access

Special features: Beach fishing

This access offers seclusion on an untouched beach. There's a small, paved parking lot, no facilities, and no handicapped access.

Beach Length: 150-foot access to miles and miles of beach.
Pets: Not allowed.
Directions: 5.4 miles south of the point where A1A veers south (3.5 miles north of nuclear power plant)
Hours: Sunrise to sunset.
Fee: None.
Contact: St. Lucie County Recreation Office, 772-462-1521; Marine Safety, 772-462-2355
www.stlucieco.gov/leisure/beaches.htm

Blind Creek Park

Special features: Portable toilets only · Beach fishing · Nature trails

This park straddles both sides of A1A, with access to the ocean and the Intracoastal Waterway, where there's a sand boat ramp on Little Mud Creek. The nature trail goes south along the ICW to Blind Creek. On the ocean side is a sheltered lagoon.

Beach Length: 2,000 feet.
Pets: Not allowed on beach.
Directions: 6.7 miles south of the point where A1A veers south.
Hours: Sunrise to sunset.
Fee: None.
Contact: St. Lucie County Recreation Office, 772-462-1521; Marine Safety, 772-462-2355
www.stlucieco.gov/leisure/beaches.htm

Turtle Beach

Special features: Beach fishing

The dirt road is gated and only a few cars have room to park (do not block gate). Walk five minutes on a dirt road lined with black mangrove to reach a wild beach. Except for the view of the dual towers of a nuclear power plant, Turtle Beach offers visitors a secluded, wild beach, where sea turtles are known to nest. If you see a nest, do not disturb it; some may be marked. There are no facilities, but you can use restrooms at the power plant's education/visitor center at Gate B. While there, check out the sea turtle exhibit and film. The visitor center is open Sunday through Friday, 10 a.m. to 4 p.m.

Beach Length: 1 mile.
Pets: Not allowed.
Directions: 0.5 mile north of the St. Lucie Nuclear Power Plant on A1A, 7.6 miles north of Jensen Beach Causeway.
Hours: Sunrise to sunset.
Fee: None.
Contact: 877-FPL-4FUN

Walton Rocks Beach

Special features: Outdoor shower · Picnic shelters · Beach fishing

This is St. Lucie County's only dog-friendly beach. Take the dirt road for a half mile to a large sand lot with restrooms and one picnic table under a shelter. Go another tenth of a mile to a smaller lot with more picnic tables and restrooms. Both areas have boardwalks over the dunes, with stairs.

Beach Length: 2,000 feet.
Pets: Allowed; leash not required, but they must be under voice control; waste pickup bags supplied.
Directions: 0.5 mile south of St. Lucie Nuclear Power Plant on A1A.
Hours: Sunrise to sunset.
Fee: None.
Contact: St. Lucie County Recreation Office, 772-462-1521; Marine Safety, 772-462-2355
www.stlucieco.gov/leisure/beaches.htm

Ocean Bay Natural Area

Special features: Beach fishing · Nature trails

A shady path leads through dense native trees to the Atlantic beach. A nature trail identifies trees like gumbo limbo, sea grape, and strangler fig. This 34-acre preserve continues across the highway with a hiking trail along Indian River Lagoon. Small, paved parking lot; no facilities.

Beach Length: 1,000 feet.
Pets: Not allowed.

EAST COAST

Directions: On A1A 5.5 miles north of Jensen Beach Causeway, directly across from the FPL utility plant.
Hours: Sunrise to sunset.
Fee: None.
Contact: St. Lucie County Environmental Resources, 772-462-2525
www.co.st-lucie.fl.us/erd/ocean-bay/index.htm

Herman's Bay Access

Special features: Picnic shelters · Beach fishing

This new access has a parking lot, but no facilities. There's a handicapped-accessible overlook, with stairs leading to the beach.

Beach Length: 150-foot access to miles of beach.
Pets: Not allowed.
Directions: 5 miles north of Jensen Beach Causeway on A1A.
Hours: Sunrise to sunset.
Fee: None.
Contact: St. Lucie County Recreation Office, 772-462-1521; Marine Safety, 772-462-2355
www.stlucieco.gov/leisure/beaches.htm

Normandy Beach Access

Special features: Beach fishing

There's a small paved parking lot and benches under a shelter, but no facilities.

Beach Length: 150-foot access to miles of beach.
Pets: Not allowed.
Directions: 4 miles north of Jensen Beach Causeway on A1A.

Hours: Sunrise to sunset.
Fee: None.
Contact: St. Lucie County Recreation Office, 772-462-1521; Marine Safety, 772-462-2355
www.stlucieco.gov/leisure/beaches.htm

Dollman Park

Special features: Outdoor shower · Beach fishing

From the paved parking lot, a sand path leads over the dunes through saw palmetto to a half mile of undeveloped, almost wild beach nestled between condominiums. There are no facilities. A half mile north on the west side of A1A, Dollman Riverside Park's half-mile-long Maritime Hammock Nature Trail identifies 13 native plants and trees. There are no facilities at the nature trail.

Beach Length: 0.5 mile.
Pets: Not allowed.
Directions: 2.8 miles north of Jensen Beach Causeway on A1A.
Hours: Sunrise to sunset.
Fee: None.
Contact: St. Lucie County Recreation Office, 772-462-1521; Marine Safety, 772-462-2355
www.stlucieco.gov/leisure/beaches.htm

Waveland Beach

Special features: Outdoor shower · Beach fishing

There's a large paved parking lot with restrooms that are slightly run down. A handicapped ramp leads to an overlook, with stairs down to beach.

EAST COAST

Beach Length: 300 feet.
Pets: Not allowed.
Directions: 1.5 mile north of Jensen Beach Causeway.
Hours: Open 24 hours.
Fee: None.
Contact: St. Lucie County Recreation Office, 772-462-1521; Marine Safety, 772-462-2355
www.stlucieco.gov/leisure/beaches.htm

Glasscock Beach

Special features: Beach fishing

This access point has a small dirt parking lot, no facilities, and stairs to the beach. Despite these drawbacks, you have now entered the county of pet-friendly beaches!

Beach Length: 100-foot access to miles of beach.
Pets: Allowed on a leash.
Directions: 0.4 mile north of Jensen Beach Causeway on A1A, just south of the Martin County line.
Hours: Sunrise to sunset.
Fee: None.
Contact: Martin County Parks Department, 772-221-1418
www.martincountyfla.com/beaches.asp

Jensen Sea Turtle Beach

Special features: Outdoor shower · Picnic shelters · Beach fishing

This park has a very long parking lot with several access points to the beach. The snack bar serves breakfast and lunch, 8 a.m. to 3:30 p.m.

There are volleyball nets and sheltered picnic tables. Across A1A, Island Shoppes has an arcade, pharmacy, and restaurant.

Beach Length: 0.3 mile.
Pets: Allowed on a leash outside of area with lifeguard.
Directions: At the end of the Jensen Beach Causeway (SR 732) on A1A.
Hours: Open 24 hours.
Fee: None.
Contact: Martin County Parks Department, 772-221-1418
www.martincountyfla.com/beaches.asp

Bob Graham Beach

Special features: Outdoor shower · Beach fishing

Named for the longtime U.S. senator and former Florida governor, this park has a large, paved lot, native plant restoration, and a handicapped ramp to an overlook with stairs down to the beach. There are no facilities.

Beach Length: 500 feet.
Pets: Allowed on a leash.
Directions: 0.7 mile south of Jensen Beach Causeway (SR 732) on A1A.
Hours: Open 24 hours.
Fee: None.
Contact: Martin County Parks Department, 772-221-1418
www.martincountyfla.com/beaches.asp

EAST COAST

Beachwalk/Pasley Park

Special features: Beach fishing

This access has native plant restoration and interpretive signs about turtles, dunes, and shorebirds. There's a dirt parking lot and handicapped ramp to the beach. No facilities.

Beach Length: 100-foot access to miles of beach.
Pets: Allowed on a leash.
Directions: 0.9 mile south of Jensen Beach Causeway (SR 732) on A1A.
Hours: Open 24 hours.
Fee: None.
Contact: Martin County Parks Department, 772-221-1418 www.martincountyfla.com/beaches.asp

Bryn Mawr Beach Access

Special features: Beach fishing

Known by locals as Alex's Beach. A large dirt parking lot has stairs to the beach. The land was donated in 1973 by Bryn Mawr Group. There are no facilities.

Beach Length: 100-foot access to miles of beach.
Pets: Allowed on a leash.
Directions: 1 mile south of Jensen Beach Causeway (SR 732) on A1A.
Hours: Open 24 hours.
Fee: None.
Contact: Martin County Parks Department, 772-221-1418 www.martincountyfla.com/beaches.asp

Virginia Forrest Access

Special features: Beach fishing

Named for the woman who donated the land in 1973, it has a large dirt parking lot, no facilities, and no handicapped accessibility.

Beach Length: 50-foot access to miles of beach.
Pets: Allowed on leash.
Directions: 1.5 mile south of Jensen Beach Causeway (SR 732) on A1A.
Hours: Open 24 hours.
Fee: None.
Contact: Martin County Parks Department, 772-221-1418
www.martincountyfla.com/beaches.asp

Tiger Shores Beach

Special features: Outdoor shower · Beach fishing

There is free parking in a dirt lot with stairs to the beach.

Beach Length: 50-foot access to miles of beach.
Pets: Allowed on leash.
Directions: 2 miles south of Jensen Beach Causeway (SR 732) on A1A. From Stuart, take A1A North over bridge on A1A, go 0.7 mile past turn for McArthur Boulevard.
Hours: Open 24 hours.
Fee: None.
Contact: Martin County Parks Department, 772-221-1418
www.martincountyfla.com/beaches.asp

Stuart Beach

Special features: Outdoor shower · Picnic shelters Beach fishing

This large park has plenty of recreational resources to enjoy: volleyball and basketball courts, boogie board, and umbrella and chair rentals. There's a handicapped-accessible ramp to the beach and beach wheelchairs are for rent. Adjacent to the park is Elliott Museum, which houses Martin County history, art galleries, and an antique car gallery (www.elliottmuseumfl.org). Across A1A is the Florida Oceanographic Coastal Center.

Beach Length: 1,000 feet.
Pets: Allowed on a leash outside of area with lifeguard.
Directions: From Stuart, take A1A North over bridge; go straight past the turn for John D. McArthur Boulevard for 0.3 mile to 825 N.E. Ocean Boulevard.
Hours: Sunrise to sunset.
Fee: None.
Contact: Martin County Parks Department, 772-221-1418
www.martincountyfla.com/beaches.asp

Santa Lucea Beach and Fletcher Beach

Special features: Outdoor shower · Beach fishing

Santa Lucea has a large paved parking lot, while adjacent Fletcher Beach has sand parking for about six cars. Both have ramps and stairs to a wild beach with coquina rock and gray sand. Surf fishing is popular. The area is known for nesting sea turtles from May through October. There are no facilities.

Beach Length: 500 feet.

Pets: Allowed on a leash.

Directions: On John D. MacArthur Boulevard, 0.3 mile south of A1A (Stuart Beach).

Hours: Sunrise to sunset.

Fee: None.

Contact: Martin County Parks Department, 772-221-1418 www.martincountyfla.com/beaches.asp

Ross Witham Beach Access (House of Refuge Beach)

Special features: Beach fishing

There's diagonal parking for about a dozen cars just off the highway. The beach is rocky and picturesque: treacherous for swimming, but fine for fishing and walking. Surfers flock here for the big waves when the wind is blowing right. Hutchinson Island is very narrow, as

House of Refuge Beach.

is the curvy road, so it is quite dangerous to back out from parking. A historic marker states that the old building here was once a house of refuge operated by the U.S. Life-Saving Service. Civilian keepers rescued shipwrecked sailors and provided them with food, shelter, and transportation. This is the last of nine such houses built on the east coast of Florida in the late 1800s (a tenth house of refuge was located on Santa Rosa Island near Pensacola). This one became the Maritime Museum in 1955 and was restored in 1976. It contains exhibits on the history of lifesaving and is administered by the Elliott Museum in Stuart. Call 772-225-1875 for hours and information.

Beach Length: 500 feet.
Pets: Allowed on a leash.
Directions: On John D. MacArthur Boulevard, 0.8 mile south of A1A (Stuart Beach).
Hours: Open 24 hours.
Fee: None.
Contact: Martin County Parks Department, 772-221-1418
www.martincountyfla.com/beaches.asp

Chastain Beach/The Rocks

Special features: Outdoor shower · Beach fishing

The parking for 20 cars fills fast with surfers. There's room for about 10 more cars across the street. There is no handicapped access.

Beach Length: 200 feet.
Pets: Allowed on a leash.
Directions: On John D. MacArthur Boulevard, 1.8 mile south of A1A (Stuart Beach).
Hours: Open 24 hours.
Fee: None.
Contact: Martin County Parks Department, 772-221-1418
www.martincountyfla.com/beaches.asp

Bathtub Reef Beach Park

Special features: Outdoor shower · Good beach for small children · Beach fishing

This unusual beach is near the southern end of Hutchinson Island at the St. Lucie Inlet. There's no surfing here because a nearshore reef dampens the surf and creates a sheltered swimming spot known as the "bathtub." The reef has been built by sabellariid (sa-bell-AIR-id) worms that construct their homes by cementing sand into tubes. This reef is *alive*, so don't stand or walk on it. There's a large parking lot with handicapped access up to a gazebo and restrooms, but stairs to the beach. Just south of the park begins the gated community of Sailfish Point, which encompasses the entire southern tip of the island. No alcohol after sunset. No fishing 9 a.m. to 5 p.m.

Beach Length: 1,000 feet.
Pets: Not allowed.
Directions: On John D. MacArthur Boulevard, 2 miles south of A1A (Stuart Beach).
Hours: Sunrise to sunset.
Fee: None.
Contact: Martin County Parks Department, 772-221-1418 www.martincountyfla.com/beaches.asp

Jupiter Island

St. Lucie Inlet Preserve State Park

Special features: Picnic shelters · Beach fishing

This isolated state park occupies the northern tip of Jupiter Island. There is no vehicular access—you can either walk 2.5 miles through Hobe Sound National Wildlife Refuge, or arrive by boat. From a kayak and canoe launch at the east end of Cove Road on the mainland, it's just a five-minute paddle straight across the Intracoastal Waterway (look both ways for traffic, and we're not kidding) to the state park boat dock. The 0.6-mile boardwalk leads through coastal hammocks of gumbo limbo, live oak, and cabbage palm to a wild, virtually deserted beach nearly three miles long. Giant leatherback turtles nest here in March and April, followed by the loggerhead and green sea turtles later in the season. At time of publication, restrooms at the dock remained closed because of storm damage, but restrooms at the beach are open. The park is not staffed.

Beach Length: 2.7 miles.
Pets: Not allowed.
Directions: The park is located on the Intracoastal Waterway, just south of St. Lucie Inlet. The GPS for the boat dock is N27 09.088, W80 09.817
Hours: 8 a.m. to sunset.
Fee: $2 per boat; $1 per canoe or kayak; honor box.
Contact: 772-219-1880
www.floridastateparks.org/stlucieinlet

Hobe Sound National Wildlife Refuge

$

Special features: Portable toilets only · Beach fishing · Nature trails

Shorebirds dodge crashing surf. Over the dunes in the pine-scrub-oak habitat live endangered scrub jays and gopher tortoise. In spring you might see a nest hole dug by a sea turtle; do not disturb. Sea turtle walks are given in June and July. You can walk 2.5 miles on this wild beach, all the way to St. Lucie Inlet Preserve State Park, where more wild treats await.

Beach Length: 2.5 miles.
Pets: It's a very rare national wildlife refuge that allows pets. Let's keep it that way by keeping them leashed and picking up after them. Don't let your dog dig; he may destroy a sea turtle nest.
Directions: From Route 1 in Hobe Sound, take Route 708 east (Bridge Road) to Jupiter Island, turn left on A1A (North Beach Road), and go 1.7 mile to refuge entrance. Exclusive homes along the way.
Hours: Sunrise to sunset.
Fee: $5 per vehicle
Contact: 772-546-6141
www.fws.gov/hobesound

Hobe Sound National Wildlife Refuge Headquarters

Special features: Picnic shelters · Beach fishing · Nature trails

A small, shallow beach on the Intracoastal Waterway at the bottom of 50 wooden steps, visitor center, and 0.4-mile Sand Pine Scrub nature trail can be found at the refuge headquarters.

Beach Length: 500 feet.
Pets: Allowed on a leash.
Directions: 2 miles south of the town of Hobe Sound on Route 1.
Hours: Sunrise to sunset.
Fee: None.
Contact: 772-546-6141
www.fws.gov/hobesound

Hobe Sound Beach

Special features: Picnic shelters · Outdoor shower · Beach fishing

Bridge Road, the entrance to exclusive Jupiter Island, is lined with huge strangler fig trees. The county has one small park on this millionaires' enclave. It is free and allows pets. Pro golfer Tiger Woods purchased a home on this island in 2006 for a reported $38 million, a record even for this exclusive zip code. The park has a handicapped ramp to the beach, where surf fishing is very popular (not allowed in the area where lifeguard is located).

Beach Length: 300-foot access to miles of beach.
Pets: Allowed on a leash, outside of area with lifeguard.
Directions: From Route 1 in Hobe Sound, take Route 708 east (Bridge Road) to Jupiter Island; park is straight ahead at the junction with A1A.
Hours: Sunrise to sunset.
Fee: None.
Contact: Martin County Parks Department, 772-221-1418
www.martincountyfla.com/beaches.asp

Blowing Rocks Preserve

$ ⚦ ⛱ 🚫 🚳

Special features: Outdoor shower · Nature trails

This wonderful Nature Conservancy preserve straddles Jupiter Island, with ocean on one side and Intracoastal Waterway on the other. The blowing rocks are an exciting attraction at high tide, when waves pound into eroded rock and shoot up through blow holes of sea caves. Walk 100 yards on a sand path to beach walkways with stairs. A sandy nature trail goes a half mile north under an arbor of sea grape. Swimming is quite treacherous because of the rocks, and is at your own risk. Coolers and food are not allowed. There's parking for about 20 cars here. Across Beach Road is more parking at the Education Center, which has restrooms and nature trails that follow the ICW. The Mangrove Trail is a short and handicapped-accessible boardwalk with overlooks on the ICW.

Beach Length: 1 mile.
Pets: Not allowed.
Directions: From Route 1 in Tequesta, go east on CR 707 over the bridge to Jupiter Island. Road veers left and becomes S. Beach Road. Go 1.8 mile to the preserve.

Sea grape covers the dunes at Blowing Rocks Preserve.

Hours: 9 a.m. to 5 p.m. (parking lot and education center close at 4:30 p.m.).
Fee: $2, free for ages 12 and under.
Contact: 561-744-6668
www.nature.org

Coral Cove Park

Special features: Outdoor shower · Good beach for small children · Beach fishing

This ocean beach on the southern end of Jupiter Island has some of the same rock formations as Blowing Rocks Preserve to the north, but views of them are more accessible, with a paved pathway up to and along the top of the dune (there are stairs down to the beach, however). Surfing and fishing are not allowed in the swim area watched over by lifeguards. Plenty of free parking.

Beach Length: 600 feet on ocean; 600 feet of shoreline on the Intracoastal Waterway.
Pets: Allowed in park on a leash, but not on beach or shoreline.
Directions: From Route 1 in Tequesta, go east on CR 707 over the bridge to Jupiter Island. Road veers left and becomes S. Beach Road. Go 0.8 mile to the park entrance, on the right. For handicapped access: upon entering the park, continue straight up a slightly inclined access road and park on the right.
Hours: Sunrise to sunset.
Fee: None.
Contact: Palm Beach County Parks, 561-966-6600
www.co.palm-beach.fl.us/parks

> Across the road from Coral Cove Park is the county's Shoreline Restoration Project, providing free street parking and several accesses to a narrow beach on the Intracoastal Waterway. You can wade and fish here or park a lawn chair to view the sunset. It's a nice place to hang out if the wind is blowing hard off the Atlantic.

South Florida

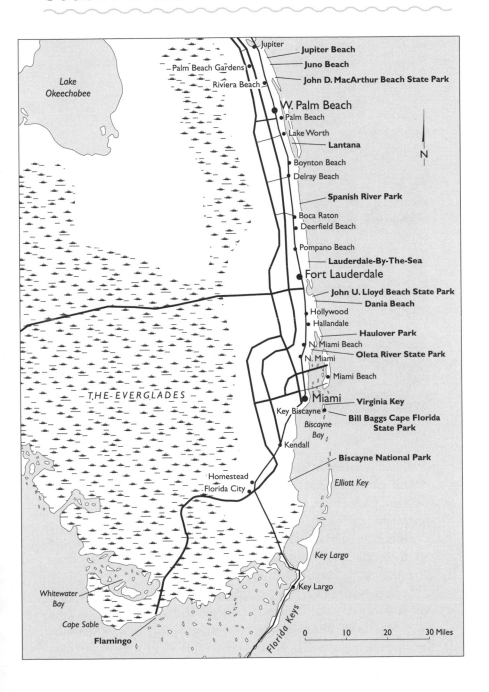

Lake
Okeechobee

Jupiter
Jupiter Beach
Palm Beach Gardens
Juno Beach
Riviera Beach
John D. MacArthur Beach State Park

W. Palm Beach
Palm Beach
Lake Worth
Lantana
Boynton Beach
Delray Beach
Spanish River Park
Boca Raton
Deerfield Beach
Pompano Beach
Lauderdale-By-The-Sea
Fort Lauderdale
John U. Lloyd Beach State Park
Dania Beach
Hollywood
Hallandale
Haulover Park
N. Miami Beach
Oleta River State Park
N. Miami
Miami Beach

- THE EVERGLADES -
Miami
Virginia Key
Key Biscayne
**Bill Baggs Cape Florida
State Park**
Biscayne
Bay
Kendall

Biscayne National Park

Homestead
Florida City
Elliott Key

Key Largo

Whitewater
Bay
Key Largo
Cape Sable

Flamingo

Florida Keys

N

0   10   20   30 Miles

Relaxing near the lighthouse at Bill Baggs Cape Florida State Park in South Florida.

A stream of white limos and lowriders crawls up Ocean Drive past bubble-gum-pink Art Deco hotels. Girls with navel rings and guys with six-pack abs parade in front of Armani, Polo, and Versace's storefront windows.

Hey, is that Uma Thurman walking by? As the sun sets, Miami's South Beach scene really heats up. Nightclubs pulse a steady bass. The Atlantic surf is audible from across the street.

Such is Miami Beach, seemingly the center of the universe on a hot summer day and unquestionably South Florida's most exciting strip of sand. If you're looking for action, family fun, or solitude, here's the scoop on all of South Florida's places to wiggle your toes in the sand.

Palm Beach Area

Dubois Park

Special features: Outdoor shower · Good beach for small children · Fishing jetty

This historic park on the south side of Jupiter Inlet has a small beach right on the inlet, and sheltered swimming on a lagoon. The inlet is a fine place to sit and watch boats with a view of the historic red Jupiter Inlet Lighthouse. The Dubois Pioneer Home, built on an ancient Indian shell mound, is open for tours Tuesday and Wednesday, 1–4 p.m. (561-747-6639).

Beach Length: 1,200 feet.
Pets: Allowed in the park on a leash, but nowhere near the beach.
Directions: From A1A (S. Ocean Drive) in Jupiter, turn east on Jupiter Beach Road, then immediate left on Dubois Road.
Hours: Sunrise to sunset.
Fee: None.
Contact: Palm Beach County Parks, 561-966-6600
www.co.palm-beach.fl.us/parks

Jupiter Beach County Park

Special features: Outdoor shower · Good beach for small children · Fishing jetty · Beach fishing

Like Dubois, this park is on Jupiter Inlet, but offers a beach on the Atlantic. Continue past the first parking lot along a winding lane with shady picnic spots. The inlet is at the end. There's no swimming

SOUTH FLORIDA

on the inlet, but fishing is allowed 24 hours a day. Surfing and fishing are not allowed in the swim area where lifeguard is located. Surf wheelchair available.

Beach Length: 1,700 feet.
Pets: Allowed in the park on a leash, but not on the beach.
Directions: From A1A (S. Ocean Drive) in Jupiter, go 0.3 mile east on Jupiter Beach Road to Ocean Trail Way and turn left into park.
Hours: Sunrise to sunset; inlet fishing 24 hours.
Fee: None.
Contact: Palm Beach County Parks, 561-966-6600
www.co.palm-beach.fl.us/parks

Carlin Park

Special features: Outdoor shower · Picnic shelters · Beach fishing

This park has 3,000 feet of sparkling white ocean beach watched over by lifeguards. The Lazy Loggerhead Café serves breakfast and lunch on an open-air deck just off the beach. The 120-acre park has plenty of free parking, playing fields, and tennis, volleyball, and bocce courts as well as an amphitheater for outdoor performances. Surfing and fishing are not allowed in the swim area watched over by lifeguards. A surf wheelchair is available.

Beach Length: 3,000 feet.
Pets: Allowed in the park on a leash, but not on the beach.
Directions: Located on Old A1A in Jupiter.
Hours: Sunrise to sunset.
Fee: None.
Contact: Palm Beach County Parks, 561-966-6600
www.co.palm-beach.fl.us/parks

Jupiter Beach

Special features: Outdoor shower · Picnic shelters · Beach fishing

The spectacular white beach runs south from Carlin Park all the way to Juno Beach, with free on-street parking, a smooth bike path/sidewalk, bike racks, outdoor showers, and water fountains at numerous dune boardwalks. There's no development on the oceanside, so the views are gorgeous.

Beach Length: 2.5 miles.
Pets: Allowed on a leash on the sidewalk (pickup bags are provided), but not on the beach.
Directions: Along A1A from Jupiter south to Juno.
Hours: Sunrise to sunset.
Fee: None.
Contact: Palm Beach County Parks, 561-966-6600
www.co.palm-beach.fl.us/parks

SOUTH FLORIDA

Juno Beach Park and Pier

Special features: Outdoor shower · Picnic shelters · Fishing pier

This five-acre park has a huge parking lot on the west side of A1A, which may be more for the accommodation of the 24-hour fishing pier than the small ocean beach. Fishing is allowed only from the 990-foot pier, which has a bait shop and snack bar. There's a designated surfing area. Use caution crossing the highway from the parking lot.

Beach Length: 300 feet.
Pets: Not allowed on beach.
Directions: Between US 1 and A1A at Seaview Drive.

Hours: Sunrise to sunset; fishing pier is open 24 hours except during sea turtle nesting season (March–October), when it opens an hour before sunrise and closes at sunset.

Fee: None.

Contact: Palm Beach County Parks, 561-966-6600
www.co.palm-beach.fl.us/parks

Loggerhead Park

Special features: Outdoor shower · Beach fishing · Good beach for small children · Nature trails

The entrance to this wooded park is on US 1, although the beach is across A1A. The park is home to the Marinelife Center, a sea turtle rehabilitation and education center with exhibits, live sea turtles, and other marine animals. Night turtle walks are given in June and July. There's volleyball, horseshoes, and a bike and nature trail. Fishing and surfing are not allowed in the area with lifeguards. Surf wheelchair available.

Beach Length: 900 feet.

Pets: Allowed in park on a leash, but not on beach.

Directions: On Route 1, 0.2 mile north of Donald Ross Road in Juno Beach.

Hours: Sunrise to sunset; the Marinelife Center is open 10 a.m. to 4 p.m. Tuesday through Saturday, and noon to 3 p.m. Sunday (www.marinelife.org).

Fee: None.

Contact: Palm Beach County Parks, 561-966-6600
www.co.palm-beach.fl.us/parks

John D. MacArthur Beach State Park

Special features: Outdoor shower · Picnic shelters · Beach fishing · Nature trails

Unique along South Florida's developed coast, this 438-acre park preserves the largest remaining example of tropical maritime hammock in Palm Beach County. The two-mile beach is pristine, and, just offshore, a worm reef is great for snorkeling. The Nature Center has exhibits and aquariums. Here you can rent kayaks for a paddle out to Munyon Island, which has a small beach on the Intracoastal Waterway. A tram runs across the estuary on a 1,600-foot bridge to the beach, where there's a handicapped-accessible ramp right to the sand. No lifeguards. Fish in the lagoon or nonswimming areas of the beach.

Beach Length: 2 miles.
Pets: Allowed in the park, but not on the beach.
Directions: From Riviera Beach, take E. Blue Heron Boulevard (A1A) to Singer Island. Veer north on A1A, 1 mile to the park, in North Palm Beach.
Hours: 8 a.m. to sunset; Nature Center open 9 a.m. to 5 p.m. daily.
Fee: $4 per vehicle.
Contact: 561-624-6950
www.floridastateparks.org/macarthurbeach
www.Macarthurbeach.org

Ocean Reef Park

Special features: Outdoor shower · Picnic shelters

This festive beach is popular for parasailing, and the snorkeling on the offshore reef is wonderful. Fishing and surfing are not allowed.

There's a small dune ecosystem with an overlook and plenty of free parking. Surf wheelchair available.

Beach Length: 700 feet.
Pets: Allowed in the park on a leash, but not on the beach.
Directions: From Riviera Beach, take E. Blue Heron Boulevard (A1A) to Singer Island. Veer north on A1A, go 1 mile to the park.
Hours: Sunrise to sunset.
Fee: None.
Contact: Palm Beach County Parks, 561-966-6600
www.co.palm-beach.fl.us/parks

Riviera Municipal Beach

Special features: Outdoor shower · Beach fishing

Public parking is at a mall parking lot, giving access to a quarter mile of sandy fun with lifeguards, volleyball nets, picnic tables, and showers. Fishing is allowed outside the areas with lifeguards.

Beach Length: 1,000 feet.
Pets: Not allowed.
Directions: On Singer Island, at Blue Heron Boulevard and Ocean Drive (A1A), behind Ocean Mall.
Hours: Sunrise to sunset.
Fee: None.
Contact: Riviera Beach Municipal Beach, 561-845-4070
www.rivierabch.com

Palm Beach Shores Park

Special features: Outdoor shower · Beach fishing

The community's lone public beach access has parking for residents only. Outsiders can park at Town Hall for free and walk a block and a half to the beach. Once there you can walk the beach between Bamboo Road and Lake Worth inlet.

Beach Length: 2,000 feet.
Pets: Allowed in the park, but not on the beach.
Directions: Take E. Blue Heron Drive across to the island, turn south on South Ocean Drive, then go 0.5 mile to Edwards Lane.
Hours: Sunset to sunset.
Fee: Annual beach sticker is $30 and available to residents only.
Contact: Palm Beach Shores Town Hall, 561-844-3457
townhall.ci.palm-beach-shores.fl.us/

Midtown Beach

Special features: Outdoor shower

Even though it's much smaller, ritzy Palm Beach rivals Miami Beach for upscale shopping, with Worth Avenue establishments like Saks, Neiman, Jimmy Choo, and Chanel. But the public beach is available to anyone no matter wallet size or zip code. There's metered street parking on South Ocean Boulevard (A1A) from Royal Palm Way to a half mile south of Worth Avenue. There's handicapped access at Chilean and South Ocean, and public restrooms at the Town Hall on South County Road, about a block off the beach. Fishing is not allowed.

Beach Length: 0.5 mile.
Pets: Not allowed.

Directions: Access the island on Royal Palm Way to A1A in Palm Beach.
Hours: 8 a.m. to 10 p.m.
Fee: Metered parking.
Contact: Palm Beach Beach Rescue, 561-838-5483

Phipps Ocean Park

Special features: Outdoor shower · Picnic shelters · Beach fishing

North of the busy Lake Worth Beach is this quiet park with picnic tables, a tennis center, and tiki huts up on a bluff. Tennis courts are located between two parking lots, both with restrooms. The north lot has handicapped access to the beach. The south lot has stairs up and over a steep dune.

Beach Length: 0.25 mile
Pets: Not allowed.
Directions: 1.5 mile north of Lake Worth Beach on A1A.
Hours: 8 a.m. to sunset.
Fee: There are about 24 free two-hour spaces with metered parking for overflow.
Contact: Palm Beach Beach Rescue, 561-838-5483

Richard G. Kreusler Park

Special features: Outdoor shower

This small county park is a tad quieter than the municipal beach just south of it, but gives access to the same stretch of beach. There's a grassy picnic area and an artificial reef offshore for snorkeling.

Beach Length: 450 feet.

Pets: Not allowed.

Directions: From Lake Worth, take Lake Avenue (Route 802) onto the island. The road ends at the park on A1A.

Hours: Sunrise to sunset.

Fee: Pay machine for metered parking.

Contact: Palm Beach County Parks, 561-966-6600 www.co.palm-beach.fl.us/parks

Lake Worth Municipal Beach

Special features: Outdoor shower · Fishing pier

The barrier island offshore of Lake Worth is a lively scene, with shops, a casino, 1,200-foot fishing pier, and a popular seafood restaurant, Benny's at the Beach. A trolley brings beachgoers to these two adjacent parks. On a nice day, the huge parking lot is nearly full and the white beach a sea of umbrellas. Beware a steep drop-off just offshore.

Fishing pier at Lake Worth Municipal Beach.

Beach Length: 1,200 feet.

Pets: Not allowed.

Directions: From Lake Worth, take Lake Avenue (Route 802) onto the island. The road ends at the beach on A1A.

Hours: Sunrise to sunset.

Fee: Pay machine (attendants quickly ticket cars not displaying the receipt).

Contact: Lake Worth Municipal Beach, 561-533-7367 www.lakeworth.org

Lantana Public Beach

$

Special features: Outdoor shower · Picnic shelters

The Dune Deck Café, on a high dune covered with native vegetation, is a great place for beer and burgers. There are volleyball nets and an offshore reef. Nonresidents have access to a small metered parking lot; a larger free lot is available for residents with permits. Fishing is not allowed on the beach.

Lantana Beach dune crossover.

Beach Length: 750 feet.
Pets: Not allowed.
Directions: On A1A at E. Ocean, next to the Ritz-Carlton Hotel.
Hours: One hour before sunrise to one hour after sunset; lifeguard on duty 9 a.m. to 5 p.m.
Fee: Metered parking or resident beach sticker.
Contact: 561-540-5731
recorded beach report: 561-540-5735
www.lantana.org

Ocean Inlet Park

Special features: Outdoor shower · Picnic shelters · Good beach for small children · Fishing jetty

This 11-acre park has a small beach with lifeguard on the Intracoastal Waterway side of the island, a marina and boat slips, fishing jetty, playground, and picnic pavilions (a wedding was being performed on the day we visited).

Beach Length: 600 feet.
Pets: Allowed on a leash in grassy areas, but not on beach.
Directions: On the west side of A1A (N. Ocean Boulevard), just south of the inlet.
Hours: Sunrise to sunset; 24-hour inlet fishing.
Fee: None.
Contact: Palm Beach County Parks, 561-966-6600
www.co.palm-beach.fl.us/parks

Ocean Ridge Hammock Park

Special features: Outdoor shower · Beach fishing

From the free parking lot on the west side of A1A, walk across the road and through a shady and intimate hammock forest preserve to the beach. No restrooms or lifeguards.

Beach Length: 1,100 feet.
Pets: Allowed on a leash on trails, but not on beach.
Directions: On N. Ocean Boulevard (A1A) at Inlet Cay Drive, about a half mile north of E. Ocean Drive, the access road to the island.
Hours: Sunrise to sunset.
Fee: None.
Contact: Palm Beach County Parks, 561-966-6600
www.co.palm-beach.fl.us/parks

Boynton Beach Oceanfront Park

Special features: Outdoor shower · Beach fishing

This gorgeous beach below native vegetated dunes would probably be your favorite spot—if you lived here. But if you're not a resident and don't want to pay $10, the free beaches at Ocean Ridge Hammock Park, just to the north, or Gulfstream County Park to the south are just as nice. Fishing is allowed outside areas with lifeguards.

Beach Length: 965 feet.
Pets: Not allowed.
Directions: On N. Ocean Boulevard (A1A) in Ocean Ridge, about 0.25 mile north of E. Ocean Drive, the access road to the island.
Hours: Sunrise to sunset.

Fee: $10 per vehicle for nonresidents; free to residents with permit ($30 per year).
Contact: Boynton Beach Leisure Services, 561-742-6565
www.boynton-beach.org

Gulfstream County Park

Special features: Outdoor shower · Beach fishing

This park has landscaped grounds with native plants and a board-walk to a beach with lifeguard. The free parking lot fills quickly on nice days.

Beach Length: 600 feet.
Pets: Not allowed.
Directions: From Boynton Beach, take E. Woodbright Avenue across the ICW to the island; go south on N. Ocean Boulevard (A1A) for 1 mile to the park at Bel Air Drive.
Hours: Sunrise to sunset.
Fee: None.
Contact: Palm Beach County Parks, 561-966-6600
www.co.palm-beach.fl.us/parks

Delray Municipal Beach

Special features: Outdoor shower

A sign for this Village by the Sea welcomes visitors to the friendly beach town's two miles of sand. Park on Ocean Boulevard (A1A) or at one of these parks with restrooms: Sarah Gleason Park (2 S. Ocean Boulevard), Sandoway Park (200 block on west side of A1A), and Anchor Park (340 S. Ocean Boulevard). By the way, Sarah Gleason

Friendly Delray Beach.

was the visionary landowner who deeded her oceanfront property as a public park way back in 1871. Fishing is prohibited in the areas with lifeguards.

Beach Length: 2 miles.
Pets: Not allowed.
Directions: Take E. Atlantic Avenue to the island and look for on-street parking 0.5 mile north and 0.5 mile south on Ocean Boulevard (A1A).
Hours: Beach open 5 a.m. to 11 p.m. Parks open 8 a.m. to dusk.
Fee: Metered parking; annual resident parking permit is $63.60.
Contact: 561-243-7352; recorded beach conditions: 561-27BEACH
www.mydelraybeach.com

Atlantic Dunes Park

Special features: Outdoor shower · Picnic shelters · Nature trails

This shady, serene park has handicapped parking right at the beach, and a metered parking lot on the other side of A1A. There's a boardwalk over the dunes, which are covered in sea grape, and a hard-packed trail, accessible via handicapped surf chair.

Beach Length: 350 feet.
Pets: Not allowed.
Directions: On A1A, one block north of E. Linton Boulevard at 1600 S. Ocean Boulevard.
Hours: 8 a.m. to dusk.
Fee: Metered parking for up to four hours.
Contact: Delray Beach Parks and Recreation, 561-243-7260; recorded beach conditions: 561-27BEACH
www.mydelraybeach.com

> *Expensive Sand*
>
> The city of Boca Raton has three miles of gorgeous beach, but its parks have the highest entrance fees of any in Florida, topping out at $18. Since entry is free to residents with a permit, the hefty nonresident fees would seem intended to keep outsiders away.

Spanish River Park

Special features: Beach fishing · Nature trails

This expansive 100-acre wooded park on the west side of A1A extends for half a mile along the highway. Three pedestrian tunnels go under A1A to the beach. There's fishing and a kayak launch on the Intracoastal Waterway. Surf fishing on the ocean is allowed only outside of lifeguard hours of 9 a.m. to 5 p.m. There's free on-street parking for about 30 cars on Spanish River Road, just west of A1A. Walk across the highway to the boardwalk (no facilities).

Beach Length: 0.5 mile.
Pets: Not allowed.

Directions: Just south of Route 800 (Spanish River Road), on Route A1A.

Hours: 8 a.m. to sunset.

Fee: $16 weekdays; $18 weekends; annual residential permit is $31.25.

Contact: Boca Raton Parks and Recreation, 561-393-7810

www.ci.boca-raton.fl.us/parks/Spanishriver.cfm

Red Reef Park

Special features: Outdoor shower · Beach fishing · Nature trails

This 67-acre park has an offshore manmade reef of limestone boulders, popular with tropical fish and snorkelers alike. Surf fishing is also popular, but is prohibited in the swimming area between 9 a.m. and 5 p.m. There's also an executive golf course.

Beach Length: 0.5 mile.

Pets: Not allowed.

Directions: From Boca Raton, cross to the island on E. Palmetto Park Road; go north on N. Ocean Boulevard (A1A), 1 mile to the park.

Hours: 8 a.m. to 10 p.m.

Fee: $16 weekdays; $18 weekends; annual residential permit is $31.25.

Contact: 561-393-7806

www.ci.boca-raton.fl.us/parks/redreef.cfm

Nearby: when you've had enough sun, head across the highway from Red Reef Park to the Gumbo Limbo Nature Center to see live marine animals and take a walk on a shady nature trail. Suggested donation: $3. 1801 N. Ocean Boulevard, Boca Raton, 561- 338-1473, www.gumbolimbo.com

South Beach Park

Special features: Outdoor shower · Beach fishing · Nature trails

This large and shady park has three beach accesses, all with parking lots. The restrooms are at the center access. Surf fishing is popular, but not allowed in the swimming area from 9 a.m. to 5 p.m.

Beach Length: 0.5 mile.
Pets: Not allowed.
Directions: On Ocean Boulevard (A1A) at NE 4th Street in Boca Raton.
Hours: 8 a.m. to sunset.
Fee: $15 weekdays; $17 weekends; annual residential permit is $31.25.
Contact: 561-393-7806
www.ci.boca-raton.fl.us/parks/southbeachpark.cfm

South Beach Pavilion

Special features: Beach fishing

This pavilion on a tall bluff overlooking the ocean is a favorite local gathering spot. Free one-hour parking for about 20 cars fills up fast. Fishing is not allowed from 9 a.m. to 5 p.m., when lifeguard is on duty.

Beach Length: Access to South Beach Park's half mile of beach.
Pets: Not allowed.
Directions: Located just south of South Beach Park on A1A.
Hours: 6 a.m. to 11 p.m.
Fee: None.
Contact: 561-393-7974
www.ci.boca-raton.fl.us/parks/southbeachpark.cfm

SOUTH FLORIDA

South Inlet Park

Special features: Outdoor shower · Fishing jetty · Beach fishing

This nice shady park on the south side of Boca Inlet has sand volley-ball, a fishing jetty, and picnic tables with grills. No fishing or surfing within the area with lifeguards. A surf wheelchair is available.

Beach Length: 850 feet.
Pets: Allowed on a leash in the park, but not on the beach.
Directions: On the south side of Boca Inlet at S. Ocean Boulevard (A1A) and Ponce de Leon Road.
Hours: Sunrise to sunset.
Fee: $4 weekdays; $6 weekends.
Contact: Palm Beach County Parks, 561-966-6600
www.co.palm-beach.fl.us/parks

Fort Lauderdale Area

Deerfield Public Beach

Special features: Outdoor shower · Picnic shelters · Fishing pier

The mile-long public beach extends north and south of the 900-foot International Fishing Pier, with a nicely landscaped boardwalk. No swimming is allowed in the surfing area on the north side of the pier and south of tower #9. Lifeguards are on duty year-round, 9 a.m. to 5 p.m. There are several sand volleyball courts, and a beach wheelchair is available.

Beach Length: 1 mile.
Pets: Not allowed.
Directions: The fishing pier is at the east end of 2nd Street on A1A.
Hours: 6 a.m. to 11 p.m.
Fee: Metered street parking.
Contact: Deerfield Beach Parks and Recreation, 954-480-4433; recorded beach conditions: 954-480-4413
www.deerfield-beach.com

North Ocean Park

Special features: Outdoor shower · Beach fishing

This small park is nestled between condos and hotels, but gives access to the same stretch of beach as Pompano Public Beach to the south. There are picnic tables and a boardwalk ramp over the dunes.

Beach Length: 0.6 mile.
Pets: Not allowed.

Directions: At NE 16th and A1A in Pompano Beach.
Hours: Sunrise to sunset.
Fee: Metered parking.
Contact: Pompano Beach Parks and Recreation, 954-786-4111
recorded beach report: 954-786-4005
www.mypompanobeach.org

Pompano Public Beach

Special features: Picnic shelters · Outdoor shower · Fishing pier

This city is named after a fish for good reason. Book a charter, cast a line from pier or beach, or simply watch the tropical fish by snorkeling the large artificial reef of sunken freighters. Pompano Beach Boulevard, east of A1A, runs parallel to it. It has metered parking from E. Atlantic Boulevard to several blocks north. There's a fishing pier at 222 North Pompano Beach Boulevard, open 24 hours. Surfing is restricted to the north side of the pier. Fisherman's Wharf restaurant is at NE 2nd. Restrooms and beach wheelchairs are available at 10 N. Pompano Beach Boulevard. The beach has a lifeguard year-round, 9 a.m. to 4:45 p.m.

Beach Length: 0.6 mile.
Pets: Not allowed.
Directions: At the east end of E. Atlantic Boulevard and N. Pompano Boulevard.
Hours: 6 a.m. to 11 p.m.
Fee: Metered parking.
Contact: Pompano Beach Parks and Recreation, 954-786-4111
recorded beach report: 954-786-4005
www.mypompanobeach.org

Lauderdale-By-The-Sea Public Beach

Special features: Outdoor shower · Fishing pier · Beach fishing

A mile-long beach, 24-hour fishing pier, pubs, and shops can be found in this beautiful beach community. A living coral reef, a snorkel trail, and the wreck of the SS *Copenhagen* lure both snorkelers and divers. There's metered parking along El Mar Drive (one block east of A1A), a metered lot at El Rado, and handicapped beach accesses at Washingtonia and Datura.

Beach Length: 1 mile.
Pets: Not allowed.
Directions: At the east end of Commercial Boulevard along El Mar Drive.
Hours: Open 24 hours.
Fee: Metered parking lots and on-street parking.
Contact: Lauderdale-By-The-Sea Public Works, 954-776-0576 www.lauderdalebythesea-fl.gov

Fort Lauderdale City Beach

Special features: Outdoor shower · Beach fishing

The city where Spring Break was invented in the 1950s has been toning down that image to appeal to a slightly older, more well-heeled, and less rowdy clientele. That said, this is still a very fun, very happening beach town with miles of uninterrupted sand. Rent a small sailboat or personal watercraft, or go parasailing. Restaurants, bars, and shops are just steps off the sand. Surf fishing is allowed anywhere, but only from dusk to dawn.

Details: Four miles of public beach line A1A, from the border of Lauderdale-By-The-Sea to Port Everglades, with metered street parking and bus service the entire length. The Strip, from Sunrise Boulevard south to Las Olas, is the busiest section. North and south of here you're likely to find a bit more peace and quiet. There are beach accesses at the ends of most streets. On the south end of the beach, A1A is one-way going north. Here there are no condos or hotels on the oceanside to block the view, making for a very pleasant cruise or stroll. South Beach Park has public restrooms.

Beach Length: 4 miles.

Pets: Allowed only in the Canine Beach (see below), with a permit from the Parks and Recreation Department.

Directions: From Ft. Lauderdale, take Las Olas Boulevard east to the beach and turn north or south on Atlantic Boulevard.

Hours: 6 a.m. to 6 p.m.

Fee: Free and metered street parking; $6 lot at Las Olas Boulevard.

Contact: 954-828-PARK

Beach report: 954-828-4597

http://ci.ftlaud.fl.us/beach

A freighter passes by Fort Lauderdale Beach.

Canine Beach

Hooray for Fido! The hours are restrictive, but we love that there's a special place on Fort Lauderdale Beach for pups to frolic.

Beach Length: 300 feet.
Pets: Allowed on a leash with permit.
Directions: Located along A1A, from Sunrise Boulevard north to lifeguard station #5.
Hours: Friday, Saturday, and Sunday, 3–7 p.m. in winter; 5–9 p.m. in summer.
Fee: one weekend permit: $5.65 per dog; annual permit: $25 for residents, $40 for nonresidents.
Contact: 954-828-PARK

Hugh Taylor Birch State Park

Special features: Nature trails · Beach fishing

The gift by this park's namesake means future generations can find an oasis in the middle of urban life. There's a mile-long freshwater lagoon for canoeing and fishing, a nature center, and biking and hiking trails through native Florida habitats. The visitor center is located in Birch's distinctive Art Deco home. Access the Atlantic Ocean beach via a pedestrian walkway under A1A. Fishing is allowed from the seawall on the Intracoastal Waterway.

Beach Length: 400 feet.
Pets: Allowed on a leash in the park, but not on the beach.
Directions: Sunrise Boulevard at Birch, one block off A1A in Fort Lauderdale.
Hours: 8 a.m. to sunset; beach gate open 9 a.m. to 5 p.m.

Fee: $3 single occupant vehicle; $4 per vehicle with 2–8 people; $1 per pedestrian.
Contact: 954-564-4521
www.floridastateparks.org/hughtaylorbirch

John U. Lloyd Beach State Park

Special features: Outdoor shower · Picnic shelters · Fishing jetty

It's a bit of a walk to the beach, but well worth the effort. The beach is long and wide, and you can get a whole patch of sand to yourself. It was renourished in 2006 with enough sand to fill the Empire State Building. The additional 250 feet of beach means even more room for humans as well as for nesting sea turtles. There's snorkeling and diving on the offshore reef, and fishing off the jetty. There are two boat ramps on the Intracoastal Waterway. Boaters can access the ocean or beach along the northern end of Whiskey Creek for a beach picnic. Visit the environmental education facility or watch cruise ships and container barges entering Port Everglades. There are six parking lots, all with beach access, restrooms, and showers.

Beach Length: 2.5 miles.
Pets: Allowed on a leash, but not on the beach.
Directions: From I-95, take exit 21, Sheridan Street east to A1A, and go north 1.5 miles.
Hours: 8 a.m. to sunset.
Fee: $5 per vehicle; $3 for single-occupant vehicle.
Contact: 954-923-2833
www.floridastateparks.org/lloydbeach

Dania Beach Ocean Park

Special features: Outdoor shower · Fishing pier

This small beach has the Beach Grill at the south end and a fishing pier and the new Pier Restaurant to the north. In between is a large parking lot with the beach on one side and the Intracoastal Waterway on the other. There's local bus service to the beach.

Beach Length: 0.5 mile.
Pets: Not allowed.
Directions: At the east end of Dania Beach Boulevard on A1A.
Hours: Sunrise to 10 p.m.
Fee: Pay machine in parking lot.
Contact: City of Dania Parks and Recreation, 954-924-3696
www.daniabeachfl.gov

Dania Beach fishing pier.

Hollywood North Beach Park

Special features: Outdoor shower · Beach fishing

This 56-acre county park in north Hollywood has an observation tower, natural area, handicapped boardwalk over the dunes, a bike path, and the Turtle Café. Just north of the park there's metered parking at ends of streets from Greene to Perry, about ten accesses total. Lifeguard on duty year-round.

Beach Length: 1,200 feet.
Pets: Not allowed.
Directions: North of Johnson at east end of Sheridan on A1A in Hollywood.
Hours: 8 a.m. to 6 p.m.
Fee: $5; $3 after 2 p.m.
Contact: Broward County Parks, 954-926-2444
www.broward.org/parks

Hollywood Beach

Special features: Outdoor shower · Picnic shelters · Beach fishing

There aren't many beaches where you can order a beer from a walk-up window. Yet the atmosphere here isn't typical Spring Break. You'll see all types and all ages, from deeply tanned old Russian men playing cards to girls with belly rings. You'll hear many languages as you walk along the lively "Broadwalk" lined with shops, bars, and cafés. There may be a senior citizen dance and potluck under one of the pavilions. You might hear Shakespeare, reggae, or big band music from the outdoor Beach Theater at Johnson Street, the epicenter of

SOUTH FLORIDA

Hollywood Beach's "Broadwalk."

Hollywood's beach scene. There's on-street parking where you can find it, and a parking garage on Johnson Street. There are restrooms at these parks: Harry Barry Park at Azalea Court and Surf Road, Charnow Park at Garfield Street, and Keating Park at S. Ocean Drive and Magnolia Terrace. In 2006 the Broadwalk received a $20 million facelift with new surfacing and lighting. Lifeguards watch over the entire beach year-round.

Beach Length: 4.5 miles.
Pets: Not allowed.
Directions: From I-95, take Hollywood Boulevard (Route 820) east for 3 miles to the beach.
Hours: Open 24 hours.
Fee: Metered parking.
Contact: Hollywood Beach Safety Department, 954-921-3423
www.hollywoodfl.org

Hallandale Beach

$

Special features: Outdoor shower

You can't miss this beach, crowded with high-rise condos, because of the tall, colorful water tower. There are two public beach units to the north and south of Hallandale Beach Boulevard, separated by private property. Enter the north beach behind the fire and rescue station, where a nice beachfront café is tucked away. The south beach has a small, quiet park with a shady playground among the towering condos. Both beaches have restrooms and great wave action.

Beach Length: 600 feet.
Pets: Not allowed.
Directions: From I-95 go east on Hallandale Beach Boulevard (Route 858) to A1A.
Hours: 6 a.m. to 10 p.m.
Fee: Pay machine, $1 per hour.
Contact: Hallandale Parks and Recreation, 954-457-1456 or 954-457-1452
www.ci.hallandale.fl.us/parks/beaches.html

Miami Area

Samson Oceanfront Park

Special features: Outdoor shower · Picnic shelters · Fishing pier

This tiny two-acre park squeezed between towering high-rises (including the new Miami Trump Towers) is your rabbit-hole entry to Sunny Isles' five miles of public beach. Fishing is allowed only at Pier Park, located at Sunny Isles Boulevard and Collins Avenue. The pier has 24-hour fishing and a restaurant. In addition, there are 18 beach access points along Collins Avenue (most are handicapped accessible), with metered lots or on-street parking nearby. The city's free shuttle provides beach transportation.

Beach Length: 5 miles.
Pets: Not allowed.
Directions: Take Sunny Isles Causeway (SR 826) to the island; go north on Collins Avenue 0.5 mile to the park.
Hours: Sunrise to sunset.
Fee: None for park; metered on-street parking; $6 per day to park at the pier.
Contact: Sunny Isles Beach City Hall, 305-947-0606
www.sibfl.net

Haulover Park

Special features: Outdoor shower · Picnic shelters · Beach fishing

One of Florida's only beaches where nudity is legal (by Miami-Dade County ordinance), this beach also has great surfing and swimming. The clothing-optional area is about 800 yards long on the north end of the beach. On the other side of Collins Avenue is the park's marina, with tennis courts, nine-hole golf course, and restaurant. The name of the beach comes from the time when a local fisherman used this narrow bit of island to "haul" his sponge boat from Biscayne Bay across the dunes to the ocean. Today, fishing is allowed only under the bridge, on the Intracoastal Waterway. Plenty of parking.

Beach Length: 1.5 mile.
Pets: Not allowed.
Directions: 10800 Collins Avenue, just across the inlet from Bal Harbour.
Hours: Sunrise to sunset.
Fee: $5 per vehicle.
Contact: 305-947-3525
www.miamidade.gov/parks/parks/haulover_park.asp

Oleta River State Park

Special features: Picnic shelters · Good beach for small children · Beach fishing · Fishing pier

It's not on the ocean, but don't overlook this thousand-acre park's swimming beach on a tropical lagoon, just off the Intracoastal Waterway. There's mountain biking, kayaking, plentiful bird watching, and cabins for spending the night. Fishing is from the pier or along the ICW. Bike and kayaks rental are available.

Beach Length: 1,200 feet.
Pets: Allowed in the park, but not on the beach.
Directions: Just off Sunny Isles Causeway in North Miami Beach.
Hours: 8 a.m. to sunset.
Fee: $3 for single-occupant vehicle; $5 per vehicle up to eight people.
Contact: 305-919-1846
www.floridastateparks.org/oletariver

Bal Harbour

Special features: Fishing jetty

This is a small, wealthy, and primarily private beach community. Unless you live here or are staying at one of the hotels, the only place to park is in the metered lot underneath the Haulover bridge, popular with surfers. Fishing is allowed only from the jetty or the bridge. No facilities.

Beach Length: 0.3 mile.
Pets: Not allowed.
Directions: Access the island on Broad Causeway; turn north on Bal Harbour Road and go 0.9 mile to the Haulover Bridge.
Hours: Sunrise to sunset.
Fee: Metered parking.
Contact: Bal Harbour Village, 305-866-4633
www.balharbourgov.com

Surfside

*Special features: Outdoor shower · Good beach for small children ·
Beach fishing*

The gentle waves along this small town beach are great for small children. There are pedestrian beach accesses (not handicapped accessible) and outdoor showers at the ends of 96th through 88th streets off Collins Avenue, and metered parking lots are on 93rd and 94th streets. The Oceanfront Community Center on 93rd Street has beach access with lifeguards, restrooms, snack bar, locker rooms, and a public pool (nonresidents must pay pool admission to use beach access). Fishing along the beach is allowed from dusk to dawn only.

SOUTH FLORIDA

Beach Length: 1 mile.
Pets: Not allowed.
Directions: Access the island on Broad Causeway, then turn south on A1A.
Hours: Open 24 hours.
Fee: Metered parking.
Contact: 305-866-3635, 305-861-4862
www.townofsurfsidefl.gov

North Shore Open Space Park Beach

Special features: Outdoor shower · Picnic shelters · Good beach for small children

Natural dunes covered with sea grape and sea oats make this park a jewel in urban Miami Beach. A bike path and wide beach with gentle surf add to its charm. The parking lot is on the west side of Collins Avenue. Surf wheelchairs available.

Beach Length: 0.5 mile.
Pets: Allowed in park, but not on beach.
Directions: Access Miami Beach via the North Shore Causeway and go north on Collins Avenue. The park is between 79th and 86th streets.
Hours: Sunrise to sunset.
Fee: Paid parking lot.
Contact: 305-673-7720
www.miamibeachfl.gov

North Miami Beach

$

Special features: Outdoor shower · Beach fishing

From 78th to 21st streets is the quieter, northern end of the legendary strip of sand. These cross streets off Collins, going north to south, have metered parking lots, restrooms, and outdoor showers: 72nd, 64th, 53rd, 46th, 35th, and 21st. There's also local bus service up and down Collins Avenue along the beach. Surf fishing is allowed as long as it doesn't interfere with swimmers.

Beach Length: 3.5 miles.
Pets: Not allowed.
Directions: From I-95 in Miami, take I-195 (Arthur Godfrey Road) east to Collins Avenue.
Hours: 5 a.m. to midnight; meters operate 9 a.m. to midnight.
Fee: Metered parking.
Contact: Miami Beach Parks and Recreation, 305-673-7730; Miami Beach Patrol, 305-673-7714
www.miamibeachfl.gov

Lummus Park

 $

Special features: Outdoor shower

This is the heart of South Beach: hip sidewalk dining, pink Art Deco hotels, expensive cars cruising Ocean Drive. The beach is wide and white and the water is fine. The park is shaded by palms and chickee huts. Topless sunbathing is not uncommon here. There's a small metered lot at 5th Street and on-street metered parking all along Ocean (you can pay with a credit card at handy machines). There are restrooms at 5th and 14th. Note: north of here, hotels block public access from 15th to 20th.

Ocean Drive, South Beach.

Beach Length: 0.75 mile.

Pets: Not allowed.

Directions: Access South Beach on MacArthur Causeway (5th Street) and go north on Ocean Drive. The park runs between 5th and 15th.

Hours: Sunrise to sunset.

Fee: Metered parking.

Contact: Miami Beach Parks, 305-673-7720; Miami Beach Patrol, 305-673-7714

www.miamibeachfl.gov

Marjory Stoneman Douglas Ocean Beach Park

Located south of much of the SoBe craziness, this beach is more family oriented (i.e., topless sunbathing is really not evident). There's a metered lot between 2nd and 3rd streets.

Beach Length: 400 feet.
Pets: Not allowed.
Directions: From MacArthur Causeway, turn south on Collins Avenue to 3rd Street.
Hours: Sunrise to sunset.
Fee: Metered parking.
Contact: Miami Beach Parks and Recreation, 305-673-7730; Miami Beach Patrol, 305-673-7714
www.miamibeachfl.gov

SOUTH FLORIDA

South Pointe Park

Special features: Picnic shelters · Fishing jetty · Fishing pier

This park has an enviable spot at the southern tip of Miami Beach on the Government Cut to Biscayne Bay. It was rough around the edges when we visited, but is slated for major improvements with new restrooms and facilities. A very nice restaurant called Smith & Wollensky has outdoor dining right on Government Cut, a great spot for cruise ship watching. There's swimming on the ocean beach, and fishing from the Sunshine Pier and mile-long jetty. Pier Park at South Pointe Drive and Ocean Boulevard has metered parking. Note: The park is closed for renovations; no projected opening date at press time. Call ahead for status.

Beach Length: 300 feet.
Pets: Allowed in park on a leash, but not on beach.
Directions: Access South Miami Beach via MacArthur Causeway; go south on Washington Avenue. The park is along Washington, between 5th and 1st.
Hours: Sunrise to sunset.
Fee: $2 for Miami residents with photo ID; $5 for nonresidents.
Contact: 305-673-7730
www.miamibeachfl.gov

Rickenbacker Causeway/Hobie Beach

Special features: Outdoor shower · Fishing pier · Beach fishing

The two islands along the causeway to Virginia Key draw windsurfers by the dozens on windy days. Because it's the only pet-friendly beach between Fort Lauderdale and the Florida Keys, lots of pups frolic in the surf (keep them leashed; the highway is very close). The rules are a little lax here, so there may be some partying or an occasional nude sunbather. It's also not the cleanest beach because of the pets and partying, so it's not the best beach for toddlers to play in the sand. You can rent windsurfers and kayaks or even take a ride in an ultralight. There are 24-hour fishing piers parallel to the bridge and restrooms on the south side. The north side of the causeway is shaded by Australian pines, and the shore is coarse gravel and rocks. Hence, it's a quiet place to park a lawn chair and admire the Miami skyline. There's bus service along the causeway out to Key Biscayne, as well as a nice bike path.

Dog-friendly Hobie Beach on Rickenbacker Causeway.

Beach Length: 1.5 mile combined.
Pets: Allowed on a leash.
Directions: From Route 1 in Coral Gables, take the Rickenbacker Causeway toward Virginia Key and Key Biscayne.
Hours: Sunrise to sunset.
Fee: None, except for $1.25 toll to access the causeway.
Contact: Miami-Dade County Causeway Public Works, 305-361-2833.

Virginia Key Beach

Special features: Outdoor shower · Nature trails

There's a lot of fun going on at this locals' beach where we witnessed frolicking dogs (technically not allowed), beer drinking (ditto), and basketball playing on a beachside court. The facilities are a tad rough and there's a solid waste composting facility nearby. But none of this affects the beauty of an interpretive trail through the Virginia Key Hammock, an ecological restoration of native plants and trees.

Beach Length: 3 miles.
Pets: Not allowed.
Directions: From Route 1 in Coral Gables, take the Rickenbacker Causeway to Virginia Key.
Hours: 9 a.m. to 8 p.m.
Fee: $3 per car.
Contact: City of Miami Parks and Recreation, 305-960-3000
http://ci.miami.fl.us/cms/parks

Historic Virginia Key Beach Park Trust

Special features: Good beach for small children

This historic African American beach, closed for the last 20 years, reopened in early 2008, thanks to the efforts of one local woman. When the concessions and amusement buildings were slated for demolition in 2005, Athalie Range petitioned the city to create a trust to restore the park. The trust has since reacquired the mini train that once ran through the park and refurbished the carousel. The 82-acre park is open for swimming and picnicking. A South Florida Human Rights Museum is also planned. Sadly, Mrs. Range passed away in 2006 at the age of 91, but her dream is being carried on. No fishing allowed.

Beach Length: 1 mile; there are lifeguards on about a third of it.
Pets: To be determined.
Directions: Just south of the city's Virginia Key Beach on Rickenbacker Causeway
Hours: 8 a.m. to dusk.
Fee: None.
Contact: Virginia Key Beach Park Trust, 305-960-4600
www.virginiakeybeachpark.net

Crandon Park

Special features: Outdoor shower · Picnic shelters · Good beach for small children · Nature trails

Toward the north end of Key Biscayne on the Atlantic lies one of South Florida's most beautiful and popular beaches. This huge county park has a parking lot that could be an airstrip, with parking for 3,000 cars. A sandbar offshore creates sheltered, low-wave swimming along 2 miles of beach. It's a great place to bring the family, with a merry-go-round, amusement center, bike rentals and bike path, and a nature center that interprets the legacy of naturalist Marjory Stoneman Douglas. On the bay side of the island, the park has a golf course, marina, kayak rentals, eco-tours, and tennis courts.

Beach Length: 2 miles.
Pets: Not allowed.
Directions: From Coral Gables, take Rickenbacker Causeway to Key Biscayne and go to 4000 Crandon Boulevard.
Hours: 8 a.m. to sunset.
Fee: $5 per vehicle.
Contact: 305-361-5421
www.miamidade.gov/parks/parks/crandon_beach.asp

Bill Baggs Cape Florida State Park

Special features: Outdoor shower · Picnic shelters · Nature trails · Beach fishing

This park on the south end of Key Biscayne claims to be "15 minutes from downtown Miami, but a world apart." You leave traffic behind for one of Florida's most beautiful beaches, but Bill Baggs still has much of the liveliness and color that make Miami exciting. The beach is busy on weekends, with families serving up paella and barbecue while kids ride boogie boards and fly kites. When we were there, a Hindu wedding was taking place at the lighthouse. Built in 1825 and reconstructed in 1846, it is the oldest structure in Miami-Dade County. Climb to the top Thursday through Monday (tours at 10 a.m. and 1 p.m.). There's a nice bike path and bike rentals (try one of those made for two with a sun canopy on top) along with kayak, beach chair, and umbrella rentals. There's a café near the beach and the Boater's Grill, overlooking No Name Harbor, serves authentic Cuban food. There's no fishing from the beach, but it is popular on the seawall along Biscayne Bay.

Lighthouse at Bill Baggs Cape Florida State Park.

Beach Length: 1.2 mile from the lighthouse north.

Pets: Allowed on a leash in picnic areas and along the seawall, bike trails, and hiking trails, but not on the beach.

Directions: From I-95 in Miami, take the Rickenbacker Causeway all the way to the end of Key Biscayne.

Hours: 8 a.m. to sunset.

Fee: $5 per vehicle.

Contact: 305-361-5811
www.floridastateparks.org/capeflorida

From the seawall at Bill Baggs Cape Florida State Park you can see Stiltsville. The Prohibition-era houses were built on stilts a mile offshore, just beyond the reach of the law.

Matheson Hammock County Park

$

Special features: Picnic shelters · Outdoor shower · Good beach for small children · Beach fishing · Nature trails

This beautifully landscaped park has an unusual atoll beach, a lagoon circled with sand, and an elegant restaurant, the Red Fish Grill, inside a historic coral stone building. There's a marina with boat rentals. A curious "wading beach" right on Biscayne Bay has a sign warning of crocodiles! Fishing is allowed only on Biscayne Bay.

Beach Length: 200 feet.
Pets: Not allowed.
Directions: From Route 1, go west on Kendal Drive 2.25 miles to end, turn right on Old Cutler Road and go 0.75 mile to the park. It is just north of Fairchild Tropical Gardens in S. Coral Gables.
Hours: Sunrise to sunset.
Fee: $4 per vehicle.
Contact: 305-665-5475
www.miamidade.gov/parks/parks/matheson_beach.asp

SOUTH FLORIDA

Homestead Area

Biscayne National Park

Special features: Nature trails · Developed campground

The park has no beach on the mainland, but Elliott Key, accessible only by boat, has a very small wading beach, boat dock, and camping. Fishing is from your boat or wading along mangrove lined shorelines. Homestead Bayfront Park, adjacent to the visitor center, has a boat ramp where you can launch.

Beach Length: 150 feet.
Pets: Allowed on a leash only in the developed areas of Elliott Key, not on beach.
Directions: From Homestead, take SW 328th St. east for 6 miles until it ends at the park visitor center. Elliott Key is 8 miles offshore.
Hours: Elliott Key is open 24 hours.
Fee: None for day use. $10 to camp; $15 for overnight docking on Elliott Key.
Contact: 305-230-7275
www.nps.gov/bisc
Boat tours: 305-230-1100.

Homestead Bayfront Park

Special features: Outdoor shower · Picnic shelters · Good beach for small children · Beach fishing

This family park has a pleasant saltwater lagoon for swimming. The full-service Herbert Hoover Marina is the closest place to launch your boat for the offshore islands of Biscayne National Park. Fishing is allowed on the Biscayne Bay shoreline only.

Beach Length: 180 feet.
Pets: Not allowed.
Directions: From Homestead, take SW 328th Street east for 6 miles until it ends at the park, which is adjacent to Biscayne National Park visitor center.
Hours: Sunrise to sunset.
Fee: $4 per vehicle.
Contact: 305-230-3033
www.miamidade.gov/parks/parks/homestead_beach.asp

Everglades National Park

Special features: Beach fishing · Primitive camping

The few beaches of the Everglades are accessible by boat only. Go 10 miles west of Flamingo Marina to find 15 miles of sandy beach all

Beaches in the Everglades are accessible only by boat.

around the point of Cape Sable. The expansive views of Florida Bay and the Gulf of Mexico, the bird life, and the huge night sky devoid of light pollution make this a magical place. There are no facilities at the beaches, and no freshwater, but the Flamingo Marina has restrooms, showers, and a store. Primitive camping is allowed, but be sure to bring a bug shirt and all the freshwater you'll need. Out in Florida Bay, the small beach on North Nest Key is more easily accessed from Key Largo (see Florida Keys chapter).

Beach Length: 15 miles.

Pets: Not allowed anywhere in the backcountry.

Directions: From U.S. 1 in Florida City, turn west on West Palm Drive (SR9336). Go 1.6 mile to a four-way stop and turn left on Tower Road (SR 9336) (see the famous "Robert is Here" fruit and vegetable stand on the corner). Go 2 miles and turn right onto Ingraham Highway (SR 9336). Drive another 5 miles to the park entrance station, then 38 miles to the end of the road at Flamingo. GPS for marina: N25 08.541, W80 55.394

East Cape Sable is 10 miles west of Flamingo by water. GPS: N25 07.105, W81 04.797

Fee: Park entrance fee is $10 (good for seven days); launch fee is $3; backcountry camping permit (good for 14 days) is $10 plus $2 per person per night.

Contact: 305-242-7700

www.nps.gov/ever

Marina: 800-600-3813

Backcountry camping: 239-695-2945

www.nps.gov/ever/visit/campsite.htm

Florida Keys

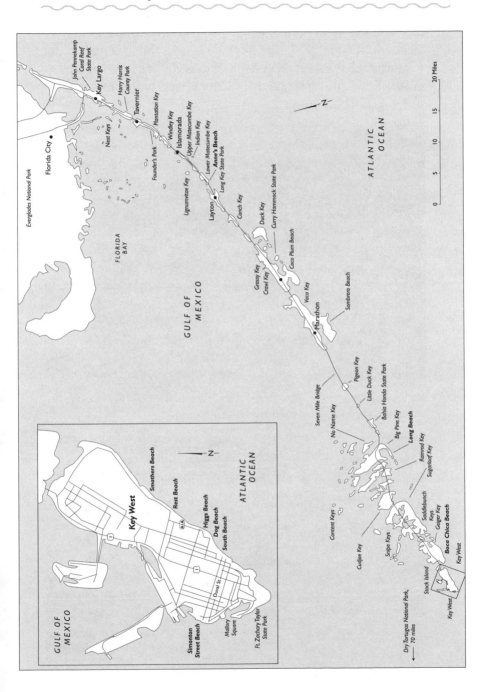

Where's the beach? That is often the first question visitors ask when they visit this coral island chain. Diving, fishing, drinking—did we mention fishing? The Florida Keys are famous for all three, but not so much for its beaches. Blame the famous 200-mile coral reef a few miles offshore, which breaks the Atlantic waves. Without a pounding surf, beaches can't form.

Many of the beaches on this string of coral islands are rocky, like this one on Indian Key (by permission of Fernando Fernandez).

This sandbar in the Dry Tortugas is an idyllic Caribbean scene.

But there are a few patches of sand, some famous, others known only to locals, and we've listed them all, including the beautiful white sands of Sombrero Beach in Marathon, Bahia Honda State Park, and Smathers Beach in Key West. In the Upper Keys, Canon Beach at John Pennekamp Coral Reef State Park is a snorkeler's delight. And while it often resembles a clayflat more than a beach, dog-friendly Anne's Beach on Lower Matecumbe seems to capture best the laid-back Keys spirit.

Beach Bumming

With the scarcity of public beaches in the Keys, it's good to know that some fun watering holes and hotels will let you enjoy their precious patch of sand for the price of a meal or cocktail.

Our favorites include the tiki bar and lunch grill at Key Largo Grande Resort (MM 97 B/S, Key Largo), Rum Runners at Holiday Isle (MM 84 O/S, Islamorada), Ocean Terrace Grill at Cheeca Lodge (MM 81.8 O/S, Islamorada), and Shula's at the elegant Reach Resort in Key West. Kick off your shoes and dance in the sand at Morada Bay's any night, but try to catch the monthly full-moon party (MM 81.6 B/S, Islamorada).

We hope our all-time favorite place to toast the sunset over Florida Bay will never change: the Caribbean Club, where scenes in Bogey and Bacall's *Key Largo* were filmed (MM 104 B/S). Next door, our friends at Florida Bay Outfitters will rent you a kayak or let you launch your own from their slip of beach (www.kayakflorida-keys.com).

The ocean beach at Cheeca Lodge in Islamorada.

Key Largo

North Nest Key

Special features: Portable toilets only · Beach fishing · Primitive camping

Play Gilligan for a day—or weekend—on this small mangrove island in Florida Bay, one of the few in Everglades National Park that allows access. It's best reached from Key Largo, eight miles by private boat or kayak. Along the way you may see dolphins, rays, sea turtles, or perhaps a manatee in the clear Caribbean-blue waters. Anchor offshore, or land on the narrow beach on the northwest side of the island. You can pitch a tent on dry land in the mangroves, but you must bring all your freshwater; a gallon per person per day is recommended. No fires allowed.

This kayak beach at Florida Bay Outfitters in Key Largo is a top spot to watch the sunset.

Beach Length: 1,000 feet.

Pets: Not allowed.

Directions: At MM 104 B/S, U.S. Route 1 in Key Largo, you can launch kayaks from Florida Bay Outfitters (no charge), or a boat from the Caribbean Club's boat ramp ($5).

GPS for N. Nest Key beach: N25 09.053, W80 30.732

GPS for Caribbean Club boat ramp: N25 08.724, W80 23.820

Hours: Sunrise to sunset.

Fee: None for day use. For camping, a backcountry permit is required from Everglades National Park: $10 plus $2 per person per night.

Contact: 239-695-2945

www.nps.gov/ever/visit/campsite.htm

Giving Directions in the Keys

U.S. Route 1 runs the length of the Keys and is marked by small green mile marker signs. MM 0 is in Key West, and MM 126 is just south of Florida City. People in the Keys also designate bayside (B/S) or oceanside (O/S) when giving a mile marker number.

KEYS

John Pennekamp Coral Reef State Park

Special features: Outdoor shower · Picnic shelters · Good beach for small children · Nature trails · Developed campground

Most of this 70-square-mile park is underwater, making this the prime headquarters for snorkeling and diving trips to the reef, three miles offshore. Fishing in the numerous mangrove creeks and flats fishing in Largo Sound is popular. There are two small manmade beaches on sheltered Largo Sound, so it's a great place for little swimmers, beginning snorkelers, or those who just want to jump in the water and easily see some fish. On Cannon Beach, you can snorkel the remains of an early Spanish shipwreck, complete with replica cannons, that attracts colorful fish and crustaceans. Far Beach is on an idyllic lagoon, complete with palm trees. Both beaches have restrooms. Swimming is allowed only within the marked areas; you must use a diver down flag when snorkeling outside the swimming areas. Take a break from the sun and explore the two nature trails, one a boardwalk through the mangroves, the other a wooded path through a tropical hardwood hammock. There are canoe/kayak trails and rentals. The park has a full-service marina, aquarium, gift shop, and snack bar. Shoreline fishing is allowed outside the swimming areas.

Beach Length: 300 feet each.

Pets: Allowed on the nature trails and in the campground, but not on the beach.

Directions: MM 102.5 O/S on U.S. Route 1, Key Largo.

Hours: 8 a.m. to sunset.

Fee: $3.50 for single-occupant vehicle; $6 for two occupants and 50¢ for each additional person in the vehicle; $1.50 for pedestrians and bicyclists.

Contact: 305-451-1202

www.floridastateparks.org/pennekamp

Harry Harris County Park

Special features: Outdoor shower · Picnic shelters · Good beach for small children · Beach fishing · Fishing jetty

This oceanside park has a tidal pool on the ocean, better for wading than swimming, a boat ramp, recreation fields, and good fishing. A coral rock barrier protects the beach from erosion and creates a nice lagoon for youngsters to splash in.

Beach Length: 100 feet.

Pets: Allowed in designated areas of the park, but not on the beach.

Directions: At MM 92.5 U.S. Route 1 O/S in Tavernier, turn east on Burton Drive and go 1.1 mile to the end.

Hours: 8 a.m. to sunset.

Fee: Free to Monroe County residents; $5 for nonresidents on weekends and holidays only.

Contact: 305-852-6188

www.monroecounty-fl.gov

Islamorada

Founder's Park

Special features: Indoor shower · Outdoor shower · Picnic shelters · Good beach for small children · Fishing jetty

This large park has much in the way of recreation, including a pool, tennis courts, playing fields, marina, skate park, and running track. The bayside swimming beach is sheltered and shallow, perfect for children or beginning kayakers. The pool has lifeguards, but the beach does not. There are indoor showers in the pool locker room, outdoor showers at the beach, and fishing off the jetty.

Beach Length: 220 feet.
Pets: There is a dog park, but dogs are not allowed on the beach.
Directions: MM 86.5 U.S. Route 1 B/S, Islamorada.
Hours: Sunrise to sunset.
Fee: None for residents of Islamorada and local hotel guests; non-residents: $2 ages 3–9; $3 students and seniors; $4 adults.
Contact: Village of Islamorada, 305-853-1685, www.islamorada.fl.us
Kayak rentals: 305-852-5633.

Islamorada Library Park

Special features: Outdoor shower · Picnic shelters

Pick out a book at the library, then walk out back to the small, quiet park on a sheltered mangrove creek. There's no swimming or wading here, but it is a rare patch of sand to lie on or launch a kayak.

KEYS

Beach Length: 50 feet.
Pets: Not allowed.
Directions: MM 81.7 U.S. Route 1 B/S, behind the Islamorada Library.
Hours: Sunrise to 5 p.m.
Fee: None.
Contact: Village of Islamorada, 305-853-1685
www.islamorada.fl.us

Robbie's Marina

Special features: Portable toilets only · Good beach for small children

This famous landmark, where you can feed giant tarpon, eat at the Hungry Tarpon, or embark on a fishing charter or ecotour to a wild island, has a tiny slip of shady beach next to the kayak shop. It's really for wading, but it's a nice spot to sit and watch the boats.

Beach Length: 100 feet.
Pets: Allowed on a leash.
Directions: MM 77.4 U.S. Route 1 B/S, at the top of lower Matecumbe Key.
Hours: 9 a.m. to 5 p.m.
Fee: $5 fee, pay in kayak shop.
Contact: Florida Keys Kayak & Ski, 305-664-4878
www.floridakeyskayakandski.com

Anne's Beach

Special features: Outdoor shower · Picnic shelters · Good beach for small children · Beach fishing · Nature trails

This is a true rarity in the Keys, a one-mile-long stretch of beach where dogs can run free. True, the narrow beach is right on the highway, the sand is more like marl clay, and the water is so shallow that true swimming is a challenge. But the laid-back Keysie atmosphere brings us back again and again to lounge in the shallow pools and gaze sleepily out over the turquoise sea.

KEYS

Indian Key Historic State Park

You won't find much sandy beach here, but there are fascinating coral rock beaches with good snorkeling on this historic island one mile off the oceanside of Lower Matecumbe. Walk the "streets" of this former capital of Dade County, then go around the eastern end of the island to find prehistoric-looking kitons embedded in the dead coral rocks. Peek into the tidal pools to see what's living in them. Launch your own kayak from Indian Key Fill, or take an ecotour from Robbie's Marina. Open 8 a.m. to sunset; ranger-led tours are given Thursday through Monday at 9 a.m. and 1 p.m. No facilities. 305-664-2540, www.floridastateparks.org/indiankey

Kayak landing on a small beach at Indian Key (by permission of Fernando Fernandez).

Details: Two parking areas are connected by a shady boardwalk through the mangroves. There are picnic pavilions along the boardwalk and restrooms and an outdoor shower at the northern parking area.

Beach Length: 1 mile.

Pets: Allowed on a leash; please pick up waste.

Directions: MM 73–74 U.S. Route 1 O/S on Lower Matecumbe.

Hours: Sunrise to sunset.

Fee: None.

Contact: Village of Islamorada, 305-664-2345
www.islamorada.fl.us

KEYS

Layton

Long Key State Park

Special features: Outdoor shower · Picnic shelters · Beach fishing · Good beach for small children · Nature trails · Developed camp-ground

"Beach" is a generous term for the park's one-mile shoreline, which is narrow, shallow, and somewhat muddy in places. But to avoid holiday and Spring Break crowds, come here to camp right on the ocean and kayak through a mangrove maze. Canoe and kayak rentals available.

KEYS

Beach Length: 1 mile.
Pets: Allowed on nature trails and in the campground, but not on the beach or any shoreline.
Directions: MM 67.5 U.S. Route 1 O/S in Layton on Long Key.
Hours: 8 a.m. to sunset.
Fee: $3.50 for single-occupant vehicle; $6 for two occupants, 50¢ for each additional; $1.50 for pedestrians and bicyclists.
Contact: 305-664-4815, www.floridastateparks.org/longkey

Curry Hammock State Park

Special features: Outdoor shower · Picnic shelters · Good beach for small children · Beach fishing · Nature trails · Developed camp-ground

Riprap protects the sand from erosion on this small undeveloped ocean beach. Rent a kayak or bring your own to explore the man-grove trails or the offshore sandbar, or hike the nature trail. Camp-

Curry Hammock State Park has a beach of riprap.

ground is open November through May. Fishing is on a channel from a small beach.

Beach Length: 0.5 mile.

Pets: Allowed on the nature trail and in the campground, but not on the beach.

Directions: MM 56.1 U.S. Route 1 O/S, Little Crawl Key.

Hours: 8 a.m. to sunset.

Fee: $3.50 for single-occupant vehicle; $6 for two occupants, 50¢ for each additional passenger; $1.50 for pedestrians and bicyclists.

Contact: 305-289-2690

www.floridastateparks.org/curryhammock

Marathon

Coco Plum Beach

Special features: Beach fishing

This long, wild beach was created by dredge and fill operations in the 1950s to build home canals. Beware of underwater debris and broken glass. It's popular with nesting sea turtles April through October, so don't let pups dig in the sand. There's a sand parking lot for about 10 cars. No facilities.

Beach Length: 1.5 miles.
Pets: Allowed; bag dispenser provided for waste pickup.
Directions: From MM 54.1 U.S. Route 1 O/S, in Marathon, turn east on Coco Plum Drive and go 1.5 mile to the park, on the right.
Hours: 7 a.m. to sunset.
Fee: None.
Contact: Marathon Parks and Recreation 305-743-6598
www.ci.marathon.fl.us

Sombrero Beach

Special features: Outdoor shower · Picnic shelters · Fishing pier

A picture postcard: white-sand beach, palm trees, azure ocean. There's a swimming beach, fishing pier, and kayak launch into Sister's Creek. From April through October, this is an important sea turtle nesting beach.

Beach Length: 0.2 mile.
Pets: Allowed; bag dispensers provided for waste pickup.

Sombrero Beach in Marathon.

Directions: At MM 50 U.S. Route 1 O/S in Marathon, go east on Sombrero Beach Boulevard, 2 miles to the end.
Hours: 7 a.m. to dusk.
Fee: None.
Contact: Marathon Parks and Recreation 305-743-6598
www.ci.marathon.fl.us

Lower Keys

Veterans Memorial Park

Special features: Outdoor shower · Picnic shelters · Beach fishing

This pleasant beach on Little Duck Key has palm trees and covered picnic tables on the oceanside with a great view of Seven Mile Bridge. It's a great place to stretch the legs or take a quick swim on a drive to Key West. There's a boat ramp and parking across the highway on the bayside.

Beach Length: 200 feet.
Pets: Not allowed.
Directions: At the west end of Seven Mile Bridge at MM 39.8 U.S. Route 1 O/S on Little Duck Key.
Hours: 7:30 a.m. to sunset.
Fee: None.
Contact: Monroe County Facilities Maintenance, 305-292-4431 www.monroecounty-fl.gov

Bahia Honda State Park

Special features: Outdoor shower · Picnic shelters · Good beach for small children · Beach fishing · Fishing pier · Nature trails · Developed campground

This island park is famous for its beaches—both ocean and bayside—and crystal-clear water. There's oceanside parking on the nearly two-mile-long Sandspur beach. Calusa, the smaller bayside beach, is shaded with palms and has picnic pavilions. There are cabins, camping, kayak rentals, a gift shop, and an interpretive center with displays about

A rocky island off Bahia Honda State Park provides good snorkeling.

KEYS

marine life. The historic railroad bridge is a great place to watch the sunset. Kayak out to an island less than a mile from the beach for good snorkeling. There's good bottom fishing from the seawalls on either side of the old bridge, and good fly-fishing in the ocean flats.

Beach Length: 2.2 miles.
Pets: Allowed in the campground, but not on the beach.
Directions: MM 36.8 U.S. Route 1 O/S on Bahia Honda Key.
Hours: 8 a.m. to sunset.
Fee: $3.50 for single-occupant vehicle; $6 for two occupants and 50¢ for each additional passenger; $1.50 for pedestrians and bicyclists.
Contact: 305-872-2353
www.floridastateparks.org/bahiahonda

Long Beach Drive

Special features: Beach fishing · Nature trails

This wild beach is a tad difficult to get to, but provides the best access for snorkeling the coral heads offshore (a kayak is recommended to get out there; be sure to have a diver down flag). A nice nature trail leads north to Big Pine Fishing Lodge and south along the beach. Limited parking for only a handful of cars. No facilities. No fires and no camping allowed.

Beach Length: 600 feet.
Pets: Allowed on a leash.
Directions: At MM 32.8 U.S. Route 1 O/S on Big Pine Key, go east on Long Beach Drive 0.4 mile to red wooden barricade on left. Walk 50 feet down the dirt road, turn left through an open area (may be ankle-high water at high tide), and look for a sandy nature trail through the mangroves to the ocean.
Hours: 30 minutes before sunrise to 30 minutes after sunset.
Fee: None.
Contact: National Key Deer Refuge 305-872-2239
www.fws.gov/nationalkeydeer/

Boca Chica Beach

Special featues: Beach fishing

This long stretch of free, public ocean beach is virtually unknown except to locals. Picnic tables and trash cans are provided, but no other facilities. There's a small parking area for two to three vehicles at the beginning of the beach on the left, some roadside parking along the way, and more at the end of the beach. Lock your car.

Beach Length: 0.5 mile.
Pets: Not allowed.
Directions: At MM 10.8 U.S. Route 1 O/S on Geiger Key, turn east on Boca Chica Road and go 3 miles to its end.
Hours: Sunrise to sunset.
Fee: None.
Contact: Monroe County Department of Public Works, 305-292-4560
www.monroecounty-fl.gov

Key West

Smathers Beach

Special features: Outdoor shower · Good beach for small children · Beach fishing

This wide, white ocean beach, popular with sunbathers and Spring Breakers, is visited by upward of 150,000 people a year. It's on the opposite side of the island from the action of Old Town Key West, but it's a Keys icon and well worth a visit. Restrooms, food vendors, kayak and personal watercraft rentals, and parasailing are located at the west end (MM 0).

Beach Length: 1 mile.
Pets: Not allowed.
Directions: MM 0–1 Route A1A O/S (South Roosevelt Boulevard). Entering Key West on Route 1, bear left onto A1A for 2.3 miles. After passing the sign for MM 1, a rocky spit marks the beginning of the swimming beach.
Hours: 7:30 a.m. to 11 p.m.
Fee: Metered on-street parking up to 12 hours, 25¢ per hour. Limited free parking across the road at east end of beach.
Contact: City of Key West Parks and Recreation, 305-293-8320 www.keywestcity.com

C. B. Harvey Rest Beach Park

Special features: Picnic shelters · Beach fishing

This park has pedestrian access to the ocean beach, with free parking and restrooms across the street at Sunny McCoy Indigenous Park.

Beach Length: 500 feet.
Pets: Not allowed.
Directions: At White Street and Atlantic Boulevard in Key West, east of the White Street Pier.
Hours: 7:30 a.m. to 11 p.m.
Fee: None.
Contact: Sunny McCoy Indigenous Park, 305-293-6418
www.keywestcity.com

Higgs Beach

Special features: Outdoor shower · Good beach for small children · Fishing pier

The sandy beach is encircled with old pier pilings that attract sea life and make for good snorkeling. Limited free parking, volleyball and tennis courts, and a sunning deck where yoga classes are sometimes held. There's a bar and restaurant right on the beach. You can rent snorkeling equipment, kayaks, beach chairs, and umbrellas. White Street Pier is on the eastern end of the beach. There's a playground across the street.

Beach Length: 1,000 feet.
Pets: Not allowed.
Directions: On Atlantic Boulevard between Reynolds and White streets, O/S, Key West.
Hours: 7 a.m. to 11 p.m.
Fee: None.
Contact: Monroe County Facilities Maintenance, 305-292-4431
www.monroecounty-fl.gov

KEYS

Beaches in the Keys backcountry are often sand bars that appear and disappear with the tide.

Dog Beach

This postage-stamp-sized beach isn't great for swimming, but dogs love it. Watch your step, and pick up your pup's waste. Limited on-street parking. No facilities. Adjacent Louie's Backyard is an excellent restaurant.

Beach Length: 50 feet.
Pets: Allowed.
Directions: At the south end of Vernon Street, O/S, Key West.
Hours: 7:30 a.m. to 11 p.m.
Fee: None.
Contact: Key West Parks Department, 305-292-8190
www.keywestcity.com

South Beach

Special features: Fishing pier

This small ocean beach has an adjacent restaurant and a fishing pier. Limited on-street parking. No facilities.

Beach Length: 150 feet.
Pets: Not allowed.
Directions: Between the south ends of Duval and Simonton streets, O/S, Key West.
Hours: 7:30 a.m. to 11 p.m.
Fee: None.
Contact: Key West Parks Department, 305-292-8190 www.keywestcity.com

Fort Zachary Taylor Historic State Park

Special features: Outdoor shower · Picnic shelters · Beach fishing · Good beach for small children · Nature trails

This park has a lovely stretch of beach facing the ocean. Rent snorkel gear or a kayak to explore offshore. Daily tours of the historic fort are offered at noon and 2 p.m. The Cayo Hueso Café serves lunch and snacks, 9 a.m. to 5 p.m.

Beach Length: 0.3 mile.
Pets: Allowed on a leash in picnic area or on the field, not on the beach.
Directions: At the southern end of Southard Street on Truman Annex, Key West.
Hours: 8 a.m. to sunset.

Fee: $3.50 for single-occupant vehicle; $6 for two occupants, 50¢ for each additional passenger; $1.50 for pedestrians and bicyclists.
Contact: 305-292-6713
www.floridastateparks.org/forttaylor

Simonton Street Beach

Special features: Picnic shelters · Beach fishing

This tiny beach nestled between two fancy hotels is the closest public beach to all the activity of Duval Street. It is frequented by the homeless and the bathrooms are a little scary. Swimming isn't really advisable because of heavy boat traffic, but this is a great place to launch a boat or kayak to see famous Mallory Square or sunsets from the water. Be sure to lock valuables.

Beach Length: 50 feet.
Pets: Not allowed.
Directions: Enter Key West on U.S. Route 1 (Truman Avenue), go right on Simonton, and follow to the end. Duval Street is one block west.
Hours: 7 a.m. to 11 p.m.
Fee: Metered parking: 25¢ for 15 minutes; up to 12 hours maximum.
Contact: Key West Parks Department, 305-292-8190
www.keywestcity.com

Dry Tortugas: The Name

First discovered by Ponce de Leon in 1513, who provisioned his ship with sea turtles, *tortuga*, these islands lack freshwater; thus the word "dry" was added to their name.

Dry Tortugas National Park

Special features: Portable toilets only · Good beach for small children · Beach fishing · Primitive camping

This cluster of seven coral islands 70 miles west of Key West in the Gulf of Mexico has pristine beaches, abundant bird life, and wonderful snorkeling. Massive Fort Jefferson, begun in 1846 but made obsolete before its completion, is open to visitors on Garden Key. There's a

Beach at Dry Tortugas National Park, Fort Jefferson in the background.

small swimming beach with good snorkeling on patch coral. Garden Key's dock is your embarkation point. There's also overnight anchorage for private vessels and a 10-site campground just outside the fort. With your own boat or kayak you can explore nearby Bush Key, a magnificent frigate bird rookery, and Loggerhead Key, which has a lighthouse, miles of beaches, and a spectacular patch coral called Little Africa just offshore. Be very careful crossing the deep and rough channel to Loggerhead Key—this is not for beginners.

Details: The only facilities are picnic tables and composting toilets (for camper use only; day visitors should use the restrooms on the ferry). The fort has a nice gift shop. Campers must bring own freshwater and take home all trash.

Beach Length: The swimming/snorkeling beach on Garden Key is 400 feet, while Dinghy Beach is about 200.

Pets: Not allowed.

Directions: It's a full-day excursion from Key West aboard a high-speed ferry (about two hours each way). There are two operators: Sunny Days Fast Cat (800-236-7937, www.sunnydayskeywest.com) and Yankee Freedom (800-634-0939, www.yankeefreedom.com). Both can take a few kayaks, but call for length restrictions and reservations.

Hours: Sunrise to sunset.

Fee: Between $139 and $150 per person for round-trip ferry, includes buffet lunch on island; additional $5 per person national park entrance fee (good for seven days); $3 per person to camp.

Contact: 305-242-7700

www.nps.gov/drto/

Panhandle

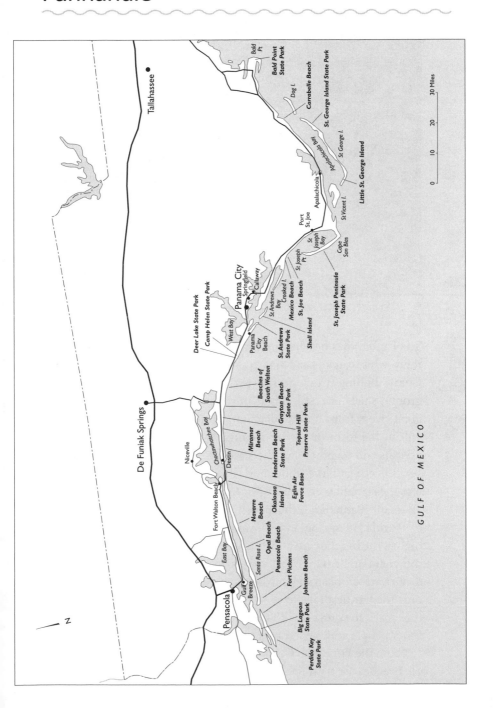

Emerald green water and sparkling white quartz sand define Panhandle beaches.

The Panhandle's beaches are unlike any other in Florida. The blindingly white sugar sand has traveled a long way to the "Emerald Coast," buffing it to a perfect texture. While most sand is of finely ground shells or coral, this is pure quartz crystal, washed down in great rivers from the Appalachian Mountains and deposited in the gulf in the form of barrier islands. When you walk on it, the tiny crystals rub together and the sand literally squeaks underfoot. The sun reflecting off the white sand through the shallow gulf waters creates the signature emerald color of this coast.

In the Panhandle, the beach season is reversed from the rest of Florida. In spring and summer, when the water temperature is higher, the beaches are more crowded with people coming from Birmingham and Atlanta. Fall comes with migrations of monarch butterflies, neotropical songbirds, hawks, and hummingbirds. In winter, only the hardiest take to the water, but you can have an entire pristine beach to yourself, with prolific shelling. The winter beach brings fewer people and, hence, more wildlife.

From the Forgotten Coast to the lively resorts of Destin, Panhandle beaches are truly sublime.

Perdido Key

Perdido Key State Park

Special features: Outdoor shower · Picnic shelters · Beach fishing ·
Nature trails

This long beach of snow white dunes is tucked between high-rises on Perdido Key. Parking lots with facilities are located at either end of the park and a boardwalk access in the middle, with parking and nature trails across the street at the Chamber of Commerce. Surf fishing is very popular for pompano, catfish, and whiting. Hurricane Ivan did a number on this island in 2004, resulting in the planting of 63,000 sea oats. Please preserve this hard work and stay off the dunes.

Beach Length: 2 miles.
Pets: Not allowed.
Directions: From Pensacola, go west on SR 292 for 15 miles.
Hours: 8 a.m. to sunset.
Fee: $1 for walk-ins; $2 per car.
Contact: Big Lagoon State Park, 850-492-1595
www.floridastateparks.org/perdidokey

PANHANDLE

> Simply Southern Fresh Market and Deli just west of Perdido Key State Park serves great seafood gumbo in a colorful café decorated with art made by the owner. Open for lunch daily (850-492-9330).

Johnson Beach

Special features: Indoor shower · Picnic shelters · Beach fishing · Nature trails · Primitive camping

This Perdido Key unit of Gulf Islands National Seashore is the last refuge for the endangered Perdido Key beach mouse. The beach was named for Rosamond Johnson, the first black serviceman from Escambia County to die in the Korean War. Before desegregation, this was the only beach in the area open to African Americans. You can walk for miles along this wild beach, which is loaded with sea-shells—mostly large cockles and sand dollars—to the remains of a pre–World War I battery fortification at the eastern end of the island. The only people you'll encounter are shell seekers and surf fishers. Look for the tracks of the tiny beach mouse around the tracking stations (aka "mice hotels"), where they get a free meal in exchange for their footprints on an ink pad. Don't want to leave? The beach is open for primitive camping 2.25 miles east of the entrance. Do not camp in the dunes or on vegetation and be sure to get a backcountry permit for your car windshield. You must bring in all your freshwater and carry out all trash.

Look up!

While you're keeping your eyes on the sand for shells, don't forget to look up once in a while. The Navy's Blue Angels fly over Perdido Key on practice flights, while migrating monarch butterflies pass closer by. The Angels are based at Naval Air Station Pensacola. The bright blue F/A-18 Hornets can often be seen practicing in the skies from March through October. To see them close up, visit the National Museum of Naval Aviation, where practices are held. You might even meet a pilot and get an autograph. 850-452-2583.

PANHANDLE

Beach Length: 6 miles.

Pets: Not allowed.

Directions: From Pensacola, go west on SR 292 for 15 miles.

Hours: 7 a.m. to sunset.

Fees: $8 per vehicle; good for seven days at all seashore units; $3 for pedestrians and bicyclists.

Contact: 850-934-2600

www.nps.gov/guis

Big Lagoon State Park

Special features: Outdoor shower · Picnic shelters · Good beach for small children · Beach fishing · Nature trails · Developed campground

The East and West beaches are half a mile apart on the Intracoastal Waterway. The West beach has sheltered swimming on a narrow beach shaded by tall pines. East Beach has a boardwalk and obser-

PANHANDLE

East Beach at Big Lagoon State Park.

vation tower, but no swimming because of the marshy and muddy shoreline. It is a critical habitat for the wintering piping plover. Both beaches have restrooms. There's a 3.5-mile loop nature trail from the entrance station to the beaches and back, and a boardwalk from the campground to beach. The many remaining downed trees from 2004's Hurricane Ivan attract numerous pileated woodpeckers. Just outside the park you'll find a 24-hour coin-op laundry, grocery store, restaurants, post office, pharmacy, and public library with free wireless Internet.

Beach Length: 1 mile.
Pets: Allowed in the campground and on the nature trails, but not on the beach.
Directions: From Pensacola take SR 292 west for 10 miles, turn left on Bauer Road, and go 1.3 miles to CR 292A.
Fee: $4 per vehicle; $1 for pedestrians and bicyclists.
Hours: 8 a.m. to sunset.
Contact: 850-492-1595
www.floridastateparks.org/biglagoon

Santa Rosa Island

Fort Pickens, Gulf Islands National Seashore

Special features: Beach fishing · Primitive camping

On the western tip of Santa Rosa Island stands the restored Civil War–era Fort Pickens, site of Geronimo's imprisonment from 1886 to 1888 and active until 1940. The seven miles of gorgeous beach are the northern extent of the Florida National Scenic Trail. Parts of the access road were washed away during Hurricane Ivan in 2004 and further damaged in 2005 by Katrina. The fort stood its ground, with minimal damage. Currently you can drive approximately two miles west of Casino Beach, park at the free county lot before the gate, then walk or bike the remaining seven miles to Ft. Pickens for a self-guided tour. Reconstruction of the access road and campground is slated for 2009.

Beach Length: 7 miles.
Pets: Allowed on leash, but not on the beach.
Directions: From Pensacola, take Pensacola Bay Bridge to Route 399 to Pensacola Beach on Santa Rosa Island. Turn right on Route 399, go approximately 2 miles to Fort Pickens Entrance Gate.
Hours: 8 a.m. to sunset.
Fee: No fees charged until road reopens.
Contact: 850-934-2600
www.nps.gov/guis

PANHANDLE

> *Santa Rosa Island*
>
> This 48-mile barrier island includes the communities of Pensacola Beach, Navarre Beach, and Okaloosa Island, and two units of the Gulf Islands National Seashore: Fort Pickens and Santa Rosa.

Quietwater Beach

*Special features: Picnic shelters · Good beach for small children ·
Beach fishing · Fishing pier*

Nestled between a go-cart place and a burger joint, this small park
offers sheltered swimming in Santa Rosa Sound. Adjacent is James
P. Morgan Memorial Park and Botanical Garden, nice for a shady
stroll.

Beach Length: 1,000 feet.
Pets: Not allowed.
Directions: From Pensacola, take Pensacola Bay Bridge to Route 399
to Pensacola Beach on Santa Rosa Island. The park is on the left just
as you access the island.
Hours: Open 24 hours.
Fee: None.
Contact: Santa Rosa Island Authority, 850-932-2257
http://sria-fla.com

A free beach trolley runs the length of Pensacola
Beach every 20 minutes, Friday through Sunday,
from Memorial Day weekend through the end of
September (www.goecat.com).

Pensacola Beach/Casino Beach

Special features: Beach fishing · Fishing pier

This small resort town is sandwiched between two units of the Gulf Islands National Seashore. Historically known as Casino Beach, this is a fun party beach where you can sip margaritas at the Dock bar, fly a kite, or walk for miles in either direction on a wide, white beach. Spring Break brings hundreds of revelers. There's an amphitheater, a fishing pier, and hot dog vendors. Nearby are hotels, shops, restaurants, and bars. West of here, you can park anywhere along Route 399 and find a pedestrian access to the beach. The road, which runs to Opal Beach and Navarre Beach, was washed out in 2004 during Hurricane Ivan but reopened in 2008. East of Casino Beach, find roadside parking with pedestrian accesses along four miles of Route 399, and a public parking lot with kayak and Hobie Cat rentals at Portofino resort (no public restrooms).

PANHANDLE

Kite flying at Pensacola Beach.

Beach Length: 2 miles west to Ft. Pickens State Park; 5 miles east to Gulf Islands National Seashore.

Pets: Not allowed.

Directions: From Pensacola, take Pensacola Bay Bridge to Route 399 to Pensacola Beach on Santa Rosa Island. Casino Beach is straight ahead.

Hours: Open 24 hours.

Fee: None.

Contact: Santa Rosa Island Authority, 850-932-2257 http://sria-fla.com

Opal Beach, Santa Rosa Unit of Gulf Islands National Seashore

Special features: Beach fishing · Picnic shelters

The beach was ironically named for the 1995 hurricane that devastated this coast; all park facilities, State Road 399, and a newly constructed bike path were virtually washed away by hurricanes in 2004 and 2005. Rebuilt in 2008, J. Earle Bowden Way provides access to the eight miles between Pensacola Beach and Navarre Beach, one of the longest continuous stretches of protected beach in Northwest Florida. You can rent a bike in the tiny resort community of Navarre Beach, ride for miles along the wild beach, plop down on the sand, and while away the day. Shelter from sun and wind and facilities can be found at Opal Beach. Stay away from damaged structures and wear shoes on the beach because of storm debris.

Hurricane damage at Opal Beach, Gulf Islands National Seashore. J. Earle Bowden Way reopened in 2008.

PANHANDLE

Beach Length: 8 miles.

Pets: Allowed on leash, but not on the beach.

Directions: From U.S. 98 in Navarre, take the Route 399 bridge across Santa Rosa Sound to Navarre Beach. Turn right on Route 399 and look for public parking at the end of it.

Hours: 8 a.m. to sunset.

Fees: None.

Contact: 850-934-2600

www.nps.gov/guis

Navarre Park's view of the bridge to Navarre Beach.

Navarre Park

*Special features: Picnic shelters · Good beach for small children ·
Beach fishing · Fishing pier*

This small county park on the mainland has sheltered swimming in
the Santa Rosa Sound. It's a good place to bring small children for a
quick dip and playing in the sand or the water play area.

Beach Length: 125 feet.
Pets: Not allowed.
Directions: Just west of the Navarre Bridge in Navarre, on U.S. 98.
Hours: 7 a.m. to 10 p.m.
Fee: None.
Contact: Santa Rosa Parks and Recreation, 850-983-1858
www.santarosa.fl.gov/parks

Eco-Beach Store is your headquarters for beach fun. Mike and Caryn Martino rent bikes and kayaks and give snorkel tours. The fishing pier, storm-damaged beyond repair, is now an underwater marine sanctuary with great snorkeling. 8460 Gulf Boulevard, Navarre Beach. 850-936-SAND, www.eco-beach.com

Navarre Beach

Special features: Outdoor shower · Beach fishing

Crossing the Navarre toll bridge is like entering another world—the barren white sand devoid of trees has been likened to the surface of the moon. It's this simple beauty that keeps tenacious residents and tourists coming back despite a barrage of hurricanes in 2004 and 2005 that leveled houses and took away tons of sand. While some might question the prudence of rebuilding, it's easy to see why people can't let go of this special place, where at certain times of the year you can watch both sunrise and sunset over the gulf. There are currently no hotels on the beach, but plenty of beach house rentals. Try www.beachhouserentals.com

PANHANDLE

Details: There are restrooms at the public park in the center of town, and lifeguards from March through October, 8 a.m. to 6 p.m. A couple of seafood restaurants and a beach shop are here. Heading west on Route 399 (J. Earle Bowden Way), there are about a dozen public access points to the beach. Route 399 continues to the Gulf Islands National Seashore, Santa Rosa Unit, also known as Opal Beach.
Beach Length: 3 miles.
Pets: Not allowed.

Directions: From U.S. 98 in Navarre, take the Route 399 bridge across Santa Rosa Sound to Navarre Beach.

Hours: Open 24 hours.

Fee: None.

Contact: Santa Rosa County, Navarre Beach Water Department, 850-936-6110

At Navarre Beach, Juana's Pagodas is a family-run restaurant that has weathered the storms for more than 15 years. In a nightly ritual, everyone at the thatched-roof, open-air bar predicts the exact time of the sunset. The closest guess wins a free drink but must stand, salute the sun, and make a toast (www.juanaspagodas.com).

Okaloosa Island

Okaloosa Island Beach Accesses

Special features: Outdoor shower · Picnic shelters · Beach fishing

This "island" is technically the western tip of Santa Rosa Island, connected by bridges to the mainland at Fort Walton Beach and to Destin at the eastern end. These sparkling white beaches are part of the same emerald coast as famous Destin, but without the towering high-rises. In addition to several public parks offering access (listed below), Santa Rosa Boulevard has seven marked and numbered accesses at these street numbers: 372, 399, 530, 600, 700, 820, and 900.

PANHANDLE

Crystal white sand on Okaloosa Island.

Beach Length: 2.5 miles total.

Pets: Not allowed.

Directions: From Fort Walton Beach, take U.S. 98 over the bridge to Okaloosa Island.

Hours: 6 a.m. to 8:30 p.m.

Fee: None.

Contact: Okaloosa County Parks, 850-651-7312 or 850-689-5772 www.co.okaloosa.fl.us/parks/parks.html

> Beach wheelchairs are available without charge at all county parks on Okaloosa Island from 7 a.m. to 2 p.m. Monday through Friday, and 8 a.m. to noon Saturday, Sunday, and holidays. To reserve one, call 850-546-0342 or 850-546-0341.

Newman C. Brackin Wayside Park and Okaloosa Pier

Special features: Fishing pier · Beach fishing

More popularly known as the Boardwalk for its honky-tonk development of bars, all-you-can-eat seafood joints, and beach shops. You can walk for miles on the wide white beach, fish on the pier, shop, eat, and party to live music.

Beach Length: 1,000 feet of park; you can walk for miles in either direction.

Pets: Not allowed.

Directions: From Fort Walton Beach, take U.S. 98 over the bridge to Okaloosa Island and go 0.75 mile to the Boardwalk.

Hours: Sunrise to midnight.

Fee: None; fee for fishing pier.

Contact: Okaloosa County Parks, 850-651-7312 or 850-689-5772 www.co.okaloosa.fl.us/parks/parks.html

John Beasley County Park

Special features: Picnic shelters · Beach fishing

It's a stone's throw from the Boardwalk and basically the same beach, but this large, quiet park seems worlds away. There's a nice dune system and lots of parking. A sign says not to leave valuables in the car.

Beach Length: 1,000 feet of park; you can walk for miles in either direction.
Pets: Not allowed.
Directions: From Fort Walton Beach, take U.S. 98 over the bridge to Okaloosa Island and go 1 mile to the park.
Hours: One hour before sunrise to one hour after sunset; cars are towed in off-hours.
Fee: None.
Contact: Okaloosa County Parks, 850-651-7312 or 850-689-5772 www.co.okaloosa.fl.us/parks/parks.html

Okaloosa Unit, Gulf Islands National Seashore

Special features: Outdoor shower · Good beach for small children · Fishing pier · Beach fishing

This park has a sheltered beach with picnic tables on the Choctawhatchee Bay side of U.S. 98.

Beach Length: 1,200 feet.
Pets: Allowed on a leash, but not on beach.
Directions: From Fort Walton Beach, take U.S. 98 over the bridge to Okaloosa Island and go 1.2 mile to the park.
Hours: Sunrise to sunset (gate is locked promptly at sunset).

Fee: None.
Contact: 850-934-2600
www.nps.gov/guis

Eglin Air Force Base

Special features: Beach fishing

A pull-off just west of the bridge to Destin is the only public access along the base's 3.5 miles of beach on Okaloosa Island. (Gated accesses are open only to military personnel.) You must obtain a permit to enter. The area near the bridge is primarily for fishing, and the beach is not so nice, with lots of trash, but walk around to the gulf side for a lovely, deserted beach. No facilities.

Beach Length: 3.5 miles.
Pets: Not allowed.
Directions: On the east end of Okaloosa Island on U.S. 98, on the west side of the bridge to Destin.
Hours: Sunrise to sunset.
Fee: $7 permit available at the Jackson Guard Station on Route 85 north in Niceville.
Contact: Natural Resources Branch, 850-882-4164
www.eglin.af.mil

Destin

Destin Public Beach Access

Special features: Outdoor shower · Beach fishing

This is a hugely popular resort destination of towering condos, hotels, and vacation homes right on the beach. The sand is crystal white and the water emerald green. From the Route 293 access to the island, cross over U.S. 98 on Hutchinson Avenue to Old Scenic Highway 98. To the right and left are six openings between the beach rentals and condos with limited on-street parking and no facilities. East of Henderson State Park on Old Highway 98, you'll find three more accesses and restrooms at June White Deck Park. Farther north, take Gulfshore Drive to find Norriego Point and O'Sheen accesses along a spit of land known as the Sand Dunes (no facilities). There's handicapped parking at Pompano Street and Shirah Street (Crystal Beach), but storm action has undercut the accesses and there are no ramps down to the beach.

Beaches of Destin.

PANHANDLE

Note: Nearly all of Destin's beachfront property is privately owned, and while some homeowners may think they own the beach, Florida law says it's public below the mean high water mark. Please respect private property.

Beach Length: 4 miles total.
Pets: Not allowed.
Directions: From Valparaiso, take Route 293 south to Destin.
Hours: Sunrise to sunset.
Fee: None.
Contact: City of Destin Public Works, 850-837-6869
www.cityofdestin.com

Clement Taylor Park

Special features: Picnic shelters · Good beach for small children · Fishing pier

At the west end of the city, this park has a small roped-off swimming beach on Choctawhatchee Bay and a gazebo and is a great place to watch the sunset.

Beach Length: 250 feet.
Pets: Not allowed.
Directions: From U.S. 98 on the west end of Destin, turn north on Calhoun Avenue and go 0.2 mile.
Hours: Sunrise to sunset.
Contact: City of Destin Public Works, 850-837-6869
www.cityofdestin.com

PANHANDLE

Henderson Beach State Park

 $

*Special features: Outdoor shower · Picnic shelters · Beach fishing ·
Nature trails · Developed campground*

This is where you get the sense of why it's called the Emerald Coast: it's an emerald oasis in the middle of busy Destin, and within these 200 acres, you'd never guess a big-box retail store is right across busy U.S. 98. Trade the high-rises and traffic for turquoise water, white quartz beach, and a healthy dune environment with a nature trail. There's more than a mile of beach, with a lifeguard in the summer and a campground to stay the night.

Beach Length: 6,000 feet.
Pets: Allowed on leash in day-use areas and campground, but not on the beach.
Directions: From Valparaiso, take Route 293 south to Destin. Turn right on U.S. 98 and go 1 mile to the park entrance.
Hours: 8 a.m. to sunset.
Fee: $4 per vehicle, or $3 for single occupant; $1 for pedestrians and bicyclists.
Contact: 850-837-7550
www.floridastateparks.org/hendersonbeach

PANHANDLE

James Lee County Park

Special features: Outdoor shower · Picnic shelters · Beach fishing

The Crab Trap Restaurant (850-654-2722) is the centerpiece of this quarter-mile county park on the gulf, with a boardwalk and parking the entire length. The open-air bar is a favorite spot for toasting the sunset.

Beach Length: 0.25 mile.

Pets: Not allowed.

Directions: Located on Old Highway 98 at the eastern end of Destin.

Hours: Sunrise to 8 p.m.

Fee: None.

Contact: Okaloosa County Parks, 850-651-7312 or 850-689-5772 www.co.okaloosa.fl.us/parks/parks.html

The Beaches of South Walton are a relatively quiet, serene jewel between the bustling—some might say overdeveloped—communities of Destin and Panama City Beach. Walton County has a four-story height restriction, so you'll never see another high-rise here. Fully 40 percent of the county's 26 miles of beach are preserved by state ownership, and all are certified "Blue Wave" by the Clean Beaches Council. Rare coastal dune lakes have been preserved, along with the towering dunes themselves, which sport colorful wildflower displays in spring and fall. If you're looking for Spring Break action, head east or west of here. If it's miles of unspoiled beach, with nearly 40 public beach accesses, then Walton County is the place (www.beachesofsouthwalton.com).

Beaches of South Walton

Miramar Beach

Special features: Beach fishing

Pompano Joe's Seafood Restaurant (850-837-2224) is a laid-back landmark perched over the beach on a high bluff. The county has three pedestrian beach accesses near the restaurant, one of them handicapped accessible. New public parking and restrooms will hopefully survive the next hurricane. This beach was severely eroded during 2004–05 storms. Since then, renourishment has added 100–150 feet to the white sand beach.

Pompano Joe's at Miramar Beach.

PANHANDLE

Beach Length: The access area is 1,100 feet, but you can walk for miles in either direction.

Pets: Only residents with permits can bring pets on the beach.

Directions: From Route 20 on the mainland, take Route 293 to Destin. Go left on U.S. 98 for 4.1 miles. Turn right on Ponce de Leon Street, which becomes Miramar Beach Road. At 0.4 mile, turn left on Scenic Gulf Drive and the restaurant is almost immediately on the right.

Hours: Open 24 hours.

Fee: None.

Contact: Beaches of South Walton, 800-822-6877 or 866-4my-beach (recorded beach info)

www.partners.beachesofsouthwalton.com

Topsail Hill Preserve State Park

Special features: Outdoor shower · Beach fishing · Nature trails · Developed campground

This huge 1,640-acre preserve has been called the most pristine undeveloped piece of Florida real estate, providing a rare glimpse of what the entire Panhandle coast once was. You can hop on the tram or bike the half mile paved route to the wide, wild beach, but if you decide to walk, you'll be rewarded with a pleasant stroll through pines and palmettos interspersed with wildflowers (a sign warns of alligators in the ponds along the way, so don't dawdle). The park is named for Topsail Hill, a 25-foot dune that resembles a ship's topsail. The once dramatic dunes have been somewhat shaved by the succession of 2004–05 storms, but it's still a spectacular environment. Seven miles of trails lead to secret spots like the three large coastal dune lakes offering freshwater fishing. In all the United States, these rare freshwater lakes exist only in the Panhandle. The endangered Choctawhatchee beach mouse depends on the sea oats here. Sea turtles crawl onto the beach at night to lay eggs. In late summer the hatchlings crawl into the sea, and in fall, swaths of yellow woody goldenrod cover the dunes.

Details: There are restrooms at the parking area and at the dune boardwalk to the beach. Stay the night in one of the comfy bungalows or the RV park.

Beach Length: 3.2 miles.

Pets: Allowed on a leash.

Directions: From Route 20, take Route 331 south to Santa Rosa Beach. Turn right on U.S. 98 and go 5 miles to Scenic Highway 30A. Turn left and go 0.25 mile to the entrance on the right. The tram to the beach runs every two hours beginning at 9 a.m.

Hours: 8 a.m. to sunset.

Fee: $2 per vehicle; $1 for pedestrians and bicyclists.

Contact: 850-267-0299

www.floridastateparks.org/topsailhill

PANHANDLE

> An 18-mile bike path runs parallel to Scenic County Road 30A through South Walton County, with intermittent views of the gulf. Pack a lunch and hit the beaches by bike.

South Walton Beach Access Points

These are the county facilities with restrooms that give access to the 4.5 miles of beach between Topsail Hill Preserve State Park and Grayton Beach. All are free and open 24 hours, and all allow pets only for residents with a permit.

Contact: Beaches of South Walton, 800-822-6877 or 866-4my-beach (recorded beach info)

www.partners.beachesofsouthwalton.com

Dune Allen Regional Access/Fort Panic Park

Special features: Outdoor shower · Beach fishing

Nestled between rental houses, limited parking. Scenic Highway 30A, west of Oyster Lake at Fort Panic Road.

Ed Walline Park

Special features: Picnic shelters · Beach fishing

Observation tower, at intersection of Scenic Highway 30A and Route 393.

Gulfview Heights Regional Access

Special features: Outdoor shower · Picnic shelters · Beach fishing

From Scenic Highway 30A in Santa Rosa Beach, turn at Goatfeathers Restaurant onto Gulfview Heights Street.

Blue Mountain Beach

Special features: Beach fishing

Off CR 30A at the southern end of CR 83 in Blue Mountain Beach.

The high dunes of Blue Mountain Beach got their name from the blue-blooming gulf coast lupine that paints the dunes in March and April. The highest dune is 70 feet, and this is also the highest point along the Gulf of Mexico within the United States.

Grayton Beach

Special features: Outdoor shower · Beach fishing

The county's oldest beach community has small bungalows and cottages and gives a nice flavor of Old Florida. The public beach access at the end of Garfield Street offers limited parking for about six cars with more parking a block away. Only residents with a permit and four-wheel-drive can drive onto the beach (permit is $105 annually, 850-267-3001). No facilities.

Grayton Beach driving access.

Beach Length: 3,000 feet.

Pets: Only residents with a permit can bring pets on the beach.

Directions: From Route 20, take Route 331 south to Santa Rosa Beach. Turn left on U.S. 98 and go 1.5 mile. Turn right on Scenic County Road 283 and go 2 miles to its end.

Hours: Open 24 hours.

Fee: None.

Contact: Beaches of South Walton, 800-822-6877 or 866-4my-beach (recorded beach info)

www.partners.beachesofsouthwalton.com

Grayton Beach's Red Bar is a circa-1938 grocery store, painted more of a brown than red. But at night it's all lit up with red lights. Inside, the funky decor includes French movie and rock posters, booths, and mismatched chairs colorfully painted and duct-taped. In adjacent Piccolo Restaurant, the waitress brings the menu on a large blackboard. The fare is seafood, creatively prepared. No credit cards accepted (850-231-1008).

Grayton Beach State Park

Special features: Outdoor shower · Picnic shelters · Beach fishing · Nature trails · Developed campground

The mile-long beach is nothing less than spectacular, and the rest of the park's 2,200 acres is fascinating, with 13 distinct habitats ranging from beach dune to tidal marsh. Three nature trails take visitors through these ecosystems. Sea turtles nest on the beach in the summer, while the endangered Choctawhatchee beach mouse lives in the dunes year-round. Camp on the banks of a rare, coastal dune lake or in one of 30 furnished cabins.

Beach Length: 1 mile.
Pets: Allowed on the nature trail, campground, and picnic area, but not on the beach.
Directions: From Route 20, take Route 331 south to Santa Rosa Beach. Turn left on U.S. 98 and go 1.5 mile. Turn right on Scenic County Road 283; go 2 miles to Scenic County Road 30A, turn left and go 0.5 mile to the park.

PANHANDLE

Rare coastal dune lake at Grayton Beach State Park.

Hours: 8 a.m. to sunset.
Fee: $4 per vehicle; $1 for pedestrians.
Contact: 850-231-4210
www.floridastateparks.org/graytonbeach

St. Joe, the giant paper company turned residential developer, operates the Watercolor Inn within its vast private beach community. Here the public—for the cost of a night's lodging in the artfully decorated inn—can partake of all the amenities that residents of this exclusive community enjoy. We're not fans of large-scale beach development, but here St. Joe appears to be doing it right, with native plantings, preservation of a rare coastal dune lake (Destin filled in theirs to build high-rises), and dimmed lighting for sea turtle nesting. They even have a full-time naturalist on staff to monitor the health and habitat of the endangered Choctawhatchee beach mouse. The only public beach access for nonguests is between the Watercolor and Seaside communities.

Van Ness Butler Regional Beach Access

Special features: Beach fishing

This small parking lot has new restrooms and is located between the private communities of Watercolor and Seaside.

Beach Length: Access is 150 feet, but you can walk for miles on the beach.
Pets: Only residents with a permit can bring pets on the beach.
Directions: From U.S. 98 in Santa Rosa Beach, go south on Route 395, then right on CR 30A.
Hours: Open 24 hours.
Fee: None.
Contact: Beaches of South Walton, 800-822-6877 or 866-4my-beach (recorded beach info)
www.partners.beachesofsouthwalton.com

The idyllic planned community of Seaside was the filming location for Jim Carey's *The Truman Show*. Unfortunately, there's no public parking at the beach accesses, which are for residents and guests only.

Seagrove Beach

Special features: Outdoor shower · Beach fishing

This small beach community dating to 1949 has 16 access points, only three with parking. There's one high-rise condo complex here, but it's the last of its kind in Walton County, which has restricted new construction to four stories. Notice the stunted and twisted live oaks along the road, adapted to the harsh beach environment. Parking lots and outdoor showers can be found at San Juan Street and adjacent to Pelayo Development; public restrooms and lifeguards are at Santa Clara Drive, an access that is handicapped accessible.

PANHANDLE

Beach Length: Nearly 2 miles.
Pets: Only residents with a permit can bring pets on the beach.
Directions: From U.S. 98 in Santa Rosa Beach, go south on Route 395 to CR 30A
Hours: Open 24 hours.
Fee: None.
Contact: Beaches of South Walton, 866-4my-beach
www.partners.beachesofsouthwalton.com

Deer Lake State Park

Special features: Portable toilets only · Picnic shelters · Beach fishing

From a small parking lot, a shady, paved footpath becomes a raised boardwalk for a 10-minute walk to the beach (no bikes allowed). This mini ecotour takes you through pine forest transitioning to dune.

The beach at Deer Lake State Park is serene and deserted.

Take your time, be silent, and you will hear beach bluestems rustling, birds singing, and crickets chirping, and see butterflies landing on the goldenrod. All this is from the boardwalk, without even getting sand in your shoes. At the end awaits the sparkling white beach and turquoise water. The park is named for the freshwater coastal dune lake.

Beach Length: 0.75 mile.
Pets: Allowed at the picnic area and on the nature trail across CR 30A, but not on the beach.
Directions: From U.S. 98 in Inlet Beach, go west on CR 30A for 5 miles.
Hours: 8 a.m. to sunset.
Fee: None.
Contact: 850-231-0337 or 850-231-4210 (Grayton Beach State Park, which manages Deer Lake)
www.floridastateparks.org/deerlake

Inlet Beach Regional Access

Special features: Outdoor shower · Beach fishing

This small parking lot should have new restrooms in 2008.

Beach Length: 1,450 feet.
Pets: Only residents with a permit can bring pets on the beach.
Directions: At the south end of Orange Street in Inlet Beach.
Hours: Open 24 hours.
Fee: None.
Contact: Beaches of South Walton, 866-4my-beach, www.partners.beachesofsouthwalton.com

PANHANDLE

Camp Helen State Park

Special features: Outdoor shower · Beach fishing · Nature trails

People have been drawn to this small peninsula for millennia, as evidenced by the 4,000-year-old middens where early Americans discarded their shells. A nature trail leads down to a long, wild beach where endangered piping plovers and sea turtles nest. It's bordered by Lake Powell, a large coastal dune lake. This park has an interesting history as a 1940s lodge with "rainbow" cottages painted different colors. The buildings are still intact and some are being restored.

Beach Length: 0.75 mile.
Pets: Allowed on leash, but not on beach.
Directions: Located on U.S. 98 in Inlet Beach, just west of the Phillips Inlet bridge.
Hours: 8 a.m. to sunset.
Fee: $2 per vehicle or $1 for pedestrians.
Contact: 850-233-5059
www.floridastateparks.org/camphelen

PANHANDLE

Panama City Beach

Panama City Beach

This city has taken the place of Fort Lauderdale as Spring Break Capital of the United States, with the world's largest beach clubs and a 26-mile sparkling white beach lined with a strip of colorful hotels and towering condos. There's everything the Spring Break crowd craves: arcades, bars, sex shops, and tattoo parlors. If you're not into intense partying, you might want to avoid late February through early April. In the relatively quieter west end of town, dozens of numbered public beach accesses can be found along Front Beach Street. The Bay Town Trolley runs the length of the beachfront (850-769-0557). Bay County Leisure Services, 850-784-4065 www.co.bay.fl.us/community/recreational.html

Pier Park in Panama City Beach.

The following free accesses have facilities, are open dawn to dusk, and do not allow pets.

Dan Russell City Pier

Special features: Fishing pier

Limited free parking at the 1,000-foot fishing pier, plenty more across the street at Aaron Bessant Park. Located in the 16,000 block of Front Beach Road. 24-hour fishing pier costs $5 to fish.
850-233-5080
www.pcbgov.com/visitors_citypier.htm

M. B. Miller Park and County Pier

Special features: Outdoor shower · Fishing pier

In the 14,000 block of Front Beach Road.

Richard Seltzer Park

Special features: Outdoor shower · Beach fishing

In the 7,000 block of Thomas Drive.

St. Andrews State Park

Special features: Indoor shower · Picnic shelters · Good beach for small children · Beach fishing · Fishing pier · Fishing jetty · Nature trails · Developed campground

This large, well-maintained park is adjacent to Panama City Beach, but has a completely different atmosphere. There are two powdery white beaches; the one on Grand Lagoon is more sheltered, while the one on the Gulf of Mexico is larger. From here you can see great Navy ships, fishing vessels, and container barges plying the shipping lane into St. Andrews Bay. Kayak rentals are available near the park's boat ramp for exploring Grand Lagoon. There are three camp stores, dive and snorkel rentals, and the Shell Island shuttle (in season). Fishing, from beach, pier, and jetty, is huge.

Beach Length: 1.5 mile.
Pets: Allowed in the campground, but not on the beach.
Directions: From U.S. 98 in Panama City, go south on Hwy 3031 (Thomas Drive) 3.5 miles; turn left on Route 392 and enter the park.
Hours: 8 a.m. to sunset.
Fee: $5 per vehicle; $1 for pedestrians and bicyclists.
Contact: 850-233-5140
www.floridastateparks.org/standrews

PANHANDLE

Shell Island

Special features: Fishing jetty · Beach fishing

This unit of St. Andrews State Park is accessible only by private boat or the Shell Island shuttle operating March through Labor Day. Walk for miles on this "island," which was attached to the St. Andrews peninsula before a shipping lane was cut in the 1930s. In 1998 Hurricane Earl made it a peninsula again by depositing sand at the other end, connecting it to Crooked Island (which is also really a peninsula). There's good snorkeling and surfing by the jetty at the western tip. Three miles from the western tip, the bayside Spanish Shanty area is very popular with the powerboat crowd, who land there and then walk over to the gulf for swimming and surf fishing. An old wooden structure is said to have been the headquarters for treasure hunters looking for Spanish treasure, hence the name Spanish Shanty. Wildlife includes the endangered Choctawhatchee beach mouse, sea turtles, a large concentration of bottlenose dolphins, and coyotes.

Details: Shell Island has no facilities and no freshwater. Please do not bring alcohol, and take home your trash. If arriving by private boat, be very alert crossing the channel to Shell Island because of large vessel traffic; we're talking giant container barges and Navy ships. Only experienced kayakers should attempt it.
Beach Length: 5 miles.
Pets: Not allowed.
Directions: Less than a mile southeast of St. Andrews State Park Boat Ramp, across the busy shipping lane.

PANHANDLE

Red Tide

These occur most commonly on the gulf coast of Florida. Despite the name, they don't always turn the water red. Areas may go for years without a "bloom," and then suffer several for no known reason. The higher-than-normal concentration of a microscopic alga produces a toxin that can kill sea life and produce a foul odor, but a mild bloom poses no problem for most beachgoers. The toxin becomes airborne and can cause coughing, sneezing, and watery eyes in some people. For this reason, small children and people with severe or chronic respiratory conditions such as emphysema or asthma should avoid areas affected by red tide. There may be a ban on eating mollusks (clams, oysters, and scallops), but it is okay to eat shrimp, crab, lobster, and fish. It's okay to swim when there's a red tide, but don't swim among dead fish (need we say this?). Visit http://research.myfwc.com or call 866-300-9399 for red tide conditions throughout the state. From outside Florida, call 727-552-2448.

Hours: 8 a.m. to sunset.
Fee: None to land on the island. $13 to launch private boat from St. Andrews State Park. The shuttle costs $11.50 for adults, $5.50 for ages 12 and under.
Contact: St. Andrews State Park, 850-233-5140
www.floridastateparks.org/standrews
www.shellislandshuttle.com

Crooked Island

Special features: Portable toilets only · Beach fishing

This is actually a long, sandy peninsula, entirely within Tyndall Air Force Base. The only access for nonmilitary personnel is at the base's eastern boundary, a dirt road marked "Crooked Island, East Beach Road." Drive 0.8 mile to an unpaved parking lot and a boardwalk to a lovely wild beach where you can walk east toward Mexico Beach, or 6.5 miles west to the tip of the peninsula. No pass is required, but be sure to carry a photo ID, and don't go wandering off the beach.

Beach Length: 7 miles.
Pets: Not allowed. A sign threatens a stiff fine and possible imprisonment for bringing dogs onto the beach, a critical wildlife habitat.
Directions: 2 miles west of Mexico Beach on U.S. 98.
Hours: Sunrise to sunset, with closures possible during times of high security alert.
Fee: None.
Contact: 850-283-2822 or 850-283-1113
www.tyndall.af.mil

PANHANDLE

St. Joseph Bay Area

Mexico Beach

Special features: Outdoor shower · Fishing pier · Beach fishing

This quiet, modest community seems to be where the regular Joe goes to vacation or to buy a vacation home. There's no towering condos to restrict the view and the three-mile beach has tons of public access at the end of nearly every street. There's good surfing, especially when a storm is coming. At the east end of town, the development is all on the land side of U.S. 98, with boardwalks going over the dunes every tenth of a mile. You'll find restrooms and outdoor showers at Canal Park, end of Canal Park Drive; 37th Street Fishing Pier; Sunset Park at 19th Street; and Wayside Park at 7th Street.

Mexico Beach pier.

PANHANDLE

Beach Length: 3 miles.
Pets: Not allowed.
Directions: From Apalachicola, take U.S. 98 west for 35 miles.
Hours: Open 24 hours.
Fee: None.
Contact: Mexico Beach Community Development Council, 850-648-8196
www.mexicobeach.com

St. Joe Beach

Special features: Picnic shelters · Beach fishing

This small community of vacation homes has only pedestrian access to the beach, but just south of the village, development falls away on both sides of U.S. 98. There are numerous access paths through the gorgeous dunes, swathed in wildflowers. Parking is along the highway. No facilities, except for Beacon Hill Park, located north of town on the inland side of U.S. 98 with a boardwalk to the beach.

PANHANDLE

Healthy dunes at St. Joe Beach.

Beach Length: 3 miles.

Pets: Allowed on leash.

Directions: From Apalachicola, take U.S. 98 west and north for 30 miles.

Hours: Sunrise to sunset.

Fee: None.

Contact: Gulf County Tourism, 850-229-7800
www.visitgulf.com

St. Joseph Peninsula State Park

Special features: Indoor shower · Picnic shelters · Beach fishing · Nature trails · Developed campground · Primitive camping

The "Forgotten Coast" has been found, and the signs—real estate, that is—are everywhere. Thus, it is all the more vital that this state park preserve the peninsula's final 10 miles, with enviable 50-foot dunes and a gorgeous beach. There are eight furnished cabins and two campgrounds on the bayside, as well as primitive camping and trails throughout the seven miles of pine flatwoods wilderness from the end of the paved road to the tip.

Beach Length: 10 miles.

Pets: Allowed on the nature trails and in the campgrounds, but not on the beach.

Directions: From CR 30A south of Port St. Joe, take CR 30E west, go 9 miles to the park at the tip of the peninsula.

Hours: 8 a.m. to sunset.

Fee: $4 per vehicle; $1 for pedestrians.

Contact: 850-227-1327
www.floridastateparks.org/stjoseph

PANHANDLE

Cape Palms Park

Special features: Outdoor shower · Beach fishing

Also on St. Joseph Peninsula, but outside the state park, this is a long, pet-friendly beach.

Beach Length: 8 miles total from Cape San Blas to the state park.
Pets: Allowed on a leash.
Directions: From CR 30A south of Port St. Joe, take CR 30E west 5 miles.
Hours: Sunrise to sunset.
Contact: Gulf County Tourism, 850-229-7800
www.visitgulf.com

Stumphole Beach Access

Where you see large boulders alongside the road for erosion control, look for a small parking lot and boardwalk to the beach.

Beach Length: 8 miles total from Cape San Blas to the state park.
Pets: Allowed on a leash.
Directions: From CR 30A south of Port St. Joe, take CR 30E west 4 miles.
Hours: Sunrise to sunset.
Contact: Gulf County Tourism, 850-229-7800
www.visitgulf.com

PANHANDLE

St. Joseph Peninsula is trying to become an island, but people are fighting it. In recent storms, the road near Cape San Blas has washed over, nearly cutting off the peninsula from the mainland. Huge boulders have been deposited to try to stop the process. Whether or not it becomes an island, this peninsula has one of the best stretches of undeveloped, powdery white-sand beaches in the state.

Cape San Blas Lighthouse

Special features: Beach fishing

The sandy "elbow" of St. Joseph Peninsula, Cape San Blas is part of Eglin Air Force Base. The point erodes more with each storm and is littered with dead trees and stumps. With historically dangerous shoaling offshore, this has been the site of five lighthouses and innumerable shipwrecks. The current lighthouse was built in 1885 and made to be moved, as it was in 1918. It's behind a locked chain-link fence. Besides the lighthouse, there's little reason to use this beach as the peninsula has three public parks with nicer beaches. No facilities, dirt parking for a handful of cars.

Beach Length: 1 mile.
Pets: Allowed on leash.
Directions: From CR 30A south of Port St. Joe, take CR 30E for 3.5 miles and turn left on a dirt road marked with a sign for Eglin Air Force Base. Go 0.3 mile to the end.
Hours: Sunrise to sunset, but gate may be closed at any time for Air Force activity.
Fee: None.
Contact: Eglin Air Force Base Public Information, 850-882-3931 www.eglin.af.mil

> **Beach Riding**
>
> Five miles of beach between Indian Pass west to Salinas
> Park is open to four-wheel-drive vehicles and horses. You'll
> need a permit for each: $15 for Gulf County residents; $150
> for nonresidents. Available at the tax collector's office in the
> Gulf County Courthouse, Cecil Carlston Boulevard, Port St.
> Joe (850- 229-6116). For sunset horseback rides, call Broke-A-
> Toe, 850-899-RIDE. It's $50 for a one-hour ride.

Salinas Park

*Special features: Outdoor shower · Picnic shelters · Good beach
for small children · Beach fishing · Nature trails · Four-wheel drive
recommended*

This is a great locals' beach at the beginning of St. Joseph Peninsula where you can bring your dogs and your 4WD vehicle and even ride your horse. A nature trail winds through a shady pine hammock of mature trees with several boardwalks leading to the wide beach. Because the sand comes more from sediment of the Apalachicola River, it's not the white crystalline kind farther out on the peninsula. But it's hard packed, and a four-wheel drive isn't required. Vehicle access is just south of the park at the end of Dead Man's Curve Road.

Beach Length: 5 miles.
Pets: Allowed on leash; you must have a permit to ride horses, and they must wear waste bags.
Directions: From CR 30A south of Port St. Joe, take CR 30E for 0.25 mile to the park.
Hours: Sunrise to sunset.
Fee: None; permit required for beach driving or horseback riding (850-229-6116).
Contact: Gulf County Tourism, 850-229-7800
www.visitgulf.com

PANHANDLE

Indian Pass Beach

Special features: Beach fishing · Developed campground · Four-wheel drive recommended

There's not much beach here, but there is a boat ramp, vehicle access to the beach, and a shuttle to nearby St. Vincent Island National Wildlife Refuge. The county has an agreement with the adjacent private campground that park visitors can use the restrooms there.

Beach Length: 5 miles.
Pets: Allowed on leash.
Directions: From CR 30A, go 3 miles to the end of CR 30B on Indian Peninsula.
Hours: Sunrise to sunset.
Fee: None; permit required for beach driving or horseback riding (850-229-6116).
Contact: Gulf County Tourism, 850-229-7800
www.visitgulf.com
Indian Pass Campground, 850-227-7203
www.indianpasscamp.com

Scalloping requires snorkel gear (including a diver down flag), a mesh bag, and a saltwater fishing license. During the season, July 1 through Sept. 10, the bivalves congregate in the shallow water among the manatee and turtle grass. A small skiff or kayak helps, but in certain areas, you can simply wade out and find the little creatures. The owner of the Turtle Beach Inn near Port St. Joe (www.turtlebeachinn.com) described scalloping as being like hunting for Easter eggs: they come in a dozen hues, ranging from light pink to orange to black. Reach out and grab them quickly—they do swim! Limit: two gallons of whole scallops per person, or ten gallons per boat. Scalloping is allowed from the Mexico Beach canal east throughout the Panhandle and Big Bend.

Apalachicola Area

Four barrier islands forming Apalachicola Bay have 60 glorious miles of white sand beach, much of it preserved in perpetuity from development: St. Vincent, Little St. George, St. George, and Dog. The islands have been variously connected and separated through time and are constantly changing, particularly after violent hurricanes. Only St. George and Dog are inhabited, though large portions are preserved by the St. George Island State Park and, on Dog Island, Nature Conservancy holdings.

St. Vincent National Wildlife Refuge

Special features: Beach fishing · Nature trails

It's not hard to get to this 12,300-acre island, but you'll feel worlds away in a place where red wolves, feral hogs, elk and alligators roam. (Don't worry, you're not likely to see any of these in person, only their tracks.) Sea turtles nest here in summer, bald eagles in winter. Bring a picnic, your bike to explore the miles of forest roads, and a bag for the spectacular shelling on the 14-mile beach. On the trails you'll see a series of dune ridges, remnants of ancient beaches, and many animal tracks. This former game preserve has sheltered zebras, hogs, and sambar deer as big as elks. The latter two are still here, with organized hunts a few times a year to keep their numbers in check. Since 1990 the refuge has maintained one pair of breeding red wolves and their pups. Red wolves were once plentiful throughout Florida, but these are the only ones now living in the wild in the state. At around two years of age, the pups are taken to Alligator River National Wildlife Refuge in North Carolina, where repopulating efforts have been very successful. We saw plenty of wolf tracks, but there's little chance of seeing the animals, which are shy of humans. To see some, head to the Tallahassee Museum of Natural History, where a

PANHANDLE

Deer tracks on deserted St. Vincent Island.

half dozen live. There are no public facilities on the island, so bring your own water.

Beach Length: 14 miles.
Pets: Not allowed.
Directions: From the Indian Pass Boat Ramp (at the end of CR 30E), it's just minutes by kayak, boat, or the St. Vincent Island Shuttle.
Hours: Sunrise to sunset.
Fee: None; shuttle costs $10 for adults; $7 children under 10; $25 includes a bike rental.
Contact: St. Vincent NWR, 850-653-88080
www.fws.gov/saintvincent
Shuttle: 850-229-1065
www.stvincentisland.com

Little St. George Island

Special features: Beach fishing · Nature trails · Primitive camping

This nine-mile uninhabited barrier island of powdery white sand affords a true wilderness beach experience replete with its own challenges of mosquitoes, rattlesnakes, and exposure to sun and wind. Dolphins are numerous and you may see some rushing the shore for mullet. The shelling is out of this world: giant cockles and mussels, and scallops of every hue. About midway along the island on the gulf side is the rubble of the ill-fated Cape St. George lighthouse, which finally succumbed to erosion and toppled in October 2005. A volunteer group salvaged the rubble and rebuilt the lighthouse on St. George Island. There's primitive camping allowed at either end of the island, with no facilities or freshwater available.

PANHANDLE

Little St. George lighthouse shortly after it fell into the gulf in 2005.

Beach Length: 9 miles.

Pets: Not allowed.

Directions: Launch your own boat from Apalachicola, 8 miles north of the island, or take a guided trip from St. George Island.

Hours: Open 24 hours.

Fee: None.

Contact: The island is owned by the state, but managed by the Apalachicola National Estuarine Research Reserve, 850-653-8063 www.dep.state.fl.us/coastal/sites/apalachicola/info.htm

Tours: Journeys of St. George Island, 850-927-3259 www.sgislandjourneys.com

> St. George and Little St. George were one island until 1954, when the Army Corps of Engineers cut a narrow channel, known as the Government Cut or Bob Sikes Cut, for boats to reach the gulf.

St. George Island

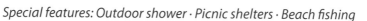

Special features: Outdoor shower · Picnic shelters · Beach fishing

Connected to Eastpoint by bridge, the 20-mile barrier island has a vacation community of many rental homes, and a handful of lodgings, stores, and restaurants. Except for the gated St. George Plantation community at the west end, much of the beach is public and you can walk for miles on the tan sand, looking for shells. There are numerous beach accesses at the ends of most cross-streets on the gulf-side (no facilities, and limited on-street parking). St. George Island Public Beach Park and has facilities. The Cape St. George lighthouse was rebuilt here in 2007. Nearby: The tiki bar on the beach at Blue

Parrot Oceanfront Café is a great spot to have a cocktail, watch the sunset, and eat seafood (68 W Gorrie Dr., 850-927-2987).

Beach Length: 3.5 miles east to the state park; nearly 2 miles west to the private St. George Plantation.

Pets: Allowed on leash; stiff fine for not picking up waste.

Directions: From Apalachicola, go east on U.S. 98 for 5 miles to the Bryant Patton Causeway (Route 300), then south for 5 miles to the island. The park is straight ahead on West Gorie Drive.

Hours: Beach open 24 hours; restrooms 9 a.m. to 8 p.m. April through Labor Day; 9 a.m. to 5 p.m. the rest of the year.

Fee: None.

Contact: Franklin County Parks and Recreation, 850-653-8277 www.franklincountyflorida.com

> St. George Island is so narrow in places that from many houses you can see St. George Bay and hear the surf on the gulf at the same time. Resort Vacation Properties manages the largest selection of homes on the island (www.ResortVacationProperties.com). The St. George Inn is a small historic hotel in the middle of town (www.stgeorgeinn.com).

PANHANDLE

St. George Island State Park

Special features: Outdoor shower · Picnic shelters · Beach fishing · Nature trails · Developed campground · Primitive camping

The park preserves nine miles on the east end of the island, with pristine beaches, dunes, and woodlands. Devastated by Hurricane Dennis in July 2005 and closed for nearly a year, facilities are now all new, including a full-service campground. The first four miles of beach are accessible by road, the last five by foot or boat only. It's a virtual wilderness, with primitive camping allowed at Gap Point. Two boat ramps provide access to Apalachee Bay, or you can launch a kayak at the sandy boat ramp to explore the bayside, land on the beach, and have a picnic.

Beach Length: 9 miles.
Pets: Allowed in the campground only, not on the beach or trails.
Directions: From U.S. 98, take the Bryant Patton Causeway (Route 300) for 5 miles to the island; turn left on Gulf Drive and drive 4 miles to the park.
Hours: 8 a.m. to sunset.
Fee: $5 per vehicle.
Contact: 850-927-2111
www.floridastateparks.org/stgeorgeisland

Dog Island

Special features: Beach fishing

Accessible only by boat, this private vacation community has no visitor facilities except for one motel, and that appears to be the way the 20 year-round residents want it to stay. There's really no public beach access, but you can take your own boat and anchor offshore, or take the shuttle boat over to stay at the Pelican Inn. The middle two-thirds of the island is owned by The Nature Conservancy, which discourages visitors, but we certainly don't begrudge one island set aside for endangered least terns and sea turtles to nest undisturbed. There are no public facilities, not even a place to buy water.

Beach Length: 6 miles.
Pets: Allowed on leash outside the refuge.
Directions: Located 3.5 miles south of Carrabelle Beach in the Gulf of Mexico.

Hours: None.
Fee: None; shuttle is $70 each way for up to six people.
Contact: GAT V Charters: 850-697-3989
The Pelican Inn: 850-697-4728
Carrabelle Area Chamber of Commerce: 850-697-2585
www.carrabelle.org

Carrabelle Beach

*Special features: Picnic shelters · Good beach for small children ·
Beach fishing*

This is a quiet, narrow roadside beach where you can walk for several miles on St. George Sound. Dog Island can be seen offshore, providing a barrier for sheltered swimming by small children.

Beach Length: 3.5 miles.
Pets: Not allowed.
Directions: On U.S. 98, 1 mile west of the small fishing town of the same name.
Hours: Sunrise to sunset.
Fee: None.
Contact: Carrabelle Area Chamber of Commerce, 850-697-2585
www.carrabelle.org

Bald Point State Park

Special features: Picnic shelters · Beach fishing · Nature trails

This new park's 4,800 acres make up the completely undeveloped eastern tip of James Island, which is really a peninsula between Ochlockonee Bay and Apalachee Bay. The park provides several accesses

PANHANDLE

Bald Point
State Park.

to a lovely white sand beach fringed by old growth oak thickets and used by migrating shorebirds and nesting sea turtles. Be sure to use boardwalks where provided to protect the dunes. Bald Point was formed 6,000 years ago, and human habitation dates to nearly 4,000 years ago. Native Americans fished and collected clams and oysters on these beaches. From the mid-1800s to the late 1900s, fishermen had seine yards at Bald Point where they hung and repaired their nets. The 4th Infantry Division, which landed on Normandy Beach, trained here during World War II.

Sunrise Beach

The best swimming. It's located 1.5 miles before the park entrance, so there's no fee. Portable toilets, picnic table, and water spigot.

North Point Beach

Restrooms, outdoor shower, and picnic shelters, but quite a bit of offshore shoaling at low tide.

Fishing Beach

Located at the end of the park road, this beach has a lot of shoaling and oyster bars and is more for fishing or walking than swimming. Wear shoes when wading. Portable toilets, fishing pier, and picnic pavilion; no freshwater.

Beach Length: 2 miles total.
Pets: Allowed on leash in part, but not on beach.
Directions: From Panacea, go south 3 miles on Route 370.
Hours: 8 a.m. to sunset.
Fee: $3 per vehicle, $1 per person, honor box; no fee at Sunrise Beach.
Contact: 850-349-9146
www.floridastateparks.org/baldpoint

PANHANDLE

Nature Coast

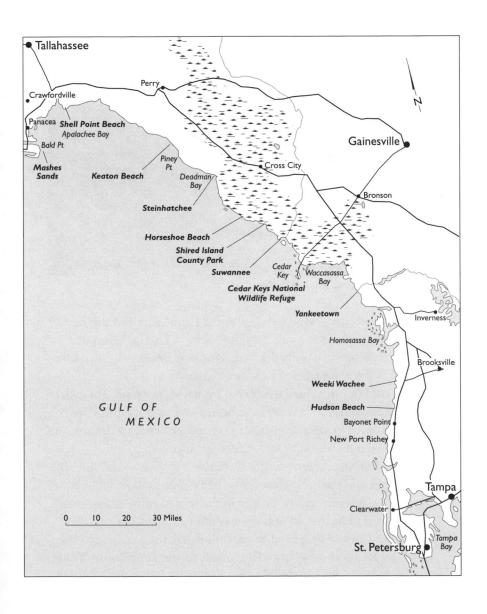

Tallahassee

Perry

Crawfordville

Panacea **Shell Point Beach**
Apalachee Bay

Bald Pt

Gainesville

Piney
Pt

**Mashes
Sands** **Keaton Beach** **Deadman
Bay**

Cross City

Steinhatchee

Bronson

Horseshoe Beach

**Shired Island
County Park**

Suwannee Cedar
Key Waccasassa
Bay

**Cedar Keys National
Wildlife Refuge**

Yankeetown Inverness

Homosassa Bay

Brooksville

Weeki Wachee

GULF OF
MEXICO **Hudson Beach**

Bayonet Point

New Port Richey

Tampa

Clearwater

0   10   20   30 Miles Tampa
Bay

St. Petersburg

Cedar Keys National Wildlife Refuge.

Between the quartz sand beaches of the Panhandle and the barrier islands of Southwest Florida arcs the Nature Coast, a region that, by and large, tourism has overlooked. Within it lies the Big Bend, so-named as the place where Florida's coast dips south.

The wild coastline here is buffered by marsh, not sand. The lack of long white-sand beaches may have been a saving grace: there's nary a high-rise hotel in sight, only miles upon miles of natural beauty, the majority of it protected by state or federal ownership.

Gulf of Mexico waters, shallow for miles offshore, are prolific with oyster bars and scallop-rich seagrass beds. This shallow water is described as "low energy," with little in the way of wave action, which is so critical in formation of barrier islands and beaches.

In those areas where sand has accumulated, the beaches are cherished by locals and visitors alike. Small towns like Keaton Beach, Hudson Beach, and Cedar Key are festive and friendly, while the islands of Cedar Keys National Wildlife Refuge offer long stretches of wild island beach.

NATURE COAST

Wakulla County

Mashes Sands County Park

Special features: Portable toilets only · Fishing pier · Beach fishing · Nature trails

This is a small crescent of sand at the mouth of a creek on Ochlockonee Bay. There's limited parking at the beach, with more on the road at the boat ramp and restrooms on Route 372.

Beach Length: 1,000 feet.
Pets: Allowed on leash.
Directions: From Panacea, take U.S. 98 south for 3 miles, go west on Mashes Sands Road (Route 372) 1.9 mile, and turn right into the park.

Mashes Sands County Park is a crescent of beach.

NATURE COAST

Hours: Sunrise to sunset.
Fee: None.
Contact: Wakulla County Parks and Recreation, 850-926-7227
www.wakullacountyfla.com

Shell Point Beach

Special features: Outdoor shower · Beach fishing

This is a fairly long beach for the region, located in a residential community on the tip of a peninsula between Oyster and Apalachee bays. At low tide, a mudflat is exposed, and there's a boat channel just offshore. No facilities at the beach, but there is a marina nearby.

Beach Length: 400 feet.
Pets: Allowed on leash.
Directions: From SR 365 north of Spring Creek, take SR 367 south for 4.5 miles until it ends at the park.
Hours: Sunrise to sunset.
Fee: None.
Contact: Wakulla County Parks and Recreation, 850-926-7227
www.wakullacountyfla.com

NATURE COAST

Taylor County

Hodges Park at Keaton Beach

Special features: Outdoor shower · Good beach for small children · Fishing pier

On our 10-day kayaking trip along the Big Bend Saltwater Paddling Trail, this place was a sliver of paradise. We pulled up onto the sandy beach of this pleasant county park and headed for Keaton Beach Hot Dog Stand for the best grouper sandwiches in the county (they'll also cook your catch for you). We ran into Sandy Beach here (her real name), the unofficial ambassador of this friendly town. She gave us a lift in her golf cart a quarter mile to the store and campground, where they let us take much-needed showers. The park also has a 700-foot fishing pier and is a great place to dig for scallops (the season runs July 1 through September 10). There's a boat ramp and a motel across the road from the campground. Thanks, Sandy. We'll be back!

Beach Length: 400 feet.
Pets: Not allowed.
Directions: From Perry, take CR 361 south for 14 miles.
Hours: 9 a.m. to 10 p.m.
Fee: None.
Contact: Taylor County Chamber of Commerce, 850-584-5366 or 850-578-2850 www.keatonbeach.org

Scalloping is a unique outing requiring only snorkel gear, diver down flag, mesh bag, and saltwater fishing license. During the season, July 1 through Sept. 10, the colorful bivalves congregate in the shallow water among manatee and turtle grass. A small skiff or kayak helps, but certain places like Hagen's Cove and Keaton Beach are "sweet spots" where you can simply wade out and catch them—but grab quickly, because they do swim! Getting them out of the shell is the hardest part. You might find a local at the docks who will open them for a fee.

Limit: Two gallons of whole scallops per person; or ten gallons per boat.

NATURE COAST

Dixie County

Butler and Douglas Community Park/ Horseshoe Beach

Special features: Indoor shower · Picnic shelters · Beach fishing · Developed campground

The "beach" has oyster rocks and at low tide is a mudflat, but in this region of few beaches, it's a nice place to picnic, launch a boat, camp, and watch the sunset on the Gulf of Mexico. The Horseshoe Café, on Main Street, is a walk of about half a mile.

Beach Length: 500 feet.
Pets: Not allowed.
Directions: At the end of W. 8th Avenue in Horseshoe Beach.
Hours: Open 24 hours.
Fee: None for day use; fee for camping.
Contact: Dixie County Public Works, 352-498-1239
www.dixie.fl.gov

Shired Island County Park

Special features: Picnic shelters · Beach fishing · Developed campground

Adjacent to the Lower Suwannee National Wildlife Refuge, it's technically not an island, but this remote, sandy beach with palm trees has an island feel. It's a tad shallow for swimming, however, and at low tide, a mudflat is exposed. It's a good place for scalloping, even without a boat. You can camp here, or launch a canoe or kayak and head to nearby Big Pine and Little Pine islands just offshore to the south. These wild, sandy beaches have Caribbean-like stretches of natural white sand and picturesque sabal palms. They are for day use only. CAUTION: Water from the park's spigots is not drinkable.

Beach Length: 0.5 mile.
Pets: Not allowed.
Directions: From Cross City, take CR 357 south for 20 miles.
Hours: Open 24 hours.
Fee: None for day use; fee for camping
Contact: Dixie County Public Works, 352-498-1239
www.dixie.fl.gov

NATURE COAST

Levy County

Cedar Key City Park

Special features: Outdoor shower · Picnic shelters · Good beach for small children

This small city park in the heart of downtown Cedar Key has all the amenities, including a small sandy beach that is very nice. Kayak rentals are available, and this is a good place to launch to the outlying islands of Cedar Keys National Wildlife Refuge. Within walking distance are the waterfront seafood restaurants and boutiques that give this island community its charm.

Beach Length: 300 feet.
Pets: Allowed on leash.
Hours: Sunrise to sunset.
Fee: None.
Contact: Cedar Key City Hall, 352-543-5132
www.cedarkey.org

Cedar Keys National Wildlife Refuge

Special features: Portable toilets only · Beach fishing · Nature trails

Several islands, all within a mile or two of Cedar Key, have wild beaches to explore, accessible only by private boat or tour boat. Seahorse Key and Atsena Otie have nice long beaches, while North Key and Snake Key each have small stretches of beach.

Beach Length: Varies
Pets: Allowed on leash.

Directions: 50 miles southwest of Gainesville at the end of State Road 24. Access is from Cedar Key boat ramp or by private tour operator.
Hours: Sunrise to sunset. Seahorse Key is closed for bird nesting from March 1 through June.
Fee: None.
Contact: Lower Suwannee National Wildlife Refuge, 352-493-0238
www.fws.gov/cedarkeys/
For boat tours and kayak outfitters: 352-543-5600
www.cedarkey.org/fishing.php

The dunes on Seahorse Key in Cedar Keys National Wildlife Refuge.

NATURE COAST

Seahorse Key

Cedar Keys National Wildlife Refuge
Walk along this wild 1.5-mile beach and you'll pass a huge dune ridge covered with palms and ancient live oaks. At 52 feet, it's the highest point on the entire gulf coast of Florida. Local lore holds that pirates buried treasure here, and millennia of native Americans fished and deposited shells in middens. While you can take dead shells from the beach—and they're plentiful—you can't take artifacts of any kind.

You'll see lots of bird life, including bald eagle, white ibis, and the relatively rare white pelican. About 20,000 birds nest on the refuge islands each year, which is why all of Seahorse Key and a 300-foot buffer zone around it are closed to visitors during nesting season, March 1 through June.   The rest of the year, you can walk the beach, but not the interior. That's just as well, because you'd likely run into water moccasins that are plentiful under the trees. There are no public facilities, and the lighthouse is not open to the public.

> ### *Atsena Otie*
>
> Cedar Keys National Widlife Refuge
> This is the only island in the refuge where you can leave the shore
> and enter the interior. A nature trail interprets the town and the
> cedar mills that once thrived here, with a population of 300 people.
> The E. Faber pencil mill was destroyed in a hurricane in 1896, and
> only a few piles of bricks and a cemetery among oaks draped in
> Spanish moss remain. There's a nice beach on the east side, acces-
> sible only by private boat, not by the nature trail, and a boat dock
> and portable toilet on the west side. There is no freshwater.

Yankeetown Park

Special features: Picnic shelters · Beach fishing

This park has a tiny little patch of sand, but it still qualifies, and, as
we said, beaches are scarce on this coast.

Beach Length: 100 feet.
Pets: Not allowed.
Directions: From Yankeetown, go west on CR 40 for 3.2 miles. The
park is just before the end of Follow That Dream Parkway, on the
right.
Hours: Sunrise to sunset.
Fee: None.
Contact: Levy County Mosquito Control, 352-486-5127

NATURE COAST

Citrus County

Fort Island Gulf Beach

Special features: Outdoor shower · Picnic shelters · Fishing pier

This is a nice long stretch of quiet beach where you can sit under a shelter and watch the birds. Fishing is prohibited on the beach and jetties but allowed from the pier. There is a boat ramp nearby.

Beach Length: 600 feet.
Pets: Not allowed.
Directions: From U.S. 19 in Crystal River, turn west on Fort Island Turnpike (Route 44) and go 9.5 miles.
Hours: Sunrise to sunset.
Fee: None.
Contact: Citrus County Parks and Recreation, 352-527-7677
www.bocc.citrus.fl.us/parks/parks_recreation.htm

NATURE COAST

Fort Island Gulf Beach is a nice spot for bird watching.

Hernando County

Alfred A. McKethan Pine Island Park

Special features: Outdoor shower · Picnic shelters · Fishing pier

This is a rarity on the Nature Coast: a natural sand beach with water deep enough for swimming. As such, it's very popular in season, so arrive early; the 143 parking spaces fill up quickly. Willy's Tropical Breeze Café serves tasty treats. After you've traveled miles through marsh-grass prairie, the sand, palm trees, and festive blue roofs of the park are like a little oasis.

Beach Length: 300 feet.
Pets: Not allowed.
Directions: From Weeki Wachee, go 5 miles west on Cortez Boulevard (CR 550). Turn right on Pine Island Drive (CR 495) and go 2.4 miles to the park.
Hours: 8 a.m. to 7 p.m. (November through March); open until 9 p.m. the rest of the year.
Fee: $2 per car; no fee Nov. 15 to Feb. 14.
Contact: Hernando County Parks and Recreation, 352-754-4027 www.co.hernando.fl.us/Parks_Rec/parks/index.htm

Rogers Park

Special features: Outdoor shower · Picnic shelters · Fishing pier

Located on the quiet Weeki Wachee River, this park is frequented by manatees. There's a very small swimming area on a manmade beach with a seawall.

Beach Length: 200 feet.
Pets: Not allowed.
Directions: From Weeki Wachee, go west on Cortez Road (CR 550) 2.7 mile, left on Shoal Line Boulevard (CR 597) for 1.1 mile to the park.
Hours: Open 24 hours.
Fee: $2 per car, charged April through September only
Contact: Hernando County Parks and Recreation, 352-754-4027

NATURE COAST

Pasco County

Robert J. Strickland Memorial Park

Special features: Outdoor shower · Picnic shelters · Beach fishing

Hudson Beach is a resort town with a festive atmosphere. Along the white-sand beach there's a boardwalk, open-air restaurants, and tiki bars.

Beach Length: 700 feet.
Pets: Not allowed.
Directions: 1 mile west of U.S. 19 at the end of Clark Street in Hudson.
Hours: Dawn to dusk.
Fee: None.
Contact: Pasco County Parks, 813-929-1260
www.pascocountyfl.net/menu/index/parkindex.htm

Robert K. Rees Park

Special features: Picnic shelters · Beach fishing · Nature trails

This park has a nice white-sand beach and boardwalk nature trail through mangroves, great for bird watching. There's a kayak launch into the gulf.

Beach Length: 500 feet.
Pets: Not allowed.

Robert K. Rees Park.

Directions: From U.S. 19 in New Port Richey, travel west on Green Key Road for 1.7 mile.
Hours: Dawn to dusk.
Fee: None.
Contact: Pasco County Parks, 813-929-1260
www.pascocountyfl.net/menu/index/parkindex.htm

NATURE COAST

Southwest Coast

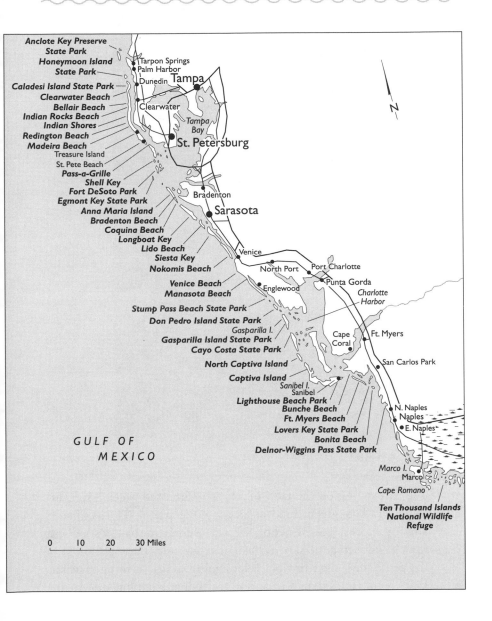

Anclote Key Preserve
State Park
Honeymoon Island
State Park
Caladesi Island State Park
Clearwater Beach
Bellair Beach
Indian Rocks Beach
Indian Shores
Redington Beach
Madeira Beach
Treasure Island
St. Pete Beach
Pass-a-Grille
Shell Key
Fort DeSoto Park
Egmont Key State Park
Anna Maria Island
Bradenton Beach
Coquina Beach
Longboat Key
Lido Beach
Siesta Key
Nokomis Beach
Venice Beach
Manasota Beach
Stump Pass Beach State Park
Don Pedro Island State Park
Gasparilla I.
Gasparilla Island State Park
Cayo Costa State Park
North Captiva Island
Captiva Island
Sanibel I.
Sanibel
Lighthouse Beach Park
Bunche Beach
Ft. Myers Beach
Lovers Key State Park
Bonita Beach
Delnor-Wiggins Pass State Park

Tarpon Springs
Palm Harbor
Dunedin   Tampa
Clearwater

Tampa
Bay
St. Petersburg

Bradenton
Sarasota

Venice
North Port   Port Charlotte
Englewood   Punta Gorda
Charlotte
Harbor

Cape
Coral   Ft. Myers

San Carlos Park

N. Naples
Naples
E. Naples

Marco I.
Marco
Cape Romano

Ten Thousand Islands
National Wildlife
Refuge

GULF OF
MEXICO

N

0   10   20   30 Miles

Bird life on a gulf coast beach.

The sun setting on the Gulf of Mexico turns the water a soft, luminescent blue green, and the sand a glowing pink. Flocks of gulls and royal terns, like the people who have come to soak in some last rays, stand facing the sun. Terns and sanderlings dart in and out of the gentle surf, their tiny black legs going so fast as to be invisible. Like them, children run in and out, playing, laughing, and racing the surf.

Whether sitting on a lively resort beach on Anna Maria Island or having remote Cape Romano all to yourself, be sure to enjoy at least one beach sunset on the Gulf of Mexico.

Tarpon Springs Area

Anclote River Park

Special features: Outdoor shower · Picnic shelters · Beach fishing · Good beach for small children

At the mouth of the river where it empties into the gulf, this large, pleasant park is popular with boaters. There are two sheltered swimming areas with nice white sand.

Beach Length: 1,200 feet.
Pets: Not allowed.
Directions: From Alt 19 in Holiday, go east on Anclote Boulevard for 2 miles to Bailies Bluff Road.
Hours: 6 a.m. to sunset.
Fee: None.
Contact: Pasco County Parks, 813-938-2598
www.pascocountyfl.net/menu/index/parkindex.htm

Anclote Key Preserve State Park

Special features: Portable toilets only · Picnic shelters · Beach fishing · Nature trails · Primitive camping

This four-mile-long barrier island, about three miles off the coast, is accessible only by private boat or kayak. The island's bayshore is covered with mangrove trees, great for bird watching but not beachcombing, with only one or two places to land a kayak. The gulf side, however, is one long stretch of wild beach. The shelling is mythical, with huge sand dollars, cockles, whelks, and a kaleidoscope of scallops. It's one of the state's most important nesting habitats for shore-

Shady camping area on Anclote Key Preserve State Park.

birds like the piping plover, so from March through August be very careful not to disturb feeding or resting birds.

Details: There's a working 1887 lighthouse staffed by a ranger, picnic shelters, and portable toilets at the southern end of the island, but it's much easier to land a boat at the northern end, so that's where most people camp. The boat dock is for government use only; land your boat on the beach, or anchor offshore and walk in.
Beach Length: 4 miles.

SOUTHWEST

Camping on Anclote Key

To camp, you must obtain an overnight parking permit from Anclote River Park, then check in with Honeymoon Island State Park by phone. Keep fires contained to grills, and secure food from racoons. You must bring your own freshwater; a gallon per person per day is recommended. The Australian pine trees provide nice cover for camping, but these nonnatives have pushed out native species and are being treated for removal, so you may see dead standing trees.

Pets: Not allowed.

Directions: Launch a boat or kayak from Anclote River Park in Holiday, head due west into the gulf for approximately 3 miles.

Hours: 8 a.m. to sunset.

Fee: None.

Contact: Honeymoon Island State Park, 727-469-5942

www.floridastateparks.org/anclotekey

Fred H. Howard Park

Special features: Outdoor shower · Picnic shelters · Good beach for small children · Beach fishing · Nature trails

This huge wooded park in Tarpon Springs has winding drives and a kayak trail through mangroves. Enter another world when you travel over a causeway to the beach, an oval "island" of palms and white sand. Beach wheelchairs available on request. Those familiar with open water crossings can launch a kayak here to visit Anclote Key State Park, 2.5 miles to the north.

Beach Length: Along the 0.5-mile causeway and another 0.5 mile around the island

Pets: Not allowed.

Directions: From downtown Tarpon Springs, take Riverside Drive to Sunset Drive, which ends at the park. From U.S. Alt. 19, just south of Tarpon Springs, turn west on Klosterman Road, right on Carlton, left on Curlew Place, right on Florida Avenue, left on Sunset Drive to the park.

Hours: 7 a.m. to sunset.

Fee: None.

Contact: 727-943-4081

www.pinellascounty.org/park/06_Howard.htm

Sunset Beach

Special features: Picnic shelters · Outdoor shower

This small, quiet park in Tarpon Springs, a mini version of Howard Beach, is a small island oasis connected to the mainland by a causeway.

Beach Length: 900 feet.
Pets: Not allowed.
Directions: From U.S. Alt. 19, turn west on Martin Luther King Jr. Drive, left on Whitecomb Boulevard to the west end of Gulf Road.
Hours: Sunrise to 10 p.m.
Fee: None.
Contact: City of Tarpon Springs Parks Department, 727-942-5610 www.tarponsprings.com/florida_parks_recreation.html

Crystal Beach Live Oaks Park

Special features: Picnic shelters · Fishing pier

There's not a lot of beach, and it's certainly not crystal, but there are beautiful live oaks in this shady, quiet, dog-friendly park with a shallow wading beach. It's a serene place to watch the sunset, with benches looking out over the gulf and a fishing pier (open 6 a.m. to 10 p.m.). No facilities.

Beach Length: 1,200 feet.
Pets: Allowed on a leash.
Directions: At the west end of Crystal Beach Avenue, 2 blocks west of U.S. Alt. 19.
Hours: 7 a.m. to dark.
Fee: None.
Contact: Pinellas County Parks, 727- 464-3347 www.pinellascounty.org/park

SOUTHWEST

Dunedin Area

Dunedin Causeway

Special features: Beach fishing

On the way to Honeymoon Island State Park, this long narrow strip of sand is a festive locals' hangout for fishing, kayaking, and sailing (rentals available). You can drive onto the beach, launch a kayak to Caladesi Island, watch the sunset, or play football. Different activities are informally grouped on different patches of beach.

Beach Length: 1 mile.
Pets: Not allowed.
Directions: From U.S. Alt. 19 in Dunedin, take the causeway (SR 586) toward Honeymoon Island State Park; the best beach is on the left side of the causeway.

Boat rentals on Dunedin Causeway beach.

Hours: Sunrise to sunset.
Fee: None.
Contact: City of Dunedin Parks, 727-298-3278
www.dunedingov.com

Honeymoon Island State Park

Special features: Outdoor shower · Beach fishing · Nature trails

This lovely island has two rarities for a state park: a dog beach and a café that sells alcohol (must be consumed on premises). Originally called Hog Island, it was renamed in 1939 by a New York developer who built thatched bungalows to attract newlyweds. The large park has secluded nature trails, mangrove swamps, and a nature center. Surfing is good near the north end of the park. Sea turtles and shorebirds nest on these beaches, so be aware of roped-off areas. Café Caladesi is open 10:30 a.m. to 4 p.m.

Beach Length: 3 miles.
Pets: Allowed on leash at the pet beach on the island's southern tip and on nature trails.
Directions: From U.S. 19, take the Dunedin Causeway (SR 586) to the park.
Hours: 8 a.m. to sunset.
Fee: $5 per vehicle; $3 with a single occupant.
Contact: 727-469-5942
www.floridastateparks.org/honeymoonisland

Caladesi Island State Park

Special features: Picnic shelters · Indoor shower · Outdoor shower · Beach fishing · Nature trails

Caladesi Island State Park.

Thanks to the natural depositing of sand, Caladesi is now connected to North Clearwater Beach to the south, from which the hardy can walk. However, the advisable way to get here is by private boat or ferry from Honeymoon Island State Park. The beach is sublime, rated #2 in the nation by Dr. Beach in 2006.

Details: Use the 108-slip marina if you come with your own boat. From the dock, it's a five-minute walk to the beach on one of two trails that lead to bathhouses. Both are handicapped accessible by either boardwalk or concrete path. You'll find chairs and kayak rentals on the beach.

Off the Beach

Since it's quite old for a barrier island (about 3,000 years), Caladesi has an enchanting, unique mix of pine and live oak forest. Along the 3.5 miles of hiking trails, you'll see relic dunes running through the middle of the island and the remains of an old homestead. Look for the Twin Pine, where early settler Myrtle Scharrer was photographed sitting in the crook (the old photo is in the ranger station). Stay on the trails to avoid rattlesnakes and poison ivy.

SOUTHWEST

Beach Length: 1.8 mile.

Pets: Not allowed on the ferry or on the beach. If brought by private boat, they must be leashed.

Directions: The ferry leaves from Honeymoon Island State Park on the hour, departs Caladesi on the half hour, and takes about 15 minutes. The last one leaves the island at 5:30 p.m.

GPS for channel entrance: N28 01.985, W82 48.893; for dock: N28 01.922, W82 49.148.

Hours: 8 a.m. to sunset.

Fee: Entrance fee to Honeymoon Island State Park: $5 per vehicle; $3 with a single occupant. Ferry is $9 for adults.

Contact: 727-469-5918

www.floridastateparks.org/caladesiisland

Three Rooker Bar

Special features: Beach fishing

This crescent-shaped sandbar is one of Florida's top five spots for nesting shorebirds, and as such should be treated with care. The mainland side is grass and mud, so land on the gulfside beach. Steer clear of two large areas at either end posted "no entry" for protection of bird nesting activity. Please tread lightly, if at all.

Beach Length: 2 miles.

Pets: Not allowed.

Directions: 2 miles north of Honeymoon Island State Park.

Hours: Sunrise to sunset.

Fee: None.

Contact: Honeymoon Island State Park, 727-469-5942

www.floridastateparks.org/honeymoonisland

Clearwater–St. Petersburg Area

North Clearwater Beach

The stretch of beach on the north end of the island would seem to be for residents only, with scarce parking and signs like "no outlet," "no through streets," and "dead end." But the Jolley Trolley makes stops at four numbered pedestrian beach accesses along Eldorado Drive at Bohenia, Manog, Gardenia, and Juniper (heading south to north). No facilities.

Beach Length: 1.7 miles.
Pets: Allowed; clean up after them (bags provided).
Directions: From Clearwater Beach, follow Mandalay Avenue north to a small rotary at Acacia. Go left to reach Eldorado; turn right and look for accesses on left, but there is no parking.

Pedestrian beach access at North Clearwater Beach.

SOUTHWEST

Hours: Sunrise to sunset.
Fee: None.
Contact: Clearwater Beach Lifeguard Station, 727-462-6963

The Jolley Trolley runs the length of Clearwater Beach, between downtown Clearwater and the beach, and to Sand Key. It costs $1. 727-445-1200.

Clearwater Beach

Special features: Outdoor shower · Good beach for small children · Fishing pier

Top off a day of play on this sparkling white-sand beach with the nightly sunset celebration at Pier 60, featuring local artists and performers (starts two hours before sunset). Restrooms are located at Pier 60 and the south beach pavilion, where you can rent cabanas and chairs. There are public beach accesses at the west end of most

Clearwater Beach.

streets off Mandalay. Some have a few parking spaces, or you can park a very short block away on Mandalay (some metered, some free). There is a metered parking lot (#37) at Kendall (no facilities), and the lot at the west end of Bay Esplanade has beach grills and outdoor showers.

Beach Length: 1.3 mile.
Pets: Not allowed.
Directions: From Clearwater, take the Memorial Causeway to the island, with beach access to the north on Mandalay Avenue and to the south on S. Gulfview Boulevard. The park is south, just past Pier 60.
Hours: The beach and Pier 60 are open 24 hours, with lifeguards from 9:30 a.m. to 4:30 p.m.
Fee: South Beach pay parking lot $1.50 per hour, up to $10 per day maximum; metered street parking all along beach.
Contact: Clearwater Beach Lifeguard Station, 727-462-6963
www.clearwater-fl.com

Sand Key County Park

Special features: Outdoor shower · Picnic shelters · Beach fishing · Nature trails

This lovely wide beach is a quiet respite between condo developments. The popular park has a long meandering fitness trail, picnic areas, and a Paw Park. The sand is composed of ground-up shells, not very fine, but good for exfoliating the feet. South of the park, there are some pedestrian beach accesses between the hotels and condos, but no parking to speak of. Beach wheelchairs are available at the park.

Beach Length: 0.3 mile
Pets: Allowed in the Paw Park, but not on the beach.

SOUTHWEST

Directions: Access Sand Key via Route 416 (Bellair Beach Causeway), go north on Gulf Boulevard for 2.5 miles to the park.
Hours: Sunrise to sunset
Fee: Metered parking, $1 per hour
Contact: 727-588-4852
www.pinellascounty.org/park/15_Sand_Key.htm

> Suncoast Beach Trolley runs along the beach communities from Clearwater Beach south to Pass-a-Grille. It runs every 20 to 30 minutes from 5 a.m. to 10 p.m. and costs $1.25 per ride. 727-530-9911, www.psta.net/beachtrolley.htm

Bellair Beach Access

This beach community has pedestrian access at 6th, 13th, and 19th streets. A parking lot is at 19th, but it is only for Bellair Shores residents with decals. Limited street parking where you can find it.

Beach Length: 1 mile.
Pets: Not allowed.
Directions: Access Sand Key via Route 416 (Bellair Beach Causeway); beach accesses are off Gulf Boulevard to the north and south.
Hours: Sunrise to sunset.
Fee: None.
Contact: Bellair Beach Public Works Department, 727-595-4646

Indian Rocks Beach Access

Special features: Outdoor shower · Beach fishing

This community has much better access than its neighbor to the north, with impressive public access at the ends of nearly every ave-

Indian Rocks Beach.

nue from 1st through 28th. Most have outdoor showers and parking, although a few are pedestrian only. Pinellas County operates a park at 18th Avenue with a metered lot, restrooms, and outdoor showers.

Beach Length: 2 miles.
Pets: Not allowed.
Directions: From the mainland, access Sand Key via Walsingham Road; along Gulf Boulevard find accesses at the west ends of avenues 1 through 28.
Hours: Open 24 hours.
Fee: Metered lot is $1 per hour.
Contact: City of Indian Rocks Beach, 727-595-2517
www.indian-rocks-beach.org

SOUTHWEST

Indian Rocks Beach

Special features: Outdoor shower

This residential community has accesses at the west ends of nearly every street off Gulf Boulevard. The park at 1700 Gulf Boulevard has facilities.

Beach Length: 3 miles.
Pets: Not allowed.
Directions: Access Sand Key via Walsingham Road, turn south on Gulf Boulevard.
Hours: Sunrise to sunset.
Fee: Metered parking: 50¢ per hour
Contact: Pinellas County, 727-588-4852
www.pinellascounty.org/park

Indian Shores

Special features: Outdoor shower

Tiki Gardens park at 196th Avenue is on the inland side of the highway, so you have to walk across Gulf Boulevard at the light. Use the pedestrian walkway with traffic button. There are also public accesses with limited parking at the ends of 186th, 190th, 193rd, 197th, and 198th avenues (portable toilet at 197th).

Beach Length: 1 mile.
Pets: Not allowed.
Directions: Access Sand Key via Walsingham Road, turn south on Gulf Boulevard to Tiki Gardens at 196th Avenue.
Hours: Sunrise to sunset.
Fee: Metered parking: 50¢ per hour
Contact: Pinellas County, 727-588-4882
www.pinellascounty.org/park

SOUTHWEST

Redington Shores Beach Access

Special features: Outdoor shower · Fishing pier

There's a 3.5-acre county park with lots of parking, beach access, and facilities one mile north of Gulf Boulevard at 182nd Street. At 175th Street is a privately operated fishing pier with parking strictly for the pier and no beach access.

Beach Length: 1 mile.
Pets: Not allowed.
Directions: From St. Petersburg, take Tom Stuart Causeway (Route 666) to the island. Turn north on Gulf Boulevard and go 2.5 miles. The park is at 18200 Gulf Boulevard.
Hours: Sunrise to sunset.
Fee: Prepay machine to park: $1 per hour.
Contact: Redington Shores Town Hall, 727-397-5538 www.pinellas-county.org/park/13_Redington.htm

North Redington Beach Access

Special features: Beach fishing

This mile-long beach has six pedestrian accesses with street parking along Gulf Boulevard. There's only one beach parking lot, but it is for residents only. Limited on-street parking.

Beach Length: 1 mile.
Pets: Not allowed.
Directions: From St. Petersburg, take Tom Stuart Causeway (Route 666) to the island. Turn north on Gulf Boulevard and go 1 mile.
Hours: Open 24 hours.
Fee: None.

SOUTHWEST

Contact: Town of North Redington Beach, 727-391-4848
www.townofnorthredingtonbeach.com

Madeira Beach

Special features: Picnic shelters · Outdoor shower · Beach fishing

You can rent lounge chairs, umbrellas, kayaks, and aqua cycles along this beach strip, dubbed Mad Beach. The city operates Archibald Memorial Beach between Madeira Way and 153rd Street. There are also public lots with restrooms at 141st and 144th streets and limited free parking at the ends of 130th through 136th (no facilities).

Beach Length: 3.5 miles.
Pets: Not allowed.
Directions: From St. Petersburg, take Tom Stuart Causeway (Route 666) to the island. Turn north on Gulf Boulevard to Archibald Memorial Beach, or south to the other accesses.
Hours: 6 a.m. to 10 p.m.
Fee: Metered parking lot, $1 per hour.
Contact: City of Madeira Beach, 727-391-9951
www.ci.madeira-beach.fl.us

John's Pass Park

Special features: Outdoor shower · Picnic shelters · Fishing pier · Beach fishing

This historic fishing village and beach at the south end of Sand Key is a major commercial fishing hub where a lot of groupers are landed. Try for your own at the public fishing pier. Note: Replacement of the John's Pass Bridge will be ongoing for several years. The park is open, but be aware that it may be used as a staging area for construction vehicles.

Beach Length: 500 feet.
Pets: Not allowed.
Directions: From St. Petersburg, take Tom Stuart Causeway (Route 666) to the Madeira Beach. Turn south on Gulf Boulevard, go 2 miles to the pass at 129th Street.
Hours: 6 a.m. to midnight.
Fee: Metered parking, $1 per hour.
Contact: City of Madeira Beach, public works: 727-391-1611
www.ci.madeira-beach.fl.us

> Treasure Island is about three miles long, narrow at the top at John's Pass, wider in the middle, and tapering to Blind Pass at the southern end. These three gulf beach areas have distinct personalities. Sunshine Beach, to the north, and Sunset Beach, to the south, are residential and quieter than the middle section, where the hotels, restaurants, and tourists are. Sunshine Beach has pedestrian beach access, but no public facilities at this time.

City of St. Petersburg Municipal Beach

Special features: Picnic shelters · Beach fishing

Technically outside St. Pete limits, this northern Treasure Island property was purchased years ago by the city for its residents to enjoy the beach. This pleasant park has grills, a snack bar, and volleyball nets. A beach wheelchair is available. There's also public parking at the west ends of most streets from 121th through 127th.

Beach Length: 500 feet.
Pets: Not allowed.
Directions: From St. Petersburg take Treasure Island Causeway to the island, turn north on Gulf Boulevard to 112th Street.
Hours: 5 a.m. to 1 a.m.

SOUTHWEST

Fee: Pay machine to park.
Contact: St. Petersburg Recreation Department, 727-893-7441
www.stpete.org/fun/parks/parks.htm

Treasure Island Beach Accesses

Special features: Outdoor shower · Beach fishing

The county operates two accesses on Treasure Island, one at 104th Avenue with free, limited parking, and a metered lot at 100th, both with restrooms. There are pedestrian accesses at the ends of streets. The beach is very wide here, a pleasure to run or walk on.

Beach Length: 0.8 mile.
Pets: Not allowed.
Directions: Gulf Boulevard at 100th and 104th avenues on Treasure Island.
Hours: 5 a.m. to 1 a.m.

Treasure Island.

Fee: Some free parking; Sandpiper Lot is $1 per hour.
Contact: Pinellas County, 727-943-4081
www.pinellascounty.org/park

Sunset Beach

Special features: Outdoor shower · Picnic shelters · Good beach for small children · Beach fishing

The beach becomes narrower as you go south on Treasure Island, but quieter, too, except on Thursday evenings, when Florida folk musicians perform at the tiki bar. There's a large metered lot labeled "Tern" between 77th and 80th avenues, where you'll find Sunset Beach Pavilion and facilities. At the very southern end of the island, a boardwalk leads 0.6 mile around the point through sea grapes, past condos, and around to the canal on the other side. There are also two smaller lots north of here: Brown Pelican at 88th, and Ring Billed Gull at 81st. Neither has facilities, but there are restaurants nearby. A beach wheelchair is available.

Beach Length: 1 mile.
Pets: Not allowed.
Directions: At the south end of Gulf Boulevard on Treasure Island.
Hours: 5 a.m. to 1 a.m.
Fee: Metered parking, $1 per hour.
Contact: Treasure Island Public Works Department, 727-547-4575 X250
www.mytreasureisland.org

SOUTHWEST

Upham Beach

Special features: Outdoor shower · Beach fishing

Located at the north end of St. Pete Beach (the community officially shortened its name from St. Petersburg Beach in 1994), this quiet, pleasant park has cheery pink sidewalks and blue retaining walls. There's also a very nice café, the Seaside Grill.

Beach Length: 700 feet.
Pets: Not allowed.
Directions: From St. Petersburg, take Corey Causeway (75th Avenue) to the island and go south on Gulf Boulevard. Turn west anywhere between 67th and 70th and go 2 blocks to Beach Plaza.
Hours: Sunrise to sunset.
Fee: Pay machine in parking lot: $1.25 per hour or $5 per day.
Contact: St. Pete Beach Parks, 727-363-9247
www.stpetebeach.org/parks

St. Pete Beach Access

Special features: Outdoor shower · Beach fishing

This county access has a large metered lot and three boardwalks over lovely vegetated dunes to a gorgeous gulf beach.

Beach Length: 350 feet.
Pets: Not allowed.
Directions: From I-275 in St. Petersburg, take the Pinellas Bayway to St. Pete Beach. Go 0.8 mile north on Gulf Boulevard, just past 46th Avenue.
Hours: Sunrise to sunset.
Fee: Pay machine in parking lot: $1.25 per hour or $5 per day.

Contact: Pinellas County, 727-582-2267
www.pinellascounty.org/park/17_StPete.htm

> Suncoast Beach Trolley runs along the beach communities from Pass-a-Grille north to Clearwater Beach. It runs every 20 to 30 minutes from 5 a.m. to 10 p.m. and costs $1.25 a ride. 727- 530-9911, www.psta. net/beachtrolley.htm

Pass-a-Grille Beach

Special features: Picnic shelters · Outdoor shower · Beach fishing

When you reach the large pink 1920s Don Cesar Beach Resort, you may think you're at the end of the road, but go under the resort's garage overpass and continue on to the quiet historic beach town of Pass-a-Grille. You'll find the historic district, museum, shops, and restaurants between 7th and 10th avenues. There's diagonal and parallel parking all along the beach, and restrooms and tennis courts at 16th Avenue at Col. Frank Hurley Park. There are foot showers and prepaid parking machines at frequent walkovers.

Beach Length: 1 mile.
Pets: Not allowed.
Directions: South of St. Pete Beach, between 1st and 21st avenues along Gulf Way.
Hours: Open 24 hours (but no sleeping on the beach).
Fee: Pay machines, $1.25 per hour or $5 per day.
Contact: Contact: St. Pete Beach Parks, 727-363-9247
www.stpetebeach.org/parks

SOUTHWEST

Shell Key Preserve

Special features: Beach fishing · Primitive camping

A true rarity in this part of the coast is an undeveloped barrier island set aside for the birds. In fact, a large chunk of it is off-limits to humans, but you can picnic, snorkel, hike, primitive camp, and even bring your dog to the open beaches on the north and south ends. Get there in your own boat, or via shuttle from Pass-a-Grille. There are no facilities and no freshwater. When passing the Bird Preservation Area, walk through the shallow surf and stay off the beach.

Beach Length: 2.5 miles, with 2 miles open to the public.
Pets: Permitted only at the north and south ends of the island and must be either on a leash or under voice control. No pets are taken on the shuttle.
Directions: The island is located just north of Fort De Soto County Park. Take your own boat, or the Shell Key Shuttle, which departs daily at 10 a.m., noon, and 2 p.m. from the Merry Pier on 8th Avenue in Pass-a-Grille.
Hours: Open 24 hours.
Fee: None by private boat; shuttle is $22 for adults, $11 for children 12 and under.
Contact: Pinellas County Department of Environmental Management, 727-453-6900
www.pinellascounty.org/environment
Shell Key Shuttle, 727-360-1348. www.shellkeyshuttle.com

Fort De Soto County Park

Special features: Picnic shelters · Good beach for small children ·
Beach fishing · Fishing pier · Nature trails · Developed campground

This fantastic 1,136-acre park comprising five connected barrier islands has a historic fort and one of the nation's best-ranked beaches. There are two expansive beaches, each with restrooms and picnic shelters, and even a pet beach. The East Beach has a nice view of ships plying the shipping lane and the Sunshine Skyway Bridge. North Beach, ranked #1 in the United States by Dr. Beach in 2005, is really two beaches in one. The lagoon creates safe swimming on a wide, flat beach. It's raked daily, so the shelling isn't great. But for a wilder beach experience and more prolific beachcombing, walk around the lagoon to the exposed gulf beach on a spit of sand. The current is too strong here for swimming, especially at a tide change. (This is where local naturists are advocating for a sanctioned clothing-optional beach.) The park also has a ferry out to Egmont Key, a canoe/kayak trail, and four nature trails.

Beach Length: 7 miles.
Pets: Allowed at the 1,200-foot pet beach at Bay Pier, in designated campsites, and the Paw Playground.
Directions: From U.S. 19 in St. Petersburg, take Pinellas Bayway (Route 682) west to Route 679 and go south 6 miles to the park.
Hours: Sunrise to sunset.
Fee: None, but 85¢ in tolls to drive over the causeway (Sunpass accepted).
Contact: 727-582-2267
www.pinellascounty.org/park/05_Ft_De Soto.htm

Fort De Soto Park's East Beach has a view of the Sunshine Skyway Bridge.

SOUTHWEST

Egmont Key State Park

Special features: Portable toilets only · Beach fishing · Nature trails

This wild island is home to an 1858 working lighthouse, the remnants of 1906 Fort Dade, hundreds of endangered gopher tortoises, and myriad shorebirds under protection of a wildlife refuge. Egmont Key is a delta island formed by sediment flushed from the Hillsborough River out to the mouth of Tampa Bay. As such, it differs from other nearby islands, which are true barrier islands formed by centuries of sand deposited by wave action and storms. On the north end, hike miles of brick lanes and nature trails, then take a dip on the gulfside beach. During nesting season, the beach on the southern end of the island is off-limits. There is a ranger on duty, but few facilities for the public. You must bring your own drinking water.

Beach Length: 1.6 miles on gulf side; observe signs restricting access during bird nesting season.
Pets: Not allowed.
Directions: Located at the mouth of Tampa Bay, 1.5 mile southwest of Fort De Soto County Park. Access by ferry, private boat, or kayak from the county park. The dock is for government use only, so boats must anchor offshore or land on the beach. GPS for beach landing: N27 36.060, W82 45.566
Hours: 8 a.m. to sunset.
Fee: None.
Contact: 727-893-2627
www.floridastateparks.org/egmontkey

E. G. Simmons County Park

Special features: Outdoor shower · Picnic shelters · Good beach for small children Beach fishing · Fishing pier · Developed campground

SOUTHWEST

Egmont Key
State Park's
lighthouse.

This large, out-of-the-way park on the mainland has a small sheltered beach on Tampa Bay, fishing piers, and two campgrounds. The 469-acre park preserve is popular with the fishing and boating sets.

Beach Length: 300 feet.
Pets: Allowed in park, but not on beach.
Directions: From U.S. 41 in Ruskin, go west on NW 19th Avenue 2.3 miles to the end.
Hours: 8 a.m. to 6 p.m.
Fee: None.
Contact: 813-671-7655
www.hillsboroughcounty.org/parks

SOUTHWEST

Bradenton Area

Palma Sola Causeway Park

*Special features: Picnic shelters · Good beach for small children ·
Beach fishing · Fishing pier*

Located on the causeway to Anna Maria Island, this locals' park has
pink picnic shelters and grills, a bike path, and a sand boat ramp. You
can drive on the sand here, and even bring your pet.

Beach Length: 0.6 mile.
Pets: Allowed on leash.
Directions: From Bradenton, take Manatee Avenue West (Route 64)
toward Anna Maria Island. The park is on the right side of the Palma
Sola Causeway on Palma Sola Bay.
Hours: Sunrise to sunset.
Fee: None.
Contact: Manatee County, 941-742-5923
www.co.manatee.fl.us

Bayfront Park

Special features: Outdoor shower · Picnic shelters · Beach fishing

This quiet bayside beach is out of the way of the beach crowds, on
the northeastern end of Anna Maria Island. It's a nice shady place
to let the kids play or splash around. A historic marker tells about
Passage Key, a small barrier island just offshore and one of America's
first wildlife refuges. It remains an important bird nesting site and is
strictly off-limits to the public.

Beach Length: 1,200 feet.

Pets: Not allowed.

Directions: From Bradenton, take SR 64 causeway to Anna Maria Island. Turn right on N. Gulf Drive and go 2.9 miles to Anna Maria Village; turn right on Pine Avenue. Go 0.5 mile to the end and turn left on N. Bay Boulevard.

Hours: Sunrise to 10 p.m.

Fee: None.

Contact: Manatee County, 941-742-5923

www.co.manatee.fl.us

> The free Island Trolley travels the length of Anna Maria Island, making regular stops at each beach. 941-749-7116.

Anna Maria Beach Accesses

Special features: Beach fishing

The village of Anna Maria on the north end of the island is very cute; however, there's no public beach park and no public restrooms. There is a free public lot on Gulf Boulevard at Spring Street, in the middle of the village. Walk a block down Spring to the beach and the Sandbar Restaurant. There is a place to unload, but not to park, at the ends of Palm and Magnolia. Several accesses along N. Shore Drive are pedestrian only, but if you can get here, it's a great place to see shorebirds. All are handicapped accessible except the one at Willow Avenue.

Beach Length: 1,000 feet

Pets: Not allowed.

Directions: From Bradenton, take SR 64 causeway to Anna Maria Island. Turn right on N. Gulf Drive and go 2.9 miles to the city of Anna Maria.

SOUTHWEST

Hours: Sunrise to sunset.
Fee: None.
Contact: City of Anna Maria, 941-708-6130
www.cityofannamaria.com

Holmes Beach Accesses

Special features: Beach fishing

Most numbered and named streets in Holmes Beach have public access with limited parking and no facilities. These give access to nearly the entire stretch of beach, except for a few places blocked by condos and hotels.

Beach Length: 1.5 mile.
Pets: Not allowed.
Directions: From Bradenton, take SR 64 causeway to Holmes Beach on Anna Maria Island. Go north on Gulf Drive and see accesses on the left all along the beach, up to 77th Street.
Hours: Sunrise to sunset.
Fee: None.
Contact: Manatee County Parks and Recreation, 941-742-5923
www.co.manatee.fl.us

Manatee Public Beach

Special features: Outdoor shower · Fishing pier

This park has plenty of free parking and lots of activity, from volleyball to fishing from a pier. A large pipe runs along the beach for erosion control.

Beach Length: 1,000 feet.
Pets: Not allowed.

Directions: From Bradenton, take SR 64 causeway to Holmes Beach on Anna Maria Island. SR 64 becomes 40th Avenue at Gulf Boulevard. The park is straight ahead.

Hours: Sunrise to sunset.

Fee: None.

Contact: Manatee County Parks and Recreation, 941-742-5923 www.co.manatee.fl.us

Katie Pierola Park

Special features: Beach fishing

This small park with pedestrian access is located where several cottages were destroyed during Hurricane Elena in 1985. There are tiki tables, but no facilities or parking.

Katie Pierola Sunset Park on Anna Maria Island.

SOUTHWEST

Beach Length: 100-foot access to miles of beach.

Pets: Not allowed.

Directions: From Bradenton, take Cortez Road (SR 684) west to Bradenton Beach and turn north on Gulf Drive. Drive 0.8 mile to 23rd Street.

Hours: Sunrise to sunset.

Fee: None.

Contact: Manatee County Parks and Recreation, 941-742-5923 www.co.manatee.fl.us

Cortez Beach

Special features: Beach fishing

There are no public restrooms, but this stretch of beach is within walking distance of shops and restaurants. There's on-street parking where you can find it.

Beach Length: 0.75 mile.

Pets: Not allowed.

Directions: From Bradenton, take Cortez Road (SR 684) west to Bradenton Beach and turn south on Gulf Drive. Cortez Beach runs south to 13th Street.

Hours: Sunrise to sunset.

Fee: None.

Contact: Manatee County Parks and Recreation, 941-742-5923 www.co.manatee.fl.us

SOUTHWEST

Coquina Beach

Special features: Picnic shelters · Outdoor shower · Good beach for small children · Beach fishing · Fishing pier

This southern stretch of Anna Maria Island is completely undeveloped on both sides of Gulf Drive, with public access to Sarasota Bay and the Gulf of Mexico. There's plenty of unpaved parking, and picnic tables under the shade of Australian pines. It's a very pleasant place to spend a quiet day. The Coquina Beachwalk is an interpretive trail and boardwalk through the bay habitats. The beach is showing some erosion, and piers and concrete groins have been installed in an attempt to alleviate it. No swimming is permitted near the channel at the island's southern tip, but there's plenty of fishing and boat watching. There are four sets of restrooms on the gulf side, with Island Trolley stops at each, and a small café, open 10 a.m. to 4 p.m. The bay side has restrooms, picnic shelters, and a playground.

Beach Length: 1 mile.
Pets: Not allowed.
Directions: From Bradenton, take Cortez Road (SR 684) west to Bradenton Beach. Go south on Gulf Drive to the park, which runs to the end of Anna Marie Island.
Hours: 6 a.m. to 9 p.m.
Fee: None.
Contact: Manatee County Parks and Recreation, 941-742-5923 www.co.manatee.fl.us

Greer Island Beach

Special features: Beach fishing

Accessible by boat only, this spit of beach is a popular hangout for the pleasure boating crowd and nicknamed Beer Can Beach. A Longboat Key city beach access at the west end of N. Shore Road once provided pedestrian access to the island, but it has washed away with erosion. No facilities.

Beach Length: 0.5 mile.
Pets: Not allowed.
Directions: Located on the north end of Longboat Key.
Hours: Sunrise to sunset.
Fee: None.
Contact: Manatee County Parks and Recreation, 941-742-5923 www.co.manatee.fl.us

Longboat Key Accesses

Special features: Portable toilets only · Beach fishing

Longboat Key is an exclusive community of homes, condos, and resorts. There are 14 public beach accesses, but only a handful have parking. Look for the blue and white access signs between the hotels and condos. On the north end are parking lots at the ends of Broadway (has a portable toilet) and General Harris Street. On the south end there's public parking just north of Holiday Beach Resort, north of Sea Horse Beach Resort, and near Neptune Avenue (across from Buttonwood Plaza). There's also parking at Town Hall. No facilities.

Beach Length: 10 miles.
Pets: Not allowed.
Directions: From Bradenton, take Cortez Road (SR 684) west to Anna Maria Island. Go south on Gulf Drive, crossing the bridge to Longboat Key. Accesses are at street ends off Gulf of Mexico Drive.
Hours: 5 a.m. to 11 p.m.
Fee: None.
Contact: Town of Longboat Key Public Works, 941-316-1988 www.longboatkey.org

Quick Point Nature Preserve

Special features: Beach fishing · Nature trails

This nature preserve at the southern end of Longboat Key has a small beach and a couple of picnic tables on New Pass. It's nice for fishing or picnicking, but not so great for swimming, as powerboats anchor in this cove. There's much more to the preserve on the other side of the road, with nature trails and tidal lagoons, but no beach. No facilities.

Beach Length: 300 feet.
Pets: Not allowed.
Directions: From Sarasota, take the John Ringling Causeway (SR 789) west to Lido Beach; go north on Gulf of Mexico Drive (SR 789), cross the bridge to Longboat Key, and look for small beach on left, on New Pass.
Hours: Sunrise to sunset.
Fee: None.
Contact: Town of Longboat Key, 941-316-1988
www.longboatkey.org

SOUTHWEST

Sarasota Area

North Lido Beach

Special features: Outdoor shower · Beach fishing

A small parking lot on the right side of the road and street parking on the left provide access to this beach.

Beach Length: 0.5 mile.
Pets: Not allowed.
Directions: From Sarasota, take the John Ringling Causeway (SR 789) west to Lido Beach; go north on North Polk Drive 0.3 mile.
Hours: Sunrise to 11 p.m.; closes at 9 p.m. for turtle nesting season, May through October.
Fee: None.
Contact: Sarasota County Parks and Recreation, 941-861-7275 www.scgov.net

Lido Beach/Coolidge Park

Special features: Outdoor shower · Picnic shelters · Good beach for small children · Beach fishing

This is the place to go if you're looking for beach action. The large parking lot can accommodate up to 400 cars. There's also a pool, open Tuesday through Sunday, 9:30 a.m. to 4:45 p.m. (entrance fee charged), gift shop, recreation building, and more than a half mile of beach. There are handicapped-accessible observation decks and beach wheelchairs available.

SOUTHWEST

Lido Beach.

Beach Length: 0.5 mile.

Pets: Not allowed.

Directions: From Sarasota, take the John Ringling Causeway (SR 789) west to Lido Beach, go south 0.5 mile on Ben Franklin Drive.

Hours: Sunrise to 11 p.m.; closes at 9 p.m. for turtle nesting season, May through October.

Fee: None.

Contact: Sarasota County Parks and Recreation, 941-861-7275 www.scgov.net

South Lido Park

Special features: Outdoor shower · Beach fishing · Nature trails

The section of the park at the southern end of Lido Key has bay- and gulfside beaches, with fewer crowds than Lido Beach proper. The shady bayside beach is for watercraft, not for swimming. There's a large gulfside beach, but swim only in designated areas because of the danger of strong currents. The north unit of the park, 0.6 mile north, has canoe/kayak and nature trails, but no beach.

SOUTHWEST

South Lido Park, bayside.

Beach Length: 0.3 mile.
Pets: Not allowed.
Directions: From Sarasota, take the John Ringling Causeway (SR 789) west to Lido Beach, go south on Ben Franklin Drive 1.3 miles to the south end of Lido Key.
Hours: Sunrise to 11 p.m.; closes at 9 p.m. for turtle nesting season, May through October.
Fee: None.
Contact: Sarasota County Parks and Recreation, 941-861-7275 www.scgov.net

Siesta Key North Beach Accesses

Along Beach Road are public accesses with limited parking at the ends of Shell Road and Avenida Navarre. There are pedestrian accesses at the ends of Avenida Mesina and Columbus, but no parking. Where Beach Road becomes Ocean Boulevard there's a parking lot for about 20 cars, and for 20–30 cars at Calle de la Siesta and Plaza de las Palmas. No facilities.

Beach Length: 1.5 mile.
Pets: Not allowed.
Directions: From Sarasota, take Siesta Drive (Route 758) west to the north end of Siesta Key.
Hours: Sunrise to 11 p.m.; closes at 9 p.m. for turtle nesting season, May through October.
Fee: None.
Contact: Sarasota County Parks and Recreation, 941-861-7275 www.scgov.net

Siesta Key Public Beach

Special features: Outdoor shower · Picnic shelters · Beach fishing

Even this 800-space parking lot gets crowded on nice days. This is a very active beach, with parasailers, ten volleyball courts, and a sea of umbrellas on a fine white-sand beach. Beach wheelchair available.

Beach Length: 0.4 mile.
Pets: Not allowed.
Directions: From Sarasota, take Siesta Drive (Route 758) west to the north end of Siesta Key. Head south to 948 Beach Road.
Hours: Sunrise to 11 p.m.; closes at 9 p.m. for turtle nesting season, May through October.
Fee: None.
Contact: Sarasota County Parks and Recreation, 941-861-7275 www.scgov.net

Crescent Beach/Point of Rocks

Special features: Beach fishing

Point of Rocks, located on the south end of Crescent Beach, takes its name from the flat, smooth limestone rock that forms it. There are tidal pools in the rock that are quite rare in Florida. There's great diving and snorkeling on the offshore reef. This is a residential community with no public facilities and only roadside parking where you can find it.

Beach Length: Crescent Beach is 2.5 miles; Point of Rocks is about 500 feet.
Pets: Not allowed.
Directions: Take Stickney Point Road to Siesta Key; go 0.4 mile south on Midnight Pass Road to Point of Rocks Road.
Hours: Sunrise to 11 p.m.; closes at 9 p.m. for turtle nesting season, May through October.
Fee: None.
Contact: Sarasota County Parks and Recreation, 941-861-7275 www.scgov.net

Turtle Beach

Special features: Picnic shelters · Beach fishing · Developed campground

Named for the sea turtles who love to nest in the coarse sand, this park on the south end of Siesta Key has an RV campground and a narrow beach. The restrooms are a good walk from the beach to the main road, where you'll find Turtles Waterfront Restaurant and a boat ramp on the bayside.

Beach Length: 0.25 mile.

Pets: Not allowed.

Directions: From Coral Cove, go west on Route 72 (Stickney Point Road) to Siesta Key. Go south 2.5 miles on Midnight Pass Road, then turn right on Turtle Beach Road.

Hours: Sunrise to 11 p.m.; closes at 9 p.m. for turtle nesting season, May through October.

Fee: None.

Contact: Sarasota County Parks and Recreation, 941-861-7275
www.scgov.net

Nokomis Beach

Special features: Outdoor shower · Picnic shelters · Beach fishing

There are cute motels near the beach in this laid-back community. The park has a nice handicapped-accessible boardwalk to the beach, with beach wheelchairs available. Across the highway, a boat ramp gives access to the Intracoastal Waterway.

Beach Length: 400 feet.

Pets: Not allowed.

Directions: From U.S. 41 in Nokomis, go west on Albee Road (Route 789) for 1 mile. The road ends at Casey Key Road and the park.

Hours: Sunrise to 11 p.m.; closes at 9 p.m. for turtle nesting season, May through October.

Fee: None.

Contact: Sarasota County Parks and Recreation, 941-861-7275
www.scgov.net

SOUTHWEST

North Jetty Park

Special features: Picnic shelters · Fishing jetty · Beach fishing

This is a popular surfing area and fishing jetty on Venice Inlet. North Jetty Fish Camp sells beverages (alcoholic and non), bait, and snacks.

Beach Length: 450 feet.
Pets: Not allowed.
Directions: From U.S. 41, go west on Albee Road (Route 789) for 1 mile. Go left on Casey Key Road 0.6 mile to the south end of Casey Key.
Hours: 6 a.m. to midnight
Fee: None.
Contact: Sarasota County Parks and Recreation, 941-861-7275 www.scgov.net

North Jetty Park.

Venice Area

South Jetty

Special features: Fishing jetty

Fishing on the jetty and boat watching on Venice Inlet are more of an attraction than the beach, which has gray, dirtlike sand. But it's a fun, informal place to watch the sunset.

Beach Length: 400 feet.
Pets: Not allowed.
Directions: From Business 41 in downtown Venice, go west on Venice Avenue, 2 miles to the end. Turn right on Higel Drive for 0.3 mile, then left on Tarpon Center Drive for 0.7 mile to the end.
Hours: Sunrise to 11 p.m.; closes at 9 p.m. for turtle nesting season, May through October.
Fee: None.
Contact: Sarasota County Parks and Recreation, 941-861-7275 www.scgov.net

Venice Municipal Beach

Special features: Outdoor shower Beach fishing

The approach to this beach is through Venice's historic shopping district, which becomes a wide boulevard overhung with ancient live oaks. The park on the Esplanade is small, with limited parking, but the beach is huge. A fossilized reef a quarter-mile offshore is a popular diving spot. Beach wheelchairs available.

Beach Length: 900-foot park gives access to 2-mile beach.

Pets: Not allowed.

Directions: From Business 41 in downtown Venice, go west on Venice Avenue for 2 miles to the end.

Hours: Sunrise to 11 p.m.; closes at 9 p.m. for turtle nesting season, May through October.

Fee: None.

Contact: Sarasota County Parks and Recreation, 941-861-7275
www.scgov.net

Service Club Park

Special features: Outdoor shower · Picnic shelters · Beach fishing

This small park allows access to a beautiful, wide expanse of beach on which you can walk for miles in either direction. If there's no open parking spaces, don't worry. Three other parks south of here give access to the same gorgeous strand of beach.

Beach Length: 250 feet of park gives access to miles of beach.

Pets: Not allowed.

Directions: From Business 41, turn west on Airport Road, which becomes Beach Road and ends at Harbor Drive. Turn left and the park is immediately on the right.

Hours: Sunrise to 11 p.m.; closes at 9 p.m. for turtle nesting season, May through October.

Fee: None.

Contact: Sarasota County Parks and Recreation, 941-861-7275
www.scgov.net

Venice Fishing Pier

Special features: Outdoor shower · Picnic shelters · Fishing pier

The sign for Sharky's restaurant marks the entrance to the huge parking lot for this popular stretch of beach. You'll find a tiki bar, a restaurant, a fishing pier, and parking for hundreds, which actually fills up on weekends in season.

Beach Length: 750 feet.
Pets: Not allowed.
Directions: From Business 41, turn west on Airport Road, which becomes Beach Road and ends at Harbor Drive. Turn left and go 0.4 mile to the park.
Hours: Sunrise to 11 p.m.; closes at 9 p.m. for turtle nesting season, May through October.
Fee: None.
Contact: Sarasota County Parks and Recreation, 941-861-7275 www.scgov.net

Sharky's at Venice Fishing Pier.

SOUTHWEST

South Brohard Paw Park

This beach is much quieter than its neighbor to the north, so if you come to the beach for quiet and meditation, to listen to the waves, this is the better choice. A handicapped-accessible boardwalk leads to the beach.

Beach Length: 600 feet.
Pets: Allowed to run and swim in the surf.
Directions: From Business 41, turn west on Airport Road, which becomes Beach Road and ends at Harbor Drive. Turn left and go 1 mile to the park.
Hours: Sunrise to 11 p.m.; closes at 9 p.m. for turtle nesting season, May through October.
Fee: None.
Contact: Sarasota County Parks and Recreation, 941-861-7275
www.scgov.net

Caspersen Beach Park

Special features: Outdoor shower · Picnic shelters · Beach fishing · Nature trails

This park is located at the southern, undeveloped end of Venice, and is a great place to look for fossil shark teeth. From the airport southward, there's little development except for a golf course and the park. This large park has nature trails, a boat ramp, and a playground on the bayside, and a wide, white beach with restrooms on the gulfside. On approach, you get the feeling you're entering a wild beach, and unless it's a sunny day in the high season, you may have it to yourself.

Beach Length: 1.6 mile.

Pets: Not allowed.

Directions: From Business 41, turn west on Airport Road, which becomes Beach Road and ends at Harbor Drive. Turn left and go 1.3 miles to the park.

Hours: 7 a.m. to 6 p.m.

Fee: None.

Contact: Sarasota County Parks and Recreation, 941-861-7275 www.scgov.net

Manasota Beach

Special features: Picnic shelters · Outdoor shower · Beach fishing · Nature trails

This small park gives access to a beautiful stretch of beach on Manasota Key. There's a larger parking lot across the road, as well as a boat ramp on the Intracoastal Waterway. A boardwalk leads through the mangroves. Beach wheelchair available.

Manasota Beach.

SOUTHWEST

Beach Length: 1,500 feet.

Pets: Not allowed.

Directions: From CR 776 in Englewood, go west on Manasota Beach Road 2 miles to the end at Manasota Key Road.

Hours: Sunrise to 11 p.m.; closes at 9 p.m. for turtle nesting season, May through October.

Fee: None.

Contact: Sarasota County Parks and Recreation, 941-861-7275 www.scgov.net

Blind Pass Beach

Special features: Outdoor shower · Beach fishing

This beach on Manasota Key seems out of the way, but it has been discovered and you'll have plenty of company on nice days. Don't worry, there's parking for hundreds of cars.

Beach Length: 0.5 mile.

Pets: Not allowed.

Directions: From CR 776 in Englewood, go west on Manasota Beach Road 2 miles to the end, turn left on Manasota Key Road and go 4 miles to the end along a windy, narrow drive dubbed Canopy Road for the live oaks growing over it.

Hours: Sunrise to 11 p.m.; closes at 9 p.m. for turtle nesting season, May through October.

Fee: None.

Contact: Sarasota County Parks and Recreation, 941-861-7275 www.scgov.net

Port Charlotte Area

Chadwick Park at Englewood Beach

Special features: Outdoor shower · Picnic shelters · Beach fishing

This large, very popular beach gets crowded on nice days.

Beach Length: 1,200 feet.
Pets: Not allowed.
Directions: From CR 776 in Englewood, take Beach Road onto Manasota Key to the rotary. Turn right on Manasota Key Road and park is immediately on the left.
Hours: 6 a.m. to 10 p.m.
Fee: Pay machine is 50¢ per hour for a maximum of $7.50.
Contact: Charlotte County, 941-475-1265
www.charlottecountyfl.com/Parks

Stump Pass Beach State Park

Special features: Outdoor shower · Picnic shelters · Beach fishing · Nature trails

At the southern tip of Manasota Key is a new state park, run in conjunction with Charlotte County. This small but precious piece of real estate gives access to both the gulf and the bay. There's a one-mile stretch of beach where you'll find shells and shark's teeth. Use the kayak/canoe launch on the bayside to explore the channels between the park's three islands. Limited parking.

Beach Length: 1 mile.
Pets: Allowed on leash on trails, but not on the beach.

SOUTHWEST

Directions: From CR 776 in Englewood, take Beach Road onto Manasota Key to the rotary. Turn left on Gulf Boulevard and go 1 mile to the end.
Hours: 8 a.m. to sunset.
Fee: $2 per vehicle; $1 to use kayak launch; honor box.
Contact: 941-964-0375
www.floridastateparks.org/stumppass

Don Pedro Island State Park

Special features: Picnic shelters · Beach fishing · Nature trails

This small island, located between Knight Island and Little Gasparilla Island, is accessible by private boat only. From the boat dock on the bayside, walk to the gulfside for a pristine white-sand beach.

Beach Length: 1 mile.
Pets: Allowed on leash on trails, but not on the beach.
Directions: Located off the coast of Cape Haze about 9 miles south of Englewood. Access to the boat dock is through a 2.5-foot-deep channel south of the Cape Haze power line crossing.
Hours: 8 a.m. to sunset.
Fee: $1 per person; honor box.
Contact: 941-964-0375
www.floridastateparks.org/donpedroisland

Boca Grande Public Access

Special features: Beach fishing

This island of vacation homes has seven miles of beach, but aside from Gasparilla Island State Park, if you're not renting one of the homes, getting to the beach is something of a conundrum. The northern three miles of island have virtually no public access. The first real access you'll find is at 19th Street on Gasparilla Road, via a couple of stairs or a slight incline on sand (limited parking, no facilities). From here south to 1st Street, you'll see signs for public parking that state "no beach access." The reason is a high seawall, and only a handful of the street endings offer stairs down to the beach. Some do have parking, making a nice place from which to watch the sunset. In the vicinity of 4th Street, Boca Grande Village is an upscale but still quaint little town with cafés, boutiques, and galleries of local artwork. From here, take Gulf Boulevard to the southern part of the island, where there are 14 walking paths to the beach (no parking), with better access at the state parks (see below).

Beach Length: 7 miles.
Pets: Not allowed.
Directions: From Placida, take the Boca Grande Causeway (CR 775) to Gasparilla Island. Go south on Gasparilla Road about 3 miles and look for accesses on the right, beginning at about 19th Street.
Hours: Sunrise to sunset.
Fee: None.
Contact: Lee County Parks and Recreation, 941-964-2564
www.leeparks.org

Gasparilla Island State Park

Special features: Outdoor shower · Picnic shelters · Beach fishing

This park has five units along Gulf Boulevard on the southern end of the island, all with parking and restrooms or portable toilets; some have outdoor showers. The areas are named (from north to south): Sand Spur at Wheeler Road (has a Coast Guard lighthouse), Seagrape, Seawall, Dune, and Boca Grande Lighthouse, which has an elevator to the second-floor museum and visitor center. The beaches have eroded in recent storms, and lots of energy has been put into preserving them through seawalls, groins, and replenishment.

SOUTHWEST

The authors at Gasparilla Island State Park.

Beach Length: 2 miles.

Pets: Allowed on leash in the park, but not on the beaches.

Directions: From Placida, take the Boca Grande Causeway (CR 775) to Gasparilla Island. Go south on Gasparilla Road 3.5 miles and turn right on 5th Street; go 1 block to Gulf Boulevard and head south. Look for the park's four parking areas along the 2 miles of gulfside beach. The lighthouse is at the end of the road.

Hours: 8 a.m. to sunset; lighthouse is open 10 a.m. to 4 p.m. daily, November through April, and Monday through Friday the rest of the year.

Fee: $2 per day per car; honor box.

Contact: 941-964-0375

www.floridastateparks.org/gasparillaisland

Ft. Myers–Sanibel Area

Cayo Costa State Park

*Special features: Outdoor shower · Picnic shelters · Beach fishing ·
Nature trails · Primitive camping*

This wild island is accessible by private boat or ferry only. The entire
gulf side of the island is a long beach, which is narrower in some
places as a result of erosion from Hurricane Charley in 2004. The
eroded beach is lined with dead palms, but the beach is still gorgeous, and you'll likely have a long stretch of it all to yourself. The
sand is coarse as it's made up of crushed shells, and the shelling is
very good for sand dollars, fighting conches, tiger's paws, and more.
The fishing is excellent, too, especially for sheepshead.

> **Wild File**
>
> Look for wild boars on Cayo Costa's five miles
> of nature trails, and watch out for the resident
> alligator in the gulfside lagoon, unusually close
> to salt water for this freshwater species.

You can rent a bike or kayak to explore this huge island. If you stay
the night, you'll see the sunset turn the sand pink, and then get an
uninterrupted view of the starry sky.

Details: The campsites and primitive cabins are on the gulf side of
the island, while the landing dock is on the bay side, about three-
quarters of a mile away. You can walk over, or the golf-cart tram
will haul you and your gear. There are restrooms at both locations.
There's a water fountain at the dock, but you must bring all your
freshwater for camping.

SOUTHWEST

Beach Length: 7.5 miles.

Pets: Allowed on leash on nature trails, but not on the beaches.

Directions: The island is directly south of Boca Grande and west of Pine Island. The boat dock is on the sound side, about a mile from the northern tip of the island (GPS: N26 41.171, W82 14.722). The 20-minute ferry departs at 9:30 a.m. and 2 p.m. from the Pineland Marina on Waterfront Drive in Pineland. Reservations required.

Hours: 8 a.m. to sunset.

Fee: $1 per person.

Contact: 941-964-0375

www.floridastateparks.org/cayocosta

Cabin and campsite reservations: Reserve America, 800-326-3521

www.reserveamerica.com

North Captiva Island

Special features: Beach fishing

This island of vacation beach homes is accessible only by boat. There's a marina on the bay side near the northern end. Dock here and walk to the beach and a handful of restaurants. You can also land virtually anywhere along the beach on the gulf side. The southern portion is virtually undeveloped, with one entire stretch a Barrier Islands GEOpark (no facilities). At one point the island is so narrow, you can run from bay to gulf in seconds. Watch the birds in the mudflats on the bay, usually white pelicans, white egrets, and plovers, then jump into the cooling Caribbean-blue surf on the gulf. At high tide there's a small channel here that cut the island in half during Hurricane Charley in 2004. This stretch of the island actually turned over on itself during the storm, exposing great shelling.

Directions: Located between Cayo Costa and Captiva Island, which has the closest boat launches, about 3 miles south.

Beach Length: 4 miles.

North Captiva Island at its narrowest point.

Pets: Not allowed on beach.
Hours: Open 24 hours.
Fee: None.
Contact: Cayo Costa State Park, 941-964-0375
www.floridastateparks.org/cayocosta

> Get to Captiva Island via the Sanibel Causeway,
> then drive the 12-mile length of Sanibel Island.

Captiva Beach North

Special features: Portable toilets only · Beach fishing

Unless you're a resident or guest of South Seas Plantation, which owns the entire northern portion of the island, this is as far north as you can go on Captiva. The sand here is grayish, and there's better shelling on Sanibel. The pluses include shade from some Australian pines and a pet-friendly beach you can walk for miles. There's a sand parking lot for 20 cars, no handicapped parking, and the only facilities are a couple of portable toilets. There is pedestrian beach access in the middle of town at the end of Andy Rosse Lane, but scarce on-street parking.

Beach Length: 6 miles.
Pets: Allowed on leash.
Directions: From south of Ft. Myers, take the Sanibel Causeway (Route 867) to drive the 12-mile length of Sanibel Island and cross onto Captiva Island. Take Captiva Road 3 miles to the village. Just past the village, turn left on Sand-Cap Road. The access is at the end of the road.
Hours: 6 a.m. to 11 p.m.
Fee: $2 per hour to park.
Contact: City of Sanibel Public Works, 239-472-6397, or Lee County Parks and Recreation, 239-432-2006
www.leeparks.org

Turner Beach

Special features: Outdoor shower · Beach fishing · Fishing jetty

Located on the south end of Captiva Island at Blind Pass, this is a nice place to watch the sunset, then get a drink or a bite to eat across the road. The fishing is good from the beach and the rock jetty. Be very careful swimming too near the inlet because of strong currents.

Beach Length: 6 miles.
Pets: Allowed on leash.
Directions: From south of Ft. Myers, take the Sanibel Causeway (Route 867); drive the 12-mile length of Sanibel Island; cross onto Captiva Island and look for the beach immediately on the left.
Hours: Open 24 hours.
Fee: Metered 7 a.m. to dusk.
Contact: Lee County Parks and Recreation, 239-432-2006
www.leeparks.org

Skip the Traffic

Sanibel Island is a dog-friendly 12-mile beachcombing paradise, once you get through the traffic on the bridge causeway; then a bicycle is a great way to get around. You'll see the bike rental places as soon as you get on the island, with rates starting at $10 for a half day. Bike paths run parallel to nearly every road, and these are separate paved pathways, with stop signs and markings, and cars do stop for you. There are bike racks everywhere.

A new fixed span replaced the drawbridge in 2007. Check www.sanibelcauseway.com for lane closures or construction.

Bowman's Beach

Special features: Beach fishing

This isolated beach, a local favorite, is on the much less developed northern end of Sanibel Island. There is a quarter-mile walk over a bridge from the parking lot to the wide beach, but the serenity and great shelling are worth it. Some say it's the best beach on the island.

Beach Length: 1.6 mile.
Pets: Allowed on leash.
Directions: From south of Ft. Myers, take the Sanibel Causeway (Route 867) to the island and turn right on Periwinkle Way; go 2.4 miles and make a slight right on Palm Ridge Road, which becomes Sanibel-Captiva Road. Go 5 miles to Bowman's Beach Road; turn left and go 0.3 mile to the park.
Hours: Open 24 hours.

SOUTHWEST

Fee: Metered 7 a.m. to dusk.
Contact: Lee County Parks and Recreation, 239-432-2006
www.leeparks.org

Tarpon Bay Road Beach

Special features: Outdoor shower · Beach fishing

The large parking lot is a 900-foot walk on Tarpon Bay Road to its end at Casa Ybel Road. At the beach are restrooms, handicapped parking, a bike rack, and recycling receptacles. The beach is a little more eroded and narrower here than at Gulfside City Park.

Beach Length: 1,000 feet.
Pets: Allowed on leash.
Directions: From south of Ft. Myers, take the Sanibel Causeway (Route 867) to the island and turn right on Periwinkle Way. Go 2.7 miles, turn left on Tarpon Bay Road, and go 0.8 mile to the intersection of Casa Ybel Road.
Hours: The beach is open 24 hours; restrooms are open 7 a.m. to 6 p.m.
Fee: $2 per hour parking, 7 a.m. to dusk.
Contact: City of Sanibel Public Works, 239-472-6397
www.mysanibel.com

Gulfside City Park/Algier's Beach

Special features: Outdoor shower · Beach fishing · Nature trails

Houses fade to nature preserve on the way to this quiet park at the end of a dirt road. There's parking for about 40 cars, and grills, tables, and bike racks. Nearby Gulfside Park Preserve has a paved bike/

walking loop where you'll see lots of birds and perhaps an alligator in a roadside ditch. Beach wheelchair available.

Beach Length: 1,200 feet.
Pets: Allowed on leash.
Directions From south of Ft. Myers, take the Sanibel Causeway (Route 867) to Sanibel Island. Turn right on Periwinkle Way; go 1.3 miles to Casa Ybel Road; turn left and go 1.3 miles to Algiers Lane; turn left again and go to the end.
Hours: Open 24 hours.
Fee: $2 per hour charged 7 a.m. to dusk; no fee for valid handicapped parking permit.
Contact: City of Sanibel Public Works, 472-6397
www.mysanibel.com

Lighthouse Beach Park

$

Special features: Beach fishing · Fishing pier

Located on the east end of Sanibel Island, this narrow, dog-friendly beach has a historic, functioning lighthouse. On the bay side are rest-

Sanibel Lighthouse has a public beach (by permission of the Lee County Visitor and Convention Bureau/www.FortMyersSanibel.com).

SOUTHWEST

rooms, a visitor center, and fishing pier. Be sure to swim on the gulf-side beach, away from the strong currents in the channel.

Beach Length: 0.5 mile.
Pets: Allowed on leash.
Directions: From south of Ft. Myers, take the Sanibel Causeway (Route 867) to Sanibel Island. Turn left on Periwinkle Way and go 1.2 mile to the park.
Hours: Open 24 hours.
Fee: Metered parking, 7 a.m. to sunset.
Contact: City of Sanibel Public Works, 472-6397
www.mysanibel.com

Sanibel Causeway Beach

Special features: Beach fishing

The causeway island closest to Sanibel has narrow beaches on both sides, with restrooms and picnic tables on the gulf side.

Beach Length: 0.5 mile.
Pets: Not allowed.
Directions: From south of Ft. Myers, take the Sanibel Causeway (Route 867) west.
Hours: Sunrise to sunset.
Fee: None.
Contact: Lee County Dept of Parks and Recreation, 239-432-2006
www.leeparks.org

Bunche Beach

Special features: Portable toilets only · Beach fishing

This is a fun locals' beach, a little rough around the edges, but a good quick stop if you want to avoid the traffic to Sanibel. It's located on the mainland about two miles south of the Sanibel Causeway on San Carlos Bay. Be careful getting stuck in the sand parking lot, especially in the winter dry season, when the sand becomes loose and soft. In 1949, 3,000 people attended the dedication of Bunche Beach Preserve, named for Dr. Ralph Bunche, a famous African American diplomat who worked for the State Department and, later, the United Nations. Much of the 730-acre preserve is a tidal wetland harboring myriad birdlife.

Beach Length: 0.7 mile.
Pets: Not allowed.
Directions: From U.S. 41 south of Ft. Myers, take Summerlin Road (CR 869) 9.8 miles south; turn left on John Morris Road and go 1.1 mile to the end.
Hours: Sunrise to sunset.
Fee: None.
Contact: Lee County Dept of Parks and Recreation, 239-432-2006 www.leeparks.org

Bowditch Point Regional Park

Special features: Picnic shelters · Outdoor shower · Beach fishing · Nature trails

This park preserve is located on the quieter northern tip of Ft. Myers Beach, with access to the bay and gulf. Take a walk through the preserve for panoramic views of Estero Bay, then picnic in the shade.

Beach Length: 0.4 mile.
Pets: Not allowed.
Directions: At the north end of Estero Boulevard on Ft. Myers Beach.
Hours: 8 a.m. to a half hour past sunset.
Fee: Metered parking, 75¢ per hour.

SOUTHWEST

Contact: Lee County Parks and Recreation, 239-765-6794
www.leeparks.org

To avoid the traffic jam on Ft. Myers Beach, park in the free lot at the foot of Matanzas Pass Bridge (1050 Main Street). For a quarter, you can hop on the trolley that runs frequently up and down the beach.

Ft. Myers Beach

Special features: Beach fishing

This is Spring Break heaven—or hell, if you're just trying to drive through. But there are abundant public beach accesses, some a stone's throw from each other, all with limited metered parking, but no facilities. Things really get hopping around Motel Row (especially at the Lani Kai) and around the Times Square shops. There are at least 20 accesses along Estero Boulevard with parking for between three and 20 cars; most have handicapped parking. The only public restrooms are in businesses along the beach.

Beach Length: 5 miles.
Pets: Allowed on a leash (except within the county parks).
Directions: Along Estero Boulevard from Avenue A south to Flamingo Street.
Hours: Sunrise to sunset.
Fee: None.
Contact: Town of Ft. Myers Beach, 239-765-0202

Lynn Hall Memorial Park

Special features: Picnic shelters · Outdoor shower · Fishing pier · Beach fishing

This park is in the heart of Times Square action, with shopping and restaurants steps off the sand. There's a fishing pier, cooking grills, and more than 100 parking spaces.

Beach Length: 500 feet.
Pets: Not allowed.
Directions: At the west end of the Matanzas Pass Bridge on Ft. Myers Beach at 950 Estero Boulevard.
Hours: 8 a.m. to a half hour past sunset. Fishing pier open 24 hours.
Fee: Metered parking, 75¢ per hour.
Contact: Lee County Parks and Recreation, 239-765-6794

Lovers Key State Park

Special features: Outdoor shower · Beach fishing · Nature trails

This beautiful island was named when it was accessible only by boat and frequented by romancing couples. The park opened on 712 acres of reclaimed land in 1996 in cooperation with Lee County. It was disturbed by dredge and fill operations, so there are some nonnative species, but it's become an important habitat for plants, animals, and

A long white stretch of beach at Lovers Key State Park (by permission of the Lee County Visitor and Convention Bureau/www.FortMyersSanibel.com).

SOUTHWEST

humans seeking respite from city life. A boardwalk bridge crosses a mangrove-lined canal (look for manatees below) to the long white beach. There's little shade, so bring an umbrella and sunscreen. Since this is a new park, it has the latest in environmental facilities, including composting waterless toilets, and all facilities are solar powered. It's a bit of a walk to get to the beach, but there's a free tram, and the boardwalks are handicapped accessible.

Details: Lot #1 has facilities and bike and kayak rentals. Lots #2 and 3 are even farther from the beach; catch the tram if need be. There's a canoe/kayak launch at the end of lot #3, and a bike path throughout the park. A north entrance to the park is located at the bridge over Big Carlos Pass. Parking is free, with a $1 per person entrance fee. This is a beach where powerboats pull up, so do not swim in the channel. A portable toilet is the only facility.
Beach Length: 2.5 miles.
Pets: Allowed on leash, but not on beach.
Directions: Located on CR 865 between Fort Myers Beach and Bonita Beach in Lee County.
Hours: 8 a.m. to sunset. Tram runs 9 a.m. to 5 p.m.
Fee: $5 per vehicle, $3 with one occupant; $1 pedestrian or biker.
Contact: 239-463-4588
www.floridastateparks.org/loverskey

Bonita Beach Dog Park

This scene reminds us of the big fun dog party in the Dr. Seuss book *Go, Dog, Go.* You'll see dogs of every shape, size, color, and temperament, from pampered poodles to tough-guy rottweilers. It's an off-leash park past the signs, but everyone must be on his or her best behavior. At high tide, you and Fido may have to wade to the beach as it becomes more of a sandbar. No facilities. Please clean up, and have proof of license and immunization.

Beach Length: 500 feet.
Pets: Must be on leash until the off-leash sign at the beach.

Bonita Beach Dog Park.

Directions: 1 mile south of Lover's Key State Park on Estero Boulevard.
Hours: Sunrise to sunset.
Fee: None.
Contact: Lee County Parks and Recreation, 239-461-7400

Little Hickory Beach Access

Special features: Picnic shelters · Beach fishing

This is a small county park on the gulf with paid parking. For free or overflow parking, the City of Bonita Springs has two small lots across the street, Beach Park North, with picnic shelter but no facilities.

Beach Length: 500 feet.
Pets: Not allowed.
Directions: At Hickory Boulevard and Estero Boulevard in Bonita Beach.
Hours: Sunrise to sunset.
Fee: $1 per hour; pay machine.
Contact: Lee County Parks and Recreation, 239-461-7400

SOUTHWEST

Bonita Beach Public Accesses

Special features: Beach fishing

There are nine accesses along Hickory Boulevard, located about 0.2 mile apart. Each has parking for three to ten cars. There are no facilities, but access #1 is within walking distance of Bonita Beach Park.

Beach Length: 2 miles.
Pets: Not allowed.
Directions: Along Hickory Boulevard in Bonita Beach.
Hours: Sunrise to sunset.
Fee: Accesses #2–9 have free, limited parking; access #1 costs $1 per hour.
Contact: Lee County Parks and Recreation, 239-461-7400

Bonita Beach Park

Special features: Picnic shelters · Beach fishing

This park offers access to a beautiful beach with volleyball, picnic shelters, and restrooms.

Beach Length: 375 feet of park give access to miles of beach.
Pets: Not allowed.
Directions: From U.S. 41 in Bonita Springs, take Bonita Beach Road west for 2.2 miles to Hickory Boulevard.
Hours: Sunrise to sunset.
Fee: $1 per hour to park; pay machine.
Contact: Lee County Parks and Recreation, 239-461-7400

SOUTHWEST

Naples Area

Barefoot Beach Access

Special features: Beach fishing

There are no facilities at this lot, but you can walk into Lee County's Bonita Beach Park next door, which costs much less, making one wonder why you would use this lot. We guess it makes sense for county residents, who can park for free with a beach sticker.

Beach Length: 200 feet of access to miles of beach.
Pets: Not allowed.
Directions: From U.S. 41 in Bonita Springs, take Bonita Beach Road west 2.2 miles; go left on Barefoot Beach Boulevard and take an immediate right. It seems as though you're going into a condo parking lot, but keep going to the public lot.
Hours: 8 a.m. to dusk.
Fee: $6 pay machine; free to county residents with beach sticker.
Contact: Collier County Parks, 239-254-4000
www.collierparks.com

Barefoot Beach Preserve

Special features: Outdoor shower · Picnic shelters · Beach fishing · Nature trails

This long beach has three parking lots, and roadside parking when those are full. The facilities and visitor center are at lot #1. There's a marked canoe/kayak trail on Back Bay and 342 acres of what Florida used to look like: mangroves, tropical hammock, and beach unsullied by development.

SOUTHWEST

Beach Length: 1.25 mile.

Pets: Not allowed.

Directions: From U.S. 41 in Bonita Springs, take Bonita Beach Road west 2.2 miles; go left on Barefoot Beach Boulevard 1.5 mile to the end. It looks as though you're driving through a private gated community of large homes and condos, but keep going.

Hours: 8 a.m. to sunset.

Fee: $6 per day; free to county residents with beach sticker.

Contact: Collier County Parks, 239-591-8596

www.colliergov.net/parks/BarefootBeachPreserve.htm

Delnor-Wiggins Pass State Park

Special features: Outdoor shower · Picnic shelters · Beach fishing

There's swimming on the mile-long sugar-white beach, fishing on Wiggins Pass, where swimming is not allowed, and boating on Water Turkey Bay. The five parking lots at this popular park fill quickly on the weekends, and when they do, the park entrance is blocked off. You can park 0.2 mile away at a free public lot called Connor Park and walk on the paved path to Delnor-Wiggins.

Beach Length: 1 mile.

Pets: Allowed in the park, but not on the beach.

Directions: 5 miles west of I-75 exit 111, at the end of Bluebill Avenue in North Naples.

Hours: 8 a.m. to sunset.

Fee: $5 per vehicle; $3 for single occupant.

Contact: 239-597-6196

www.floridastateparks.org/delnor-wiggins

Bluebill Beach Access

Special features: Beach fishing

It is hoped that this new access will have facilities in the next few years. The small parking lot is located at the site of the former Vanderbilt Inn, just outside of Delnor-Wiggins Pass State Park. If full, park at Connor Park at 111 Avenue North.

Beach Length: 1 mile south to next access at Vanderbilt Beach Road.
Pets: Not allowed.
Directions: 5 miles west of I-75 exit 111, at the end of Bluebill Avenue at Gulfshore Drive in North Naples.
Hours: Sunrise to sunset.
Fee: Free currently; when facilities are built, $6 per day, free to county residents with beach sticker.
Contact: Collier County Parks, 239-254-4000
www.collierparks.com

Vanderbilt Beach Park

Special features: Outdoor shower · Beach fishing

This is a popular beach access among upscale hotels in North Naples. From January through March, get there before 10 a.m. to get a parking space and a spot on the beach. There's a parking lot for 120 cars and a garage for 340 just west of the Ritz-Carlton Hotel.

Beach Length: 1 mile north to Delnor-Wiggins Pass State Park; 1 mile south to end of Bay Colony Drive.
Pets: Not allowed.
Directions: From U.S. 41, go west on Route 862 for 1.3 mile to Vanderbilt Beach Road

Hours: 8 a.m. to sunset.
Fee: $6 per day; free to county residents with beach sticker.
Contact: Collier County Parks, 239-254-4000
www.collierparks.com

Clam Pass Park

Special features: Picnic shelters · Outdoor shower · Beach fishing

This 35-acre park in North Naples has a three-quarter-mile board-walk to the beach. A tram runs along the boardwalk through a mangrove forest. Even in one of the most populated areas of the county, you'll likely see shorebirds and osprey. There's a hotel and restaurant nearby.

Beach Length: 0.5 mile.
Pets: Not allowed.
Directions: From U.S. 41 go west on Seagate Drive 0.5 mile. Where the road turns left, go straight on Crayton Road.
Hours: 8 a.m. to sunset.
Fee: $6 per vehicle; free to county residents with beach sticker.
Contact: Collier County Parks, 239-254-4000
www.collierparks.com

Gulfshore Boulevard Beach Access

Special features: Beach fishing

This North Naples access is off the beaten path in a shady, residential neighborhood. There's a small, metered lot; no facilities.

Beach Length: 2 miles.
Pets: Not allowed.

Directions: From U.S. 41, go west on Seagate Drive 0.5 mile to Clam Pass Park. Seagate continues left for 0.5 mile to the end.
Hours: Sunrise to sunset.
Fee: $1 per hour to park.
Contact: Collier County Parks and Recreation, 239-254-4000
www.collierparks.com

North Gulf Shore Beach Access

Special features: Outdoor shower · Beach fishing

North Gulfshore Boulevard has a cul-de-sac at either end among high-rise condos. The north end has metered parking; the south end is pedestrian only. There is also metered parking at Via Miramar Park, 0.2 mile south of Harbour Drive, and at Vedado Way, 0.4 mile north of Harbour Drive. There are no facilities at any of the parking lots.

Beach Length: 2 miles.
Pets: Not allowed.
Directions: From 9th Street North, go west on Harbour Drive 0.6 mile to North Gulfshore Boulevard.
Hours: 8 a.m. to sunset.
Fee: $1 per hour (meters accept quarters only).
Contact: Collier County Parks, 239-254-4000
www.collierparks.com

Lowdermilk Park

Special features: Outdoor shower · Picnic shelters

This busy family park is a fun place to play volleyball, then get some hot dogs and ice cream. When sailing regattas take place, the horizon is filled with dozens of white sails.

SOUTHWEST

Lowdermilk Park in Naples, with a sailing regatta in the background.

Beach Length: 750 feet.
Pets: Not allowed.
Directions: At the west end of Banyan Boulevard on N. Gulfshore Boulevard in Naples.
Hours: Sunrise to sunset.
Fee: $1 per hour metered parking; nonmetered spaces require a residential permit.
Contact: Naples Community Services, 239-213-7120
www.naplesgov.com
www.naples-florida.com/beach.htm

Naples Beach Public Access

Special features: Beach fishing

This beautiful beach town of shady avenues has accesses at the ends of most numbered and named streets along S. Gulfshore Boulevard, south of Naples Beach Golf Club. All have metered parking and bike racks. Some have handicapped-accessible ramps, but none have facilities. North of Lowdermilk Park are condos and hotels, with only pedestrian accesses.

Beach Length: 1.5 mile.
Pets: Not allowed.
Directions: Along S. Gulfshore Boulevard in Naples.
Hours: 5 a.m. to 11 p.m.
Fee: Metered parking.
Contact: Naples Community Services, 239-213-7120
www.naples.gov.com
www.naples-florida.com/beach.htm

Naples Municipal Beach and Pier

Special features: Outdoor shower · Fishing pier

A nice Sunday morning in Naples brings people in church duds, people fishing, couples, families, and beachgoers in bikinis to stroll the fishing pier and enjoy the beach. The city has a blanket fishing license, so you don't need one on the pier, which has cleaning stations, picnic tables, and concessions. There's handicapped-only parking close to the pier, and a metered lot across the street. The historic Palm Cottage is here, open for tours 1–4 p.m. No swimming allowed within 150 feet of pier.

Beach Length: 3.6 miles.
Pets: Not allowed.
Directions: On S. Gulfshore Boulevard at 12th Avenue South in Naples.
Hours: 5 a.m. to 11 p.m.; pier is open 24 hours.
Fee: Pay-station lot and metered street parking, both $1 per hour; the pier is free.
Contact: Naples Community Services, 239-213-7120
www.naples.gov.com
www.naples-florida.com/beach.htm

SOUTHWEST

Naples Pier.

Tigertail Beach County Park

Special features: Outdoor shower · Beach fishing

Marco Island is a community of high-rise condos and hotels with few trees and not much public beach access. This park is one of the few open to the public, so it's very popular. It's a great birding spot and you may even see endangered roseate spoonbills, unmistakable for their pink color, or a bald eagle.

Beach Length: 0.5 mile.
Pets: Not allowed.
Directions: From N. Collier Boulevard, take Kendall Drive 0.5 mile and turn left on Hernando Drive; go 0.2 mile to the beach.
Hours: 8 a.m. to sunset.
Fee: $6 per day, free to county residents with beach sticker.
Contact: Collier County Parks and Recreation, 239-254-4000
www.collierparks.com

S. Marco Beach Access

$

Special features: Outdoor shower · Beach fishing

Besides Tigertail Beach County Park, this is the only public beach parking on the entire island, and it's a block from the beach. There's a one-stall bathroom and a foot shower at the parking lot. Walk between the hotels to the beach.

Beach Length: 2 miles.
Pets: Not allowed.
Directions: Go nearly to the end of S. Collier Boulevard on Marco Island, turn left on Swallow Avenue to find parking lot on right.
Hours: 8 a.m. to dusk.
Fee: $6 per day pay machine; free to county residents with a beach sticker.
Contact: Collier County Parks and Recreation, 239-254-4000
www.collierparks.com

> A half dozen crumbling white domes perch on stilts at the tip of the cape, built by hippies in the 1960s and damaged when Category 3 Hurricane Wilma made landfall here in 2005.

Cape Romano

Special features: Beach fishing · Primitive camping

On this otherworldly beach outpost just five miles south of Marco Island's high-rises, you can set up a tent to watch the sun set on one shore and rise on the other. Accessible only by private boat, this wild beach is along the eastern edge of Cape Romano Key in the Rookery

SOUTHWEST

Bay National Estuarine Research Reserve. Land your boat or kayak for a day of picnicking, fishing, shelling, and bird life. Camp overnight if you'd like and watch hundreds of shorebirds feeding. The raccoons come out in force at dusk, so be sure to stow your food and trash. There's virtually no shelter from wind and sun, but the star gazing is fabulous. There are no facilities whatsoever, so bring plenty of freshwater and pack out your trash. A marine radio is advisable.

Beach Length: 3 miles.
Pets: Allowed on leash.
Directions: Cape Romano is about 5 miles southeast of Marco Island. Launch from marinas on either Marco or Goodland. GPS for the eastern beach and good camping: N25 50.681, W81 40.765
Hours: Open 24 hours.
Fee: None; although marinas may charge a fee to launch and park overnight.
Contact: Rookery Bay National Estuarine Research Reserve, 239-417-6310
www.dep.state.fl.us/COASTAL/sites/caperomano

Domes at Cape Romano.

Ten Thousand Islands National Wildlife Refuge

Special features: Beach fishing · Primitive camping

Located between Goodland and Everglades National Park, the refuge has several remote islands with small beaches, including Whitehouse, Panther, Gullivan, and Lulu. You can land and camp pretty much anywhere you'd like, but please do not disturb vegetation. There are no facilities whatsoever, so bring freshwater and pack out your trash. A marine radio is advisable.

Beach Length: Varies.
Pets: Allowed on a leash.
Directions: Launch either from Goodland on the western side of the preserve, or from Everglades City on the northeast boundary.
Hours: Open 24 hours.
Fee: None.
Contact: Ten Thousand Islands National Wildlife Refuge, 239-353-8442
www.fws.gov/southeast/TenThousandIsland

SOUTHWEST

Index

African American beaches, historically, 21, 154, 188, 317
Alan Shepard Park, 68
Alex's Beach, 104
Alfred A. McKethan Pine Island Park, 252
Algier's Beach, 314–15
Alligators, 5–6, 208, 231, 309, 315
Amber Sands Beach access, 81
Amelia Island beaches, 15–24
Amelia Island Plantation, 22–23
Amelia Island State Park, 23–24
American Beach, 21–22
Amphitheaters, 118, 193
Anastasia Island, 38
Anastasia State Park, 38–39
Anclote Key Preserve State Park, 259–61
Anclote River Park, 259–61
Anna Maria beach accesses, 285–86
Anna Maria Island, 258, 284–89
Anne's Beach, 169
Apalachee Bay, 236–37, 244
Apalachicola area, 231–36
Apalachicola Bay, 231
Apalachicola National Estuarine Research Reserve, 234
Apollo Beach, Canaveral National Seashore, 60–61
Aquariums, 43, 121, 166
Archibald Memorial Beach, 274
Archie Carr National Wildlife Refuge, 77, 78, 80, 81
Atlantic Beach, 29–30
Atlantic Dunes Park, 130–31
Atsena Otie, 248, 250
Australian pine, 4, 260
Avalon State Park, 89

Back Bay, 323–27, 330–31
Bahia Honda State Park, 175–76
Bald eagles, 10, 249, 330
Bald Point State Park, 237–39
Bal Harbour, 147
Barefoot Beach access, 323
Barefoot Beach Preserve, 323
Barrier islands, xxi, 14; East Coast, 24, 59, 67, 79, 125; Nature Coast, 242; Panhandle, 186, 190, 231, 233–34; Southwest, 259, 265, 280–82, 284, 310
Barrier Islands GEOpark, 310
Basketball, 106, 153
Bathtub Reef Beach Park, 109
Bay County, 219
Bayfront Park, 284
Bay Town Trolley, 219
Beach accesses, protected by state law, 3, 204
Beachcombing, 9–10, 12, 17, 281, 313
Beaches of South Walton, 207–18
Beach house rentals, 198
Beach mice: Choctawhatchee, 208, 213–14, 222; Perdido Key, 188
Beach safety, 4–8
Beachwalk/Pasley Park, 104
Beacon Hill Park, 225
Bear Point Sanctuary, 95
Beer Can Beach, 289
Bellair Beach access, 270
Bellair Shores, 270
Bicentennial Park, 50–51
Big Bend, 230, 242
Big Bend Saltwater Paddling Trail, 245
Big Carlos Pass, 320
Big Lagoon State Park, 189
Big Talbot Island State Park, 25

Bike Week, 51
Biking, 28, 30, 65, 119–20, 142, 148, 152,
    155–56, 191, 194, 197, 208–9, 231, 284,
    309, 313–16, 320; bike rentals, 155, 197,
    232, 313, 320; mountain, 16, 146
Bill Baggs Cape Florida State Park, 116,
    155–56
Birds: bald eagles, 10, 249, 330; ibis, 249;
    magnificent frigate birds, 184; migra-
    tions of, 10, 186, 238; pelicans, xxiii, 10,
    83, 249; —, white, 310; piping plovers,
    190, 218, 260, 310; scrub jays, 111; song-
    birds, 10, 186; white egrets, 310
Biscayne Bay, 146, 151, 155, 157, 159
Biscayne National Park, 158–59
Blind Creek Park, 97–98
Blind Pass, 275, 313
Blind Pass Beach, 304
Blowing Rocks Preserve, 113–14
Bluebill Beach access, 325
Blue Mountain Beach, 210–11
"Blue Wave" beach, 206
Boars, wild, 309
Boat access–only beaches: East Coast, 110;
    South Florida, 158–59; Florida Keys,
    164, 183; Panhandle, 221, 231, 233, 236;
    Nature Coast, 248; Southwest, 259,
    264, 266, 280, 282, 289, 306, 309, 310,
    331, 333
Boat ramps: East Coast, 27, 40, 49, 60, 63,
    79, 83, 91, 97; Florida Keys, 165, 167, 175,
    178, 182; Nature Coast, 243, 246, 248,
    250–51, 253–54; Panhandle, 188–89,
    192, 201, 213, 221, 226, 230, 235; South
    Florida, 140, 158; Southwest, 259, 262,
    280, 282, 284, 296–97, 303, 319, 324–25
Boat rentals, 137, 157, 193, 263
Bob Graham Beach, 103
Bob Sikes Cut, 234
Boca Chica Beach, 177
Boca Grande Lighthouse, 307–8
Boca Grande public access, 306–7
Boca Grande Village, 307
Boca Inlet, 134
Boca Raton, 131–33

Bonita Beach, 320–21
Bonita Beach Dog Park, 320–21
Bonita Beach Park, 322
Bonita Beach public accesses, 322
Bonita Springs, 321–24
Bonsteel Park, 79
Boogie boards, 106, 155
Boppy's Wabasso Beach Market, 82
Bowditch Point Regional Park, 317
Bowman's Beach, 313
Boynton Beach Oceanfront Park, 128–29
Bradenton area, 284–91
Brevard County, 66–79
Broadwalk (Hollywood Beach), 142
Bryn Mawr Beach access, 104
Bunche Beach, 316
Burney Beachfront Park, 22
Bush Key, 184
Butler and Douglas Community Park
    (Horseshoe Beach), 246
Butterflies, monarch, 10, 186, 188, 217

Caladesi Island State Park, 263–66
Calusa Beach, 175
Camp Helen State Park, 218
Camping: East Coast, 15, 20, 22, 26–28, 38,
    49, 60, 64, 79; South Florida, 158–59,
    164–65, 171, 175, 183; Panhandle, 188–89,
    205, 208, 213, 221, 226, 230, 233, 235;
    Nature Coast, 246–47; Southwest, 259,
    280–82, 296, 309, 331–33
Canaveral National Seashore, 14, 60–63
Canine Beach, 139
Cannon Beach, 166
Canoeing. See Kayaking and canoeing
Canova Beach Park, 74
Cape Canaveral and Avon-by-the-Sea,
    65–66
Cape Canaveral–Cocoa Beach area, 64–71
Cape Haze, 306
Cape Palms Park, 227
Cape Romano, 258, 332
Cape Sable, 160
Cape San Blas lighthouse, 228
Cape St. George lighthouse, 233–34

Captiva Beach North, 311
Captiva Island, 312–13
Carlin Park, 118
Carrabelle Beach, 236–37
Casey Key, 297–98
Casino Beach, 191, 193–94
Caspersen Beach Park, 302
Cayo Costa State Park, 309–10
Cayo Hueso Café, 181
C. B. Harvey Rest Beach Park, 178–79
Cedar Key City Park, 248
Cedar Keys National Wildlife Refuge, 242,
    248–50
Chadwick Park at Englewood Beach, 305
Charlotte County, 305
Charleston, S.C., 24
Chastain Beach/The Rocks, 108
Cherie Down Park, 66
Children, beaches best for: East Coast,
    27, 55, 83, 109, 114; South Florida, 117,
    120, 127, 146–48, 154, 157–58; Florida
    Keys, 165, 167, 169–71, 175, 178–79, 181,
    183; Panhandle, 189, 192, 196, 201, 204,
    221, 229, 237; Nature Coast, 245, 248;
    Southwest, 259, 261, 268, 277, 280, 282,
    284, 289, 292
Choctawhatchee Bay, 201, 204
Choctawhatchee beach mouse, 208,
    213–14, 222
Citrus County, 251–53
City of St. Petersburg Municipal Beach,
    275–76
Clam Pass Park, 326
Clean Beaches Council, 206
Clearwater Beach, 267–69
Clearwater–St. Petersburg area, 267–83
Clement Taylor Park, 204
Clothing-optional beaches: Canaveral
    National Seashore, 61–63; Haulover
    Beach, Miami, 145–46; Fort De Soto
    County Park, 281
Coastal dune lakes, 12, 206, 208, 213–14,
    217–18
Cocoa Beach, 67
Cocoa Beach area, 64–71

Coconut Drive Beach, 94–95
Coconut Point Park, 77
Coco Plum Beach, 173
Col. Frank Hurley Park, 279
Collier County beaches, 323–27, 330–31
Conch Island, 38
Connor Park, 324
Coolidge Park, 292–93
Copenhagen, wreck of, 137
Coquina Beach, 289
Coquina rock, 43–44, 106
Coquina sand, 33, 37, 48, 58–59
Coral Cove Park, 114
Coral islands, 162, 183
Cortez Beach, 288
Crandon Park, 154–55
Crescent Beach Park, 41
Crescent Beach/Point of Rocks, 296
Crocodiles, 6, 157
Crooked Island, 222–23
Cross City, 247
Crystal Beach Live Oaks Park, 262
Crystal River, 251
Cuban food, 155
Curry Hammock State Park, 171–72

Dania Beach Ocean Park, 141
Dan Russell City Pier, 220
Daytona Beach, 52–53
Daytona Beach area, 14, 50–56
Deerfield Public Beach, 135
Deer Lake State Park, 216–17
Delnor-Wiggins Pass State Park, 324
Delray Municipal Beach, 129–30
Destin, 202, 203–6
Destin Public Beach access, 203
Dinghy Beach, 184
Diving. *See* Scuba diving
Dixie County, 246–47
Dog Beach, 180
Dog Island, 231, 236–37
Dollman Park, 101
Dolphins, xxiii, 10, 32, 164, 222, 233
Don Cesar Beach Resort, 279
Don Pedro Island State Park, 306

Douglas, Marjory Stoneman, 155; Marjory Stoneman Douglas Ocean Beach Park, 150
Dragonflies, 10
Dr. Beach (Stephen Leatherman), xxi, 265, 281
Driving on the beach, 19–23, 27, 34–37, 39, 40–43, 51–52, 54, 57, 58, 211, 229–30, 263, 284
Dry Tortugas National Park, 182–84
Dubois Park, 117
Dune Allen regional access, 210
Dunedin area, 263–66
Dunedin Causeway, 263–64
Duval Street, 182

Eastpoint, 234
Eco-Beach Store, 197–98
Ed Walline Park, 210
Eglin Air Force Base, 202, 228
Egmont Key State Park, 281–83
Egret, white, 310
E. G. Simmons County Park, 283
Elliott Key, 158
Elliott Museum, 106, 108
Emerald Coast, 186, 199, 205
Englewood, 305–6
Englewood Beach, 305
Estero Bay, 318
Everglades City, 333
Everglades National Park, 159–60, 164–65, 333

Far Beach, 166
Fernandina Beach, 15–19
Fernandina Main Beach, 16–18
Fish: catfish, 187; mullet, 10, 233; pompano, 136, 187; whiting, 187
Fishing Beach, 239
Flagler Avenue Park, 58
Flagler Beach, 48
Flagler Beach area beaches, 43–49
Flagler County, 43–47
Flamingo Marina, 159–60
Fletcher Beach, 106–7

Florida Bay, 160, 163–64
Florida City, 160, 165
Florida National Scenic Trail, 191
Florida Oceanographic Coastal Center, 106
Florida Power and Light, 98
Florida State Parks, xxv; East Coast, 15–17, 23, 25–27, 33, 38–39, 44–45, 49–50, 78–80, 88–90, 110–11; South Florida, 116, 121, 139–40, 146, 155–56; Florida Keys, 163, 165, 169, 171–72, 175–76, 181; Panhandle, 187, 189, 194, 203, 205, 208–9, 213, 216–18, 221–23, 226–27, 231, 234–35, 237–39; Southwest, 259–61, 263–66, 282–83, 305–11, 319–21, 325
Forgotten Coast, 186, 226
Fort Clinch State Park, 15–16
Fort Dade, 282
Fort De Soto County Park, 280–82
Fort Island Gulf Beach, 251
Fort Jefferson, 183–84
Fort Lauderdale area, 135–44
Fort Lauderdale City Beach, 137–38
Fort Panic Park, 210
Fort Pickens, Gulf Islands National Seashore, 191
Fort Walton Beach, 199–201
Fort Zachary Taylor Historic State Park, 181–82
Founder's Park, 167–68
Frank Butler Park East, 40–41
Franklin County, 235
Frank Rendon Park, 54
Frederick Douglass Memorial Beach, 96–97
Fred H. Howard Park, 261–62
Ft. Matanzas National Monument, 42
Ft. Myers Beach, 318–19
Ft. Myers–Sanibel area, 309–22
Ft. Pierce Beach public accesses, 92–93
Ft. Pierce Inlet, 91
Ft. Pierce Inlet State Park, 89–90

Gamble Rogers Memorial State Recreation area, 49

Garden Key, 183–84
Gasparilla Island State Park, 306–8
George Grady Bridge, 22–23
Glasscock Beach, 102
Golden Sands Beach Park, 82
Golf, 22–23, 46, 112, 132, 146, 155, 302, 328;
    miniature, 16
Goodland, 332–33
Gopher tortoise, 46, 111, 282
Government Cut, 151
Grayton Beach, 211–12
Grayton Beach State Park, 213–14
Greer Island Beach, 289
Guana River State Park, 33
Guana-Tolomato-Matanzas National
    Estuarine Research Reserve, 33–34
Gulf County, 226–30
Gulf Islands National Seashore, 188, 191,
    193–94, 201–2
Gulf of Mexico, xxi, xxiv, 160, 183, 211, 221,
    236, 242, 246, 258, 289
Gulfshore Boulevard Beach access, 326–27
Gulfside City Park/Algier's Beach, 314
Gulfside Park Preserve, 315
Gulfstream County Park, 129
Gulfview Heights regional access, 210
Gumbo Limbo Nature Center, 132

Hagen's Cove, 245
Hallandale Beach, 144
Harry Harris County Park, 166
Haulover Bridge, 147
Haulover Park, 145–46
Henderson Beach State Park, 205
Herbert Hoover Marina, 158
Herman's Bay access, 100
Hernando County, 252–53
Higgs Beach, 179
Hillsborough County, 283
Historic Virginia Key Beach Park Trust,
    154
Hobe Sound Beach, 112
Hobe Sound National Wildlife Refuge,
    110–12
Hobie Beach, 152–53

Hodges Park at Keaton Beach, 245
Hog Island, 264
Holiday, 259, 261
Holiday Isle, 163
Hollywood Beach, 142–43
Hollywood North Beach Park, 142
Holmes Beach accesses, 286–87
Homestead area, 158–60
Homestead Bayfront Park, 158–59
Honeymoon Island State Park, 260,
    263–66
Horseback riding: East Coast, 20, 23–24,
    60, 96–97; Panhandle, 229–30
Horseshoe Beach, 246
House of Refuge, 107–8
Howard E. Futch Memorial Park/Paradise
    Beach, 74–75
Hudson Beach, 254
Hugh Taylor Birch State Park, 139–40
Huguenot Memorial Park, 27–28
Humiston Park, 87
Hummingbirds, 186
Hurricanes: Charley, 309–10; damage
    from, 7, 82, 93, 194–95, 197, 207, 250;
    damage prevention, 6; Dennis, 235;
    Earl, 222; Elena, 285; forecasting, 10;
    Ivan, 187, 190–91, 193; Katrina, 191;
    Opal, 194–95; shipwrecks, 80; Wilma,
    331
Hutchinson Island, 91–109

Ibis, 249
Indian Key Fill, 169
Indian Key Historic State Park, 162, 169
Indian Pass Beach, 230
Indian River County, 81–85, 88–90
Indian Rocks Beach, 270–72
Indian Rocks Beach access, 270–71
Indians: Timucuan, 61. See also Native
    Americans
Indian Shores, 272
Inlet Beach regional access, 217–18
Intracoastal Waterway (ICW), 37, 40, 43,
    49, 97, 110, 111, 113, 114, 121, 127, 129, 131,
    139, 140, 141, 146, 189, 297, 303

Irene H. Canova Park, 73–74
Islamorada, 167–70
Islamorada Library Park, 167
Island Trolley, 285, 289
Isle of Eight Flags Shrimp Festival, 15

Jack Island Preserve, 90
Jacksonville area beaches, 25–32
Jacksonville Beach, 31–32
James H. Nance Park, 75–76
James Island, 237
James Lee County Park, 205–6
James P. Morgan Memorial Park and
    Botanical Garden, 192
Jaycee Park, 85–86
Jellyfish, 8–9
Jensen Sea Turtle Beach, 102–3
Jetty Park, 64–65
John Beasley County Park, 201
John Brooks Park, 95
John D. MacArthur Beach State Park, 121
John Pennekamp Coral Reef State Park,
    165–66
Johnson Beach, 188–89
John's Pass Bridge, 274
John's Pass Park, 275
John U. Lloyd Beach State Park, 140
Jolley Trolley, 267–68
Juan Ponce de Leon Landing, 78
June White Deck Park, 203
Jungle Hut Road Park, 47
Juno Beach Park and Pier, 119–20
Jupiter Beach, 119
Jupiter Beach County Park, 117–18
Jupiter Inlet, 117
Jupiter Island, 110–14

Kathryn Abbey Hanna Park, 28–29
Katie Pierola Park, 287–88
Kayaking and canoeing, xxi, xxiv, 335; East
    Coast, 26–28, 39, 43, 49–50, 63, 79, 83,
    88–89, 95, 110; Florida Keys, 164–71,
    173, 175–76, 178–79, 181–82, 184; Nature
    Coast, 245, 247–49, 254; Panhandle,
    193, 221–22, 230, 232, 236; rentals, 27,
39, 49, 152, 155, 163–64, 166, 168–71, 175,
    178–79, 181, 193, 221, 248–49, 263, 265,
    293, 309, 320; South Florida, 121, 131,
    146, 152; Southwest, 259, 261, 263–65,
    274, 281–82, 305, 309, 320, 323, 332;
    tours, 27, 79, 155, 163, 169, 234, 249
Key Biscayne, 154–56
Key Largo, 160, 164–66
Key West, 178–82
Kimberly Bergalis Memorial Drive and
    Surfside Park, 94
Kiteboarding, 91–92
Klondike Beach, Canaveral National
    Seashore, 61–62
Knight Island, 306

Lake Powell, 218
Lake Worth Municipal Beach, 125–26
Lantana Public Beach, 126–27
Largo Sound, 165
Lauderdale-By-The-Sea Public Beach, 137
Layton, 171–73
Leatherman, Stephen (Dr. Beach), xxi,
    265, 281
Leave No Trace, xxiv, 1–3, 5
Lee County, 307, 312–13, 317–22
Levy County, 248–50
Lido Beach, 291–93
Lido Key, 292–94
Lighthouse Beach Park, 315
Lighthouse Point Park, 55–56
Lighthouses, 39, 55–56, 116–17, 155–56,
    184, 228, 233, 249, 260, 282–83, 307–8,
    316
Lightning, 6–7
Little Duck Key, 175
Little Gasparilla Island, 306
Little Hickory Beach access, 321
Little Mud Creek, 97
Little St. George Island, 231, 233–34
Little Talbot Island State Park, 26–27
Loggerhead Key, 184
Loggerhead Park, 120
Long Beach Drive, 176–77
Longboat Key, 289–91

Longboat Key accesses, 290
Long Key State Park, 171
Lori Wilson Park, 69
Lovers Key State Park, 319–21
Lowdermilk Park, 327–29
Lower Keys, 175–77
Lower Matecumbe, 163, 169–70
Lower Suwannee National Wildlife Refuge, 247, 249
Lummus Park, 149–50
Lynn Hall Memorial Park, 318

Madeira Beach, 274
Magnificent frigate birds, 184
Malacompra County Park, 46
Manasota Beach, 303–4
Manasota Key, 303–6
Manatee County, 284–90
Manatee Public Beach, 286
Manatees, 11, 164, 253, 320
Marathon, 173–74
Marco Island, 330–32
Marineland, 43
Marinelife Center, 120
Maritime Hammock Nature Trail, 101
Marjory Stoneman Douglas Ocean Beach Park, 150–51
Martin County, 102–9, 112
Mary McLeod Bethune Beach Park, 59
Mashes Sands County Park, 243–44
Matanzas Beach, 42
Matanzas Inlet, 42
Matanzas Pass Bridge, 317, 319
Matheson Hammock County Park, 157
M. B. Miller Park and County Pier, 220
McLarty Treasure Museum, 80
Melbourne Beach area, 72–80
Mexico Beach, 223, 224–25
Miami area, 145–57
Miami Beach, 148–51
Miami-Dade County, 145–56
Mickler's Landing Beach, 33
Middle Cove access, 97
Midtown Beach, 123–24
Migrations, 10, 186, 188, 238

Millennium Park, 73
Miramar Beach, 207–8
Monroe County beaches, 166, 175, 177, 179
Morada Bay, 163
Munyon Island, 121

Naples area, 323–33
Naples Beach public access, 328
Naples city parks, 327–29
Naples Municipal Beach and Pier, 329–30
Nassau County, 20–23
National Key Deer Refuge, 177
National Museum of Naval Aviation, 188
Native Americans, 238; Geronimo, 191; shell mounds/middens of, 61, 177, 218, 249
Nature Conservancy, 113, 231, 236
Naval Air Station Pensacola, 188
Navarre Beach, 194, 197
Navarre Park, 196
Nease Beachfront Park, 35–36
Neptune Beach, 30–31
Newman C. Brackin Wayside Park and Okaloosa Pier, 200
New Pass, 291
New Port Richey, 255
New Smyrna Beach area, 57–59
Nokomis Beach, 297
Nonnative species, 4, 260, 319
Normandy Beach access, 100–101
Norriego Point, 203
North Beach Park, 35
North Captiva Island, 310–11
North Clearwater Beach, 265, 267–68
North Gulf Shore Beach access, 327
North Hutchinson Island, 81–90
North Jetty Park, 298
North Lido Beach, 292
North Miami Beach, 149
North Naples, 323–26
North Nest Key, 160, 164
North Ocean Park, 135
North Peninsula State Park, 50
North Point Beach, 239
North Redington Beach access, 273–74
North Shore Open Space Park Beach, 148

Ocean Avenue Park, 76
Ocean Bay Natural area, 99–100
Ocean Drive, 149–51
Oceanfront Community Center, 147
Oceanfront Park, 32
Ocean Inlet Park, 127
Ocean Reef Park, 121–22
Ocean Ridge Hammock Park, 128
Ochlockonee Bay, 237, 243
Okaloosa County, 200–201
Okaloosa Island, 199–202
Okaloosa Island beach accesses, 199–200
Okaloosa Unit, Gulf Islands National
    Seashore, 201–2
Old Salt Road Park, 46
Oleta River State Park, 146
Opal Beach, Santa Rosa Unit of Gulf
    Islands National Seashore, 194–95
Ormond Beach, 51–52
Ormond-By-The-Sea, 50–51

Palma Sola Causeway Park, 284
Palm Beach, 123–24
Palm Beach area, 117–34
Palm Beach County, 114, 117–22, 124–25,
    127–29, 134
Palm Beach Shores Park, 123
Panacea, 239, 243
Panama City Beach, 219–20
Paradise Beach, 74–75
Parasailing, 39, 121, 137, 178, 295
Pasco County, 254–55, 259
Passage Key, 284
Pass-a-Grille Beach, 279–80
Patrick Air Force Base, 70
Pelican Beach Park/Satellite Beach, 72
Pelican Inn, 236–37
Pelican Island National Wildlife Refuge, 83
Pelicans, xxiii, 10, 83; white, 249, 310
Pensacola area beaches, 187–94
Pensacola Beach/Casino Beach, 193–94
Pepper Beach Park, 89–90
Perdido Key, 187–89
Perdido Key beach mouse, 188
Perdido Key State Park, 187

Personal watercraft, 4; rentals, 137, 178
Peter's Point Beachfront Park, 20
Pet-friendly beaches: East Coast, 16, 18–22,
    27–43, 46–48, 55, 57, 99, 102–8, 111–12;
    Florida Keys, 169–70, 173, 176, 180;
    Nature Coast, 243–44, 248; Panhandle,
    208, 225, 227–30, 234, 236; South
    Florida, 139, 152; Southwest, 262, 264,
    267, 280, 284, 302, 312–16, 318, 320,
    331, 333
Phipps Ocean Park, 124
Pine Island, 310
Pinellas County, 261–62, 270–73, 277–81
Piping plovers, 190, 218, 260, 310
Plants, xxiv, 11–12, 101; allergies, 8; restora-
    tion of, 103–4, 153
Playalinda Beach, Canaveral National
    Seashore, 63
Point of Rocks, 296
Pompano Beach, 135–36
Pompano Public Beach, 136
Ponce de Leon Inlet, 55, 57
Ponce de Leon Inlet lighthouse, 55–56
Ponte Vedra–Vilano beaches, 33–37
Port Canaveral, 64–65
Port Charlotte area, 305–8
Port Everglades, 137, 140
Port St. Joe, 226–30

Quick Point Nature Preserve, 291
Quietwater Beach, 192

Range, Athalie, 154
Redington Shores beach access, 273
Red Reef Park, 132
Red tide, 7–8, 222
Richard G. Edgeton Bicentennial Park,
    72–73
Richard G. Kreusler Park, 124–25
Richard Seltzer Park, 220
Rickenbacker Causeway/Hobie Beach,
    152–53
Riomar Beach, 87
Rip currents, 4, 38
River to Sea Preserve, 43

Riviera Beach, 122
Riviera Municipal Beach, 122
Robbie's Marina, 168
Robert J. Strickland Memorial Park, 254
Robert K. Rees Park, 254–55
Robert P. Murkshe Memorial Park, 69–70
Rocks, The, 108
Rogers Park, 253
Rookery Bay National Estuarine Research
    Reserve, 332
Ross Witham Beach access (House of
    Refuge Beach), 107–8
Round Island Oceanside Park, 88
Rum Runners, 163
Ruskin, 283

Salinas Park, 229
Samson Oceanfront Park, 145
San Carlos Bay, 317
Sand Key, 268–74
Sand Key County Park, 269–70
Sandspur Beach, 175
Sanibel Causeway, 312–17
Sanibel Causeway Beach, 316
Sanibel Island, 313–16
Santa Lucea Beach and Fletcher Beach,
    106–7
Santa Rosa Beach, 209–10, 214–15
Santa Rosa County, 198
Santa Rosa Island, 191–98
Santa Rosa Sound, 192, 195–96, 198
Sarasota area, 292–98
Sarasota Bay, 289
Sarasota County, 293–304
Satellite Beach, 72
Scalloping, 230, 242, 245, 247
Scott Road Beach access, 20–21
Scrub jays, 111
Scuba diving, 4, 137, 140, 162, 165, 221,
    296, 299
Sea Grape Trail access, 84
Seagrove Beach, 215
Seagull Park, 71
Seahorse Key, 248–49
Sea islands, 24

Sea oats: protected by state law, 2, 12;
    restoration of, 17, 187
Seaside, 214–15
Seaside Park, 18
Sea turtles: Dry Tortugas, meaning of,
    182; exhibits of, 98, 120; green, 110;
    leatherback, 110; loggerhead, 78, 110;
    nature walks, 79, 111, 120; nesting season
    of, 2, 10, 33–37, 40–41, 57, 110, 120,
    292–97, 299–302, 304; nesting sites of,
    14, 59–60, 77–78, 89, 98, 106, 110–11,
    120, 142, 173, 209, 213–14, 218, 231, 236,
    238, 264, 296
Seaway Drive, 91
Sebastian Inlet, 79
Sebastian Inlet State Park, 79–80
Service Club Park, 300
Seven Mile Bridge, 175
Sexton Beach, 86
Sharks, 3, 5–6; fossils of teeth, 17, 302, 305
Shell Island, 221–23; shuttle, 221
Shell Key Preserve, 280; shuttle, 280
Shell Point Beach, 244
Shipwrecks, 80, 108, 137, 166, 228
Shired Island County Park, 247
Sidney Fischer Park, 68
Siesta Key, 294–97
Siesta Key North Beach accesses, 294–95
Siesta Key Public Beach, 295
Simonton Street Beach, 182
Sister's Creek, 173
S. Marco Beach access, 331
Smathers Beach, 178
Smith's Creek Landing, 50
Smyrna Dunes Park, 57
Snorkeling, 4; East Coast, 89; Florida Keys,
    163, 165–66, 169, 176, 179, 181, 183–84;
    Nature Coast, 245; Panhandle, 197,
    221–22, 230; South Florida, 121, 124, 132,
    136, 137, 140; Southwest, 280, 296
Sombrero Beach, 173–74
South Beach (Key West), 181
South Beach (Miami), 116, 149–51
South Beach boardwalk (Hutchinson
    Island), 93

South Beach Park (North Hutchinson Island), 88
South Beach Park (Palm Beach area), 133
South Beach Pavilion (Palm Beach area), 133
South Brohard Paw Park, 302
South Cocoa Beach, 67
South End Walkover, 23
South Fernandina Beach accesses, 19
South Inlet Park, 134
South Jetty, 299
South Jetty Park, 91–92
South Lido Park, 293–94
South Patrick Shores, 71
South Pointe Park, 151
South Walton Beach access points, 209
South Walton County, 207–18
Spanish River Park, 131
Spanish Shanty, 222
Spessard Holland North and South Beach Parks, 76–77
Spring Break, xxiv, 51–52, 137, 142, 171, 178, 193, 206, 219, 318
St. Andrews Bay, 221
St. Andrews State Park, 221–23
St. Augustine area beaches, 38–42
St. Augustine Beach, 39–40
St. George Island, 231, 234
St. George Island Public Beach Park, 234
St. George Island State Park, 231, 235–36
St. George Sound, 237
Stiltsville, 156
Stingrays, 8
St. Joe Beach, 225–26
St. Joe paper company, 214
St. Johns County, 33–42
St. Joseph Bay area, 224–30
St. Joseph Peninsula, 226–29
St. Joseph Peninsula State Park, 226
St. Lucie County, 91–102
St. Lucie County Marine Center, 91
St. Lucie Inlet, 109–10
St. Lucie Inlet Preserve State Park, 110–11
St. Pete Beach access, 278–79
St. Petersburg area, 267–83

Stuart Beach, 106
Stumphole Beach access, 227–28
Stump Pass Beach State Park, 305–6
St. Vincent Island Shuttle, 230, 232
St. Vincent National Wildlife Refuge, 230–32
Sun and heat safety, 4–5
Suncoast Beach Trolley, 270, 279
Sunny McCoy Indigenous Park, 178–79
Sunrise Beach, 239
Sunrise Park, 75
Sunset Beach (Clearwater–St. Petersburg area), 277
Sunset Beach (Tarpon Springs area), 262
Sunshine Skyway Bridge, 281
Sunshine State (film), 15, 21
Surfing, 27, 38, 67, 70, 77, 79, 90, 119, 135–36, 145, 222, 224, 264, 298
Surfside (Miami area), 147–48
Surfside (Ponte Vedra–Vilano beaches), 36–37
Surfside Park (Hutchinson Island), 94

Talbot Islands, 24–27
Tampa Bay, 282–83
Tarpon Bay Road Beach, 314–15
Tarpon Springs area, 259–62
Tavernier, 166
Taylor County, 245
Tennis, 22, 89, 118, 124, 146, 155, 157, 167, 179, 279
Ten Thousand Islands National Wildlife Refuge, 333
Theaters, outdoor, 118, 142, 193
Three Rooker Bar, 266
Tiger Shores Beach, 105
Tigertail Beach County Park, 330–31
Tiki Gardens Park, 272
Tom Renick Park, 51
Topsail Hill Preserve State Park, 208–9
Tours: by boat, 42, 158, 169, 249; by kayak, 27, 79, 155, 163, 169, 234, 249
Tracking Station Park, 85
Treasure Island, 275–77

Treasure Island beach accesses, 276–77
Treasure Shores Park, 81
Trees, 11–12; native, 47, 65, 77, 99, 101, 110; restoration of, 103, 104, 153, 214
Truman Show, The (film), 215
Turner Beach, 312
Turtle Beach (Hutchinson Island), 98
Turtle Beach (Sarasota area), 296–97
Turtle Mound Archeological Site, 60–61
Turtle Trail Beach access, 84
Tyndall Air Force Base, 223

Umbrella rentals, 4, 106, 155, 179, 274
Upham Beach, 278
Usina Beach, 34–35
U.S. Life-Saving Service, 108

Vanderbilt Beach Park, 325
Van Ness Butler Regional Beach access, 214
Varn Beach Park, 47
Venice area, 299–304
Venice Fishing Pier, 301
Venice Inlet, 298–99
Venice Municipal Beach, 299–300
Vero Beach, 85–88
Veterans Memorial Park, 175
Via Miramar Park, 327
Vilano Beach, 37
Virginia Forrest Access, 105
Virginia Key Beach, 153
Virginia Key beach accesses, 152–54
Volleyball, xxiv, 16, 32, 63, 72, 74–76, 89, 103, 106, 118, 120, 122, 126, 134–35, 179, 275, 287, 295, 322, 327
Volusia County, 50–59

Wabasso Beach, 82
Wabasso Causeway Park, 83
Wakulla County, 242–44
Walton County, 206, 215
Walton Rocks Beach, 99
Washington Oaks Gardens State Park, 44–45
Waveland Beach, 101–2
Weeki Wachee, 252, 253
Weeki Wachee River, 253
Wheelchairs, for beach use: East Coast, 17, 27–28, 32, 48–49, 52, 63, 88, 93, 106; Panhandle, 200; South Florida, 135–36; Southwest, 261, 269, 275, 277, 292, 295, 297, 299, 303, 315
Whiskey Creek, 140
Wiggins Pass, 324
Wilbur-By-The-Sea, 54
Wildlife, xxiv, 10–11, 186, 222, 223, 230
Windsurfing, 6, 152
Winterhaven Park, 55
Wolves, red, 10, 231
World War I, 188
World War II, 89, 238
Worm reefs, 109, 121
Worms: sabellariid, 109; shells of, 9

Yankeetown Park, 250

Mary and Bill Burnham are full-time travel writers who split their time between the Florida Keys and Virginia's Eastern Shore. The Burnhams have been writing together for more than a decade, blending their love of the outdoors with backgrounds in journalism and photography.

In addition to *The Complete Florida Beach Guide*, they are the authors of five guides to travel in Florida and Virginia: *Wild Florida Islands*, *Florida Keys Paddling Atlas*, *Hiking Virginia*, *Exploring Small Towns of Virginia and Maryland*, and *The Virginia Handbook*.

Their articles have been published in numerous magazines and newspapers, and they are members of the Society of American Travel Writers (SATW), the American Society of Journalists and Authors (ASJA), and the Authors Guild. They are also certified by the American Canoe Association as kayak instructors, and work as part-time guides.

Visit their Web site at www.BurnhamInk.com, sign in, and say hello. They'd love your feedback about Florida's beaches.

What's their favorite beach? Any island where they can arrive by kayak and set up a tent to face the rising or setting sun.